Analytical Legal Naturalism

Analytical Legal Naturalism

S. Zinaich Jr.

LEXINGTON BOOKS
Lanham • Boulder • New York • London

Published by Lexington Books
An imprint of The Rowman & Littlefield Publishing Group, Inc.
4501 Forbes Boulevard, Suite 200, Lanham, Maryland 20706
www.rowman.com

6 Tinworth Street, London SE11 5AL

British Library Cataloguing in Publication Information Available

Library of Congress Cataloging-in-Publication Data Is Available

Library of Congress Control Number: 2020933466
ISBN 978-1-4985-9879-8 (cloth : alk. paper) | ISBN 978-1-4985-9880-4 (ebook)

Contents

Preface

This text originated from a series of class lectures I gave at Purdue University Northwest. The class, concentrating primarily on topics of constitutional law, e.g., privacy, free speech, capital punishment, gun control, and so forth, also devoted the first five weeks to the history of natural law. Initially, I designed the course to begin with the Scholastics. After that, the focus turned to the early Modern period (roughly the early fifteen hundreds) and moved approximately to the end of the Enlightenment period. This time period is notable for the variety of natural law accounts. There are (at least) five different natural law viewpoints, and each one depends upon a justification that requires artful handling.[1] In fact, at times, the only similarity between these views is the name "natural law." Additionally, the extended justifications to champion a natural law narrative (and even those who attack it) resemble many of the analyses found within the contemporary moral realism debate.

The enquiry of natural law ended with the current legal debate between the legal positivists and natural law theorists. For example, time (certainly not nearly enough) was dedicated to the texts of Austin, Hart, and Dworkin (and to some of the scholarship surrounding the debate). Thus, it was not long before I began to formulate my own views about the debate. In fact, the issues surrounding "hard cases," that is, legal cases where close precedents for adjudication are missing, caught my attention. Unfortunately, because the issues were so complicated and arduous, defending either viewpoint seemed too difficult even under the most favorable circumstances. Not content with either side of the debate, I acted on a hunch to consider the possibility of a third (or middle) position. This view would draw from the strength of both viewpoints and avoid the drawbacks.

In time, the thesis I defend in this text emerged, but not without the help of several people who deserve recognition. The first individual that I would like to thank is Ms. Jana Hodges-Kluck, Senior Acquisitions Editor of Philosophy, Classics, Linguistics at Lexington Books. Because of her support and patience in the early stages of my text, I was able to develop a more mature and specific thesis, one that ultimately developed in the current monograph. I can say that without her support and inspiration, I do not think I would have come to develop my view.

I am also indebted to a number of people for helpful comments and criticisms. This text benefited profoundly by the independent (peer) reader for Lexington Books. It is much stronger as a result of the reader's criticisms and suggestions. Professor Frank Colucci, Associate Professor of Political Science, deserves recognition too. Professor Colucci focused on chapter 6 and provided excellent comments. Finally, I want to thank Ms. Martina S. James, who painstakingly read my text twice to comb out grammatical errors and identified clumsy paragraphs that needed clarification. Ms. James' attention to my text went beyond what anyone could expect.

Samuel Zinaich, Jr.

NOTE

1. Later I add a sixth position which I attribute to the Stoics.

Introduction

The rise of natural law begins with the ancient Greeks, comes to a crescendo in the Scholastic period, tapers off during the Enlightenment, and, essentially, disappears in the Romantic era. No doubt, pockets of scholarship dedicated to natural law appear later. Nonetheless, the efforts to breathe life back into the doctrine vary in method and success. I argue that the truth-conditions to prop up natural law fall very far afield.

My initial attention to natural law emerged from reading John Locke's *Essay Concerning Human Understanding* (*Essay*) and the *Two Treatises of Government* (*Treatises*). In the end, I yielded to the view that he was no longer wedded to a traditional doctrine of natural law. Instead, the foundation of both documents relies heavily on a corpuscular presupposition. Although such a claim seems rather odd, it sheds new light on the nominalism present in the *Essay* and his commitment to the freedom and equality of humanity in the *Two Treatises*.

Thus studying Locke's two chief documents, the metaphysical underpinnings needed to defend some sort of normative account, in particular a justification of natural law, are missing and give way to timid misgivings. This is especially apparent in Book III of Locke's *Essay*. Book III documents an early debate between the Scholastics that defended (roughly) Aristotelian substances as the basic constituents of the world and a new scientific ideal, which relies only on the assumption that there are atoms in motion. No doubt, Locke's emphasis in the *Essay* is broader than and nowhere as narrow as the interpretation of Locke who is merely identified as the defender of empiricism. The latter approach misses the main project Locke had in mind.

The explicit goal of Locke's *Essay*, in harmony with the *Treatises*, explores the ramifications of corpuscularism for morality, religion, political theory, and so forth. Such a claim does not represent an anomaly. Rather,

Locke's project represents the prevailing approach (as I will illustrate) taken by many of the texts published in the Modern era. Except for David Hume and Thomas Aquinas, the moderns remain largely ignored by philosophers and by contemporary legal theorists. This is unfortunate. Philosophers, especially with an analytical bent, see little or no value in the history of philosophy. Legal theorists or philosophers engaged in legal theory also, for the most part, ignore the history of philosophy including the Modern period.

One notable exception to this complaint comes from a (little known) text by the German scholar and lawyer, Heinrich A. Rommen (1897–1967): *The Natural Law: A Study in Legal and Social History and Philosophy.*[1] Rommen's text is unique, in many respects, because a large portion of the text reflects the strained relationship between the history of natural law and the attempts to justify human positive law. Of course, the uniqueness of Rommen's manuscript is not just a history of natural law. It is more than that. The value of *The Natural Law* resides in Rommen's ability to weave into the discussion (one that starts with the ancient Greeks) the historical context of each notable bygone figure, including an elucidation of the connection between authors, and when applicable, the concomitant scholarship of authors not generally discussed in the history of philosophy or in the specialized field of natural law.[2]

Rethinking and reinterpreting the Modern era and reading contemporary legal theory, prompted a modest version of legal naturalism developed in this text. I develop a legal concept I call Analytical Legal Naturalism (ALN). I spell out and partially defend ALN in the last chapter of this text. It is primarily designed to act as legal patch for "hard cases" in the same way a software patch is designed to fix a software problem.[3] Regrettably, at this point, it is unclear where my version of legal naturalism fits into the cornucopia of naturalistic viewpoints. First, my own view may be difficult to fit into the traditional categories of the legal debate because I come from an ethical background, with training primarily in ethical theory and, in particular, metaethics. Such an admission is not a trite comment because, as I will try to show, many of the methods employed by the major scholars in metaethics have application in the legal debate.

My view may be reasonably placed within what I call the legal realism debate. Thus, at one end of the debate, there are individuals whose positions establish the truth-values of legal statements in virtue of objective, mind-independent standards. Andrei Marmor, like many other scholars, describes Dworkin's view as an example of such an attempt.[4] These individuals often fall back on the view that morality, and in particular natural law, should play some sort of justification for the truth-values of legal statements.[5] Certainly, John Finnis would also fit this description.[6]

At the other end are those who may qualify as legal positivists. There are many versions of legal positivism developed and defended. For example,

Jules Coleman identifies inclusive (incorporationism) and exclusive positivism.[7] There is negative and positive positivism and what some call hard and soft positivism.[8] Added to this list are thin, simple, or weak versions of positivism as well.[9] Although there are too many positions to spell out here, it may be useful to focus on the traditional interpretation of John Austin's legal positivism as an early source for many of the later discussions reflecting on the viability of the same doctrine.[10] Of course, in the abundance of legal positivists' viewpoints, it is difficult to place Austin. Nevertheless, as Schaurer makes clear, all positivists share the same assumption, specifically that "all versions of legal positivism insist on the conceptual separation of law and morality."[11] Minimally, this applies to Austin as well.

Austin's view reflects what some call the "command theory of law"[12] or "political subjectivism." On this view, like Hobbes, it is the meta-legal view that the dictates of the sovereign authority on the legality of an action determine the truth-value of a legal action and its criminality. So, from this perspective, while it relies heavily on the desires and preferences of the legal authority, the desires and preferences become the truth-making conditions for legal statements (and from Hobbes' point of view, moral statements as well). Following Bentham, this view fits well with Austin's commitment to a nominalist outlook. Nominalism empties the world, so to speak, of any facts that may act as a deep, metaphysical account for the truth-making conditions of legal or moral statements.[13] Such a view, as I will argue, became prevalent during the Enlightenment period and was concomitant with the eventual demise of natural law theory. In light of this, where does my view fit?

ALN, as I label it, fits somewhere in between the two aforementioned views. It reflects the benefits and drawbacks of both the (broadly conceived) natural law and positivists camps. For example, on the one hand, it benefits from the legal positivist's insistence of distancing law and morality. It also avoids the drawbacks of subjectivism and making law relative to the desires and preference of a legal authority. On the other hand, it benefits from the natural law camps insistence that laws express cross-cultural and trans-historical significance. At the same time, it also avoids the downsides of relying on occult (transcendent) legal, moral, or modal concepts to establish the necessity of ALN.

To develop such a view, natural law must be eliminated and shown for what it really is, namely, *nonsense upon stilts.* Bentham was right. Such a viewpoint may fall like a bombshell in our midst. With that in mind, chapters 1–3 attempt to demonstrate the plausibility of this view. In order to support a natural law theory, the truth-conditions to make natural law claims true or false must be in place. This means that, in order to get the kind of cross-cultural significance and trans-historical significance we want from natural law, not to mention the necessity of such a perspective,[14] there must be the metaphysical machinery in place to support the truth-value of natural law claims. Chapters 1 and 2 describe such viewpoints we may expect to make such an endeavor come to fruition. Yet, in chapter 3, we shall see that natural law begins to lose its hegemonic position. This comes at the same time as the new scientific ideal reembraces the atom and atomism. As a result, nominalism, which was buried deeply in the recesses of the scholarly imagination, reemerges vigorously. It is not until the Utilitarians in the Romantic era (prodded, so to speak, by Hume), discussed in chapter 4, lay waste to this perspective and the numerous stilts used to prop up natural law. With natural law disposed of, it is only logical that legal positivism filled the void.

After this discussion, I take up John Austin (again), H. L. A. Hart, and Ronald Dworkin. The context in which I discuss and develop their views begins with a thought experiment. Briefly, the thought experiment creates a situation out of which a "hard case" emerges. The importance of the case does not turn upon any facts. Rather, a case must be adjudicated without any relevant case law or constitutional constraints to guide a decision. So, with the case in mind, spelling out the views of Austin's political subjectivism,[15] Hart's rule of recognition,[16] and Dworkin's constructive interpretivism,[17] I try to anticipate how they will handle the case and, eventually, show why their efforts fail. For example, I argue that Austin fails because of several problems to which his legal positivism falls prey, including the "Strange Legal Idea Objection" I develop. Hart's rule of recognition (which I describe as a form of foundationalism) ultimately fails to solve the problem of "hard cases" even though I try to buttress his view with a discussion of wide reflective equilibrium.[18] Finally, my focus turns to Dworkin. After aligning his view to a rather thin account of natural law, my arguments demonstrate that his reliance on natural law collapses under the weight of the lack of justification needed to support his view and the possibility of dealing with hard cases.

The final chapter represents my own attempt to deal with the phenomena of "hard cases." In this chapter, I develop ALN. As I made clear earlier, it fits in between a natural law explanation and legal positivism. In the end, I forge a new link in the chain of progress toward a legal concept designed to deal with hard cases, a concept that possesses necessity (conventionally conceived), analyticity, and known *a posteriori*. At the end of the chapter, I discuss several legal actions considered to be "hard cases." I deliberate about the familiar cases identified as hard and ones not so familiar. Perhaps the most famous case I review is *Griswold*. My arguments demonstrate that, using ALN, there is a way of dealing with the Connecticut laws without employing specious arguments for the conclusion that the U.S. Constitution implies a doctrine of privacy.

Finally, it is my hope that my relative anonymity among the legal community and in the scholarship of the philosophy of law will not deter potential readers from considering the arguments of this text. Perhaps the introduction of new blood into the discussion of "hard cases" will serve as a foil to develop a genuine step toward the illumination of such a fascinating problem.

NOTES

1. Heinrich A. Rommen, *The Natural Law: A Study in Legal and Social History and Philosophy*, trans. Thomas R. Hanley (Indianapolis, IN: Liberty Fund, 1998). Originally published in 1936.

2. Another notable exception is found in Hans Kelsen's work. For example, see Hans Kelsen, "Absolutism and Relativism in Philosophy and Politics," *American Political Science Review* 42, no. 5 (October, 1948).

3. Conceiving ALN as a legal patch is analogous to the reintroduction of the standard of undue burden by Justice Sandra Day O'Connor in her dissent to Akron v. Akron Center for Reproductive Health, 463 US 416 (1983). Later in the majority opinion of Planned Parenthood of Southeastern Pennsylvania v. Casey, 505 US 833 (1992), Justices O'Connor, Kennedy, and Souter, argue that, given the changing state of medical technology, instead of maintaining the outdated trimester approach to protecting the reproductive rights of women to obtain an abortion, state regulation (including the right to proscribe abortions except where the health of the mother is at stake) is set at the age of viability (roughly at 25 weeks gestation). Thus, prior to viability, although the state may regulate the abortion industry itself in terms of safe procedures and physician qualifications, such regulations may not place an undue burden upon a woman seeking an abortion prior to viability. The undue burden standard prior to viability became a "legal patch," in some respects, in order to constrain the states overreaching regulations it may have in the interest of potential life or the health and safety of the pregnant woman.

4. Andrei Marmor, "An Essay on The Objectivity of Law," in *Analyzing Law: New Essays in Legal Theory*, ed. Brian Bix (Oxford: Clarendon Press, 1998), 8–9.

5. On a tangential point of view, the term "morality" is often used in certain contexts as a device to indicate a place-holder for an autonomous discipline which, by its very existence, deserves recognition and authority. I argue that referring to "morality" does not guarantee any sort of epistemic warrant or justification for any theory the term "morality" might imply nor does the juxtaposition a view, legal or otherwise, with morality give the view epistemic authority.

6. John Finnis, *Natural Law and Natural Rights* (Oxford: Clarendon Press, 1980).

7. A view favored by Coleman, Leiter, and Hart. Jules L. Coleman and Brian Leiter, "Legal Positivism," in *A Companion to Philosophy of Law and Legal Theory*, 2nd ed., ed. Dennis Patterson (Chichester, West Sussex, UK: 2010), 230.

8. Jules L. Coleman, "Second Thoughts and Other First Impressions," in *Analyzing Law: New Essays in Legal Theory*, ed. Brian Bix (Oxford: Clarendon Press, 1998), 259.

9. Frederick Schauer, "Postivism Through Thick and Thin," *Analyzing Law: New Essays in Legal Theory*, ed. Brian Bix (Oxford: Clarendon Press, 1998).

10. John Austin, *The Province of Jurisprudence Determined*, ed. Wilfrid E. Rumble (Cambridge University Press, 1995).

11. Schauer, "Positivism Through Thick and Thin," 66.

12. Coleman and Leiter, "Legal Positivism," 231.

13. In order to distinguish legal positivism as a distinct viewpoint, one different and inconsistent with a natural law account, with its reliance on a deep, mind-independent set of moral facts, legal positivism, as I will elaborate later, must align itself with nominalism. Otherwise, a natural law account, one associated with Aquinas or Grotius could still be true even if legal positivism asserts political subjectivism.

14. Julie Dickson, *Evaluation and Legal Theory* (Oxford and Portland, OR: Hart Publishing, 2001), 17.

15. John Austin, *The Province of Jurisprudence Determined*, ed. Wilfrid E. Rumber (Cambridge University Press, 2001).

16. H. L. A. Hart, *The Concept of Law*, 3rd ed. (Oxford University Press, 2012).

17. Ronald Dworkin, *Taking Rights Seriously* (Cambridge, MA: Harvard University Press, 1978); Ronald Dworkin, "Natural Law Revisited," *University of Florida Law Review* 34, no. 2 (Winter, 1982); Ronald Dworkin, *Law's Empire* (The Belknap Press of Harvard University Press, 1986); Ronald Dworkin, *Freedom's Law: The Moral Reading of the American Constitution* (Cambridge, Mass: Harvard University Press, 1996).

18. Norman Daniels, "Wide Reflective Equilibrium and Theory Acceptance in Ethics," *The Journal of Philosophy* 76, no. 5 (May 1979).

Chapter One

The Ancient Greek Period (429 B.C.–180 A.D.)

INTRODUCTION

I begin with the Ancient Greek period, specifically with discussions about the metaphysical realism developed by Plato and Aristotle. After that, my focus turns to the Stoics. The goal of this discussion is to illuminate the metaphysical assumptions needed for the truth-making conditions associated with the Greek ontological outlook of the world. This is necessary for three reasons. First, the ontological outlook of Plato, Aristotle and the Stoics extends well into the seventeenth century. Second, the truth-making conditions associated with the Ancient Greeks serves as a (partial) foundation for a proto-scientific understanding of the world well into the seventeenth century. And, finally, the notion of the law of nature, initially coined by the Stoics, serves not only as the foundation for living a good life, it serves as the justification for human positive law, and eventually part of the justification for the origin of political authority.

PLATO OF ATHENS (429–347 B.C.)

To speak of the metaphysical realism developed by Plato is to refer to his ontology, to be precise, to his commitment to universals and particulars.[1] At first glance, such an outlook does not seem that complicated. For example, such a world appears to contain material entities and abstract entities. In fact, such an outlook is not so unfamiliar even from our contemporary point of view. For example, it is not difficult to imagine an individual who, on the one hand, endorses a contemporary scientific understanding of the world, namely, a viewpoint which studies protons, rocks, animals, and so forth, and who, on the other hand, accepts a realist account of propositions or numbers, i.e., nonmaterial objects grasped by the mind.

Thus, although it may be tempting to cast both viewpoints in the same mold, such a move would attribute undue insignificance to the views of Plato. In fact, Plato's ontological commitment brings forward not only the concept of abstract entities, e.g., his forms or universals, and material entities or what are simply called particulars, he also proposes a significant analysis of universals and the particulars, and a complicated relationship between both.

Thus, to deal adequately with Plato's doctrine of universals and particulars, three issues will be discussed in this text: 1. What are universals and what kind of universals are thought to exist? 2. What are particulars and is there knowledge of the particulars? Finally, what is the relationship between the universals and particulars? Here are partial answers to these questions.

Universals

Universals are described as transcendent, repeatable entities.[2] According to Michael J. Loux, this means that "numerically one and the same universal can be wholly and completely exhibited or . . . exemplified by several different spatially discontinuous particulars."[3] There are three different types of universals: properties, relations, and kinds.[4]

Properties are considered one-place or monadic universals. This means that they "are universals that particulars exemplify individually or one by one."[5] For example, imagine for a moment, two red balls sitting on a table together. On this view, each property, i.e., its color and shape, are universals. Thus, both possess the same color and shape because universals can be exemplified by several different particulars at the same time.[6]

Relations are considered polyadic or many-place universals.[7] Examples of relations include being a mile apart, being next to, or being the parent of, and so forth. On this view, the individuals in a relation exemplify that universal relation. While the examples demonstrate two-place examples, there are other relations that have more than two individuals.

Kinds are also universals. As Loux points out, kinds refer to things that belong to species and genera.[8] A species is an idea that represents a thing, which is subordinate to a more general idea or genus. A species applies to only individual things. The genus is an idea that refers to several different things, or species, and which differ in some respect. Universal kinds, minimally, help us to identify what a thing is or to identify what kind of thing it is.[9] As we will see, the notion of "kind" will play a significant role in Aristotle's metaphysics.

Particulars

As seen with universals, with particulars there is also the issue of their nature. No doubt, such an issue seems too simple to contemplate. That is, what are particulars except facts which take up space and exist in time? And yet, what may not be known—and certainly a topic partially neglected by the scholarly community—is what Plato takes the being of concrete particulars to be like. Thus, like the nature of universals above, the issue of the being of particulars raises several questions. First, what are the particulars and what are they made of? Second, how do organic particulars grow and develop? And, finally, what kind of justification or epistemic warrant do particulars possess? What knowledge, if any, can we claim about the particulars? Although I will briefly discuss the first two questions, my examination focuses mainly on the third question.

Plato's discussion of the particulars is focused primarily in the *Phaedo*, and in particular, it is part of Plato's defense of why the soul is deathless and indestructible.[10] As part of this debate, Plato compares two different ways to explain what particulars are like and how they develop. The first explanation Plato attributes to the "natural philosophers" before him. They pointed out necessary conditions as the cause of things, e.g., all the physical things necessary to be taller or shorter or to sit.[11] Unfortunately, they did not give *all the necessary conditions*, which would be the jointly sufficient cause of these things. What they failed to add was the role of the universals.[12] Any explanation of a cause that does not appeal to a form as part of the cause of something is false or incomplete. Thus, if something or someone is beautiful or tall, there is, of course, a physical story which is part of the explanation. The other part of the explanation involves the universals of the Beautiful or Tallness. In other words, the physical aspects of an organic being develop according to the dominant universal which it currently reflects or exhibits.[13] This leads to the following question: Is there knowledge of the particulars?

The last questions raises a difficult issue to make clear. It concerns Plato's doctrine of the Exclusion of Opposites. In the briefest of terms, this means that particular states of affairs,[14] while not being mutually opposed, always possess (immanent) contrary opposites, which likewise appear not to admit the opposite to that contained in themselves.[15] The main reason is that Plato's doctrine of the Exclusion of Opposites deeply impacts Plato's epistemic concerns for the particulars. It is precisely this doctrine which rules out our ability to know the particulars. In fact, what we are left with, when it comes to our knowledge of the particulars, is only the possibility of (at most) true beliefs. Here is a brief description of Plato's doctrine.

As I mentioned earlier, the Exclusion of Opposites is part of Plato's argument for the deathlessness and the indestructability of the soul.[16] The doctrine occurs roughly in the middle of Plato's argument for the soul. The argument for Opposites goes roughly like this. First, Plato makes clear that there is a relationship of opposites between universals and in this particular discussion, the focus turns to the universals of Tallness and Shortness. According to Plato, then, universal states of affairs, i.e., anything which we consider to be a universal fact, cannot tolerate its opposite. It must both retreat and withdraw or perish. So, the opposite itself can never become its own opposite. For example, the form of Tallness can never become the form of Shortness.[17] The second step is a little more complicated. It concerns Plato's application of the discussion of the particulars. Initially, Plato talks briefly about this part. Right after that, Socrates' companions demand a better explanation. I will discuss both but spend the most time on Plato's extended discussion.

Initially, because the point seems so obvious to Socrates, he conflates the two discussions. Like the intolerance between universals which are opposite (Tallness and Shortness), Plato explains that the "tallness in us" will never tolerate the short. Additionally, because (presumably) Socrates was short, he adds "I admit and endure shortness and still remain the same person and am this short man."[18] Thus, the implication is that while he was growing, at some point, he would never become any taller than he was then. He would remain the same height until his death. In other words, the shortness in him will never be willing to become the tall. Unfortunately, Cebes' skepticism remains in place and a better reason is demanded.

Particulars exist because of two different reasons. First, there is the physical aspect of a particular or its matter. For example, human individuals have a physical aspect, i.e., the matter. Second, there are aspects of existence of human individuals we attribute to universals. Plato makes clear that the growth and the attributes human individuals possess (or will come to possess), as do all organic beings, are guided by the way they participate in the forms.[19] So, as Plato implies, a single, individual object will exhibit clusters of contrary forms, which are not the forms themselves, but reflect the forms it exhibits.[20] Therefore, the change an object may go undergo is a story about the approach of a transcendent form and the change it causes in a physical characteristic, which reflects or is contrary to that form.

There is one last point to make which is controversial. Each object, and in this case, e.g., a human individual, will not only exhibit clusters of universals, as Socrates suggests that he reflects the universal form of shortness, but each object will exhibit or reflect opposite universals. If this is correct, then what it means is that, sticking to Socrates' comment, he reflects or exhibits the opposite forms of Tallness and Shortness at the same time. Again, this is not taken to mean that Socrates possesses the opposite forms at the same time. On the contrary, he simultaneous exhibits (contrary) physical states which reflect the forms. Because they are physical states, they are not opposites. Rather, they are causal states of the individual in question, which are connected (in some way) to the transcendent forms they reflect. Thus, on the occasion that a physical change takes place, say, a (teenage) boy who is short and who is growing taller, the young male will grow taller as the form of Tallness approaches while the form of the Short will cause the physical attributes which reflect it to retreat. This will continue until he stops growing and, as Socrates remarks, will admit and remain his height.[21]

Although this may not be apparent, this analysis become the basis for why Plato denies knowledge of the particulars. Here is what I mean. Normally, the explanation is that Plato accepts Heraclitus' notion of change, which asserts that the world is constantly in a state of (random and unpredictable) flux that occurs in the sensory world and to the sensory world. So, because of the flux of the particulars and because, for Plato, knowledge implies the impossibility of error, our sense perception will not yield knowledge of the particulars. This is because we cannot have knowledge of the things that change. While plausible, this viewpoint is problematic for two reasons. First, it ignores the role of the *logos* in Heraclitus' fragments. Second, it also ignores the kind of change Plato discusses in his dialogues, and in particular, in the *Phaedo*. I will begin by briefly discussing the former.

The enigmas and puzzles of the fragments of Heraclitus often do not lend themselves to the serious attention they really deserve. While there is substantial evidence of the notion of flux and change in the fragments, there is also no less evidence for the notion of *logos* in the fragments. This means that the *logos* will give us, as Patricia Curd makes clear, an understanding of the way things really are.[22] So, briefly, what does Curd take to be the relationship between the *logos* (the eternal, unchanging principle) and the changing and becoming nature of the world?

On the one hand, the becoming of the world is grasped by the *logos*. It reveals that change is constant and such change occasions multiplicity and diversity.[23] Second, the grasping of the *logos* also reveals something important about the change in the world: "The truth that is grasped asserts that the elements of the sensible world together are a diversity that can be and are unified, and that each object in the world is itself both a converging unity and a diverging plurality."[24] Therefore, what emerges from the fragments (and certainly anticipates Aristotle's view of the particulars), demonstrates something which distances Heraclitus from Plato. That is (unlike Plato), the fragments paint a picture of the attempt to bridge the gap between what is known about the *logos* and how the *logos* opens the door to what can be known through sense perception.

On the other hand, after distancing Plato from Heraclitus, it is important to make clear why Plato denies knowledge from sense perception. Part of the discussion occurs above, but the crucial passage which is often overlooked, is the following: "There is a further point . . . about these opposites: between each of those pairs of opposites there are two processes: from the one to the other and then again from the other to the first; between the larger and the smaller there is increase and decrease, and we call the one increasing and the other decreasing."[25] This means that, as far as all things are concerned, there is a physical process of change (or becoming) from one contrary state to another, both of which reflect or exhibit opposite universals. So, the change (unlike the unpredictable change erroneously associated with Heraclitus) articulated by Plato is localized in the causal process between the contrary states which reflect or exhibit polar opposite universals.

What is the Relationship between the Universals and Particulars?

The last topic to address is the relationship between the universals and the particulars. This analysis is built from the first two discussions above. Unfortunately, the relationship talked about here constitutes a trying ordeal, a treatment which, in many ways, defies a precise analysis. Nevertheless, there have been many attempts to spell out this relationship. For example, as Loux indicates, the relationship may be expressed in the following way: "What is being proposed here is a general schema for explaining attribute agreement."[26] So, if we suppose that there are a number of objects, which possess the same attribute, say, the color red, then there is form of Redness, which each red object is in a relationship with. The claim is that it is in virtue of standing in the relationship to the form of Redness, each object agrees in attribute by all being red.

The schema casts an informing light upon the relationship between Plato's universals and particulars. For example, (applying Loux' excellent insights) if we suppose (again) that there is the universal form of Redness, and a group of red objects, we may spell out the relationship between Plato's universals and particulars. For example, each particular red object agrees in attribute because they all *instantiate* the universal idea of Redness. Colors aside, the discussion also allows us to make more important complex statements, statements relevant to the goals of the text.

Again, if we suppose that there is the form of Justice and there are several individuals who we consider to be just individuals, then we may state that these individuals are just in virtue of *instantiating* the universal form of Justice. Be that as it may, there is an important qualification. Whereas objects may exhibit perceptible properties like color, size, shape, and so forth, justice does not qualify as a perceptible attribute. Thus, in the case of moral attributes, we are faced with the daunting question of the verification of whether an individual is just or not. Although it would take too much time to develop an adequate response to this issue (at least for now), one way to address this point is to develop an account of the inference to the best explanation. Such an account is developed against the backdrop of a contemporary debate between Gilbert Harman and Nicholas L. Sturgeon.[27]

Assuming that the verification problem can be (partially) solved, there is the issue of the truth-value of *aretaic* statements. Here is what I mean. The English language contains within it the ability to make simple statements of fact. These sentences, expressed with a subject and a modifying predicate, are in the present tense, declarative mood or the past tense, declarative mood. These sentences (or propositions) are thought to be the "bearers of truth" because we can assign the truth-value of "T" or "F" to these and only these sentences. This means that if a sentence is true, then it must *mirror* a non-linguistic reality or it must *mirror* the way the world is (or be consistent with other statements that mirror the world).[28]

From Plato's point of view, in order for a sentence to be true, or to mirror the way the world is, two things must be true: the predicate must express something true about the subject, and the subject *and* the predicate must make contact with the world by referring to or picking out an object. Let me illustrate this point with the subject-predicate statement "John R. is courageous." Suppose, then, there exists a person named John R. In order for the sentence to be true, two things must be in place. First, John R. must be courageous, and second, the terms "John R." and "courageous" must make contact with the world. In other words, according to the metaphysical realist, John R. must exist, there must exist the universal form of Courage, and the sentence must be true of John R.[29] This is the only way a sentence can be true.[30] The same story must apply equally to sentences which express other virtues endorsed by metaphysical realists. Again, why this discussion is important will be made apparent during the Modern era. This is so because Plato's metaphysical realism (among others) is used as a model for some scholars to justify moral claims including the law of nature.

ARISTOTLE OF STAGIRA (384–322 B.C.)

Although Plato never discusses the law of nature, what we glean from his writings is a deep account of the truth-making conditions for metaphysical and moral claims. Aristotle, as we shall see, does not discuss the law of nature either.[31] Nevertheless, Aristotle offers an account of the nature of reality, which is more sophisticated and intuitive than Plato's account. In fact, like Plato's moral viewpoint, Aristotle's ontological account serves as the foundation of his moral views in the *Nicomachean Ethics*. Unfortunately, this point is often overlooked. The problem is that, in many ways, the text of the *Nicomachean Ethics* does not easily lend itself to the ontological discussions we find in, say, Aristotle's *Physics* or *Metaphysics*. This is unfortunate, because nothing could be further from the truth. Part of the purpose of this section is to make this connection clear.

It follows that, to understand Aristotle's moral viewpoint, we must discuss his standpoint of particulars and universals.[32] I will begin with the former. Following Loux, Aristotle's theory of particulars may be readily understood by positioning it between two different and competing metaphysical theories: the bundle theory and the substratum theory. I will begin by discussing both theories. After that, I will discuss Aristotle's theory.[33]

Particulars

The bundle theory attempts to defend a descriptive account of concrete particulars (e.g., concrete humans, dogs, cats, trees, and so forth). According to the bundle theory, then, particular objects are made up of particular properties. In addition, there is no underlying substratum that the properties depend upon. On the contrary, in the bundle theory, particular objects are just clusters or "bundles" of *its* own properties.[34] Loux describes the bundle theory in the following way: "Bundle theorists are, we might say, *ultraessentialists*: every attribute associated with a concrete object is essential to it."[35] This means that the properties an object possesses are constituted exclusively in themselves.

Like the bundle theory, the substratum theory also attempts to give an account of what particular objects are like. It differs from the former point of view, however, to a certain extent. Although this view defends the existence of properties, the properties depend upon the existence of a substratum (or substructure), which exists independently of the properties it possesses. In contrast to the former theory, Loux calls this the *antiessentialist* theory. On this model, "nothing is essential to the literal bearers of attributes."[36] This description means that no matter what property of an object can be picked out, it will always be extrinsic to the substratum and, therefore, always incidental or accidental to the substratum. As D. M. Armstrong also explains: "These properties are rather naturally taken to be things it merely has."[37]

In contrast to both of these theories is the Aristotelian theory. Against the bundle theorist, the Aristotelian argues that not every property that an object possesses is essential. Against the substratum theory, an Aristotelian argues that not every property is accidental. So, for the Aristotelian, although particulars possess properties, some of these properties are essential to the object and some are incidental to it.[38]

Against both views, the Aristotelians argue that the particulars are basic or irreducibly fundamental entities.[39] This means that if anything counts as a living being, it is an entity that cannot be reduced to entities that are more basic. This theory is contrary to the substratum theory because particulars are reducible to something more basic than its properties. It is also contrary to the bundle theory for much the same reason. Particulars, according to the bundle theory, are, in a sense, built out of the properties from which an object is constituted. However, contrary to the bundle theory, the Aristotelians argue that none of the properties that are attributable to a particular object make sense from outside of the framework of the material particulars that they are supposed to generate.[40]

Universals

Along with particulars, like Plato, Aristotle's metaphysics contains universals including the three different types of universals—properties, relations, and kinds. Such a claim, though perfectly clear in Plato's dialogues, may not be plain to every eye. If it is true that Aristotle's metaphysics contains an account of universals, what evidence is there to warrant such a claim? To defend this point, I discuss passages in Aristotle's *Metaphysics* and, perhaps to the surprise of many scholars, an important passage often overlooked in Aristotle's *Nicomachean Ethics*.

Although there is a striking parallel between Plato and Aristotle's metaphysics, there is an undeniable difference between Plato's and Aristotle's account of kinds. As I pointed out earlier, from Aristotle's point of view, particular things found in the world have different types of properties, some are essential and others are accidental. The essential properties of, say, an organic being, mark it out as a kind of thing. So, while there may be many different looking humans—Caucasians, Africans, Asians, and so forth—each individual human possesses an essential property that makes it a human being and not a dog, geranium, or an oak tree. Again, for Aristotle, that property is the possession of rationality. For animals, it is sense perception, and for plants, it is growth and nutrition.[41] The notion of an essential property leads us to Aristotle's concept of essences.

Essences

Associated with the concept of kind is the notion of *essence*.[42] As I understand Aristotle, and as Loux makes clear, the transcendent universal kinds furnish the (corresponding) immanent essences of concrete particulars. Loux has an interesting metaphorical way of understanding this concept: "The kinds under which concrete objects fall are ontological 'cookie cutters.' They go around the universe, so to speak, partitioning it into the discrete particulars that are their instances. They cut the world up into individual human beings, individual dogs, individual oak trees, and the like."[43]

Individual human beings, dogs, plants, etc., then, in Aristotle's view, are furnished with immanent essences (the Scholatics often refer to them as substantial forms), and it is by means of these essences that concrete particulars are characterized.[44] Before I move on to discuss the normative element associated with essences, there is an important connection between the concept of essence and Aristotle's discussion of the four causes in the *Physics*.[45]

We come now to an important question. If it is true that a concrete particular is characterized by its immanent essence, what can we learn about a concrete particular from its essence? There are, at least, two things. First, as Loux points out, the essence provides us "with principles for identifying, distinguishing, and counting objects."[46] Such principles are made possible by the essential properties associated with the essence. Of the four causes discussed in the *Physics*, the essence is the formal cause. The formal cause provides the definition (the account or *logos*) of organic beings. That is, if something qualifies as a dog, then it will (minimally) have a snout and non-retractile claws. To this, the essence provides us with how things actually behave and grow.[47] This means that when we understand the essence, we also understand its function.

Unexpectedly, the essence of a concrete particular also provides something else. In addition to the illumination of various descriptive aspects of the particular object mentioned, the essence also provides a normative standard for evaluating the behavior of the concrete object. To sum up, the crucial point is this: the essence tells us not merely how a particular thing acts and develops, it also provides us a normative element, i.e., it tells us how a particular object *should* act or *should* develop.[48]

A qualifying point is necessary. Again, as I understand Aristotle, we cannot learn how an object *should* act or *should* develop just by looking at its essence or formal cause. The reason is that contained within the essence is the recipe, so to speak, of how an object will grow. Furthermore, it will grow into whatever it is supposed to be (its final cause), regardless of whether it is properly trained according to its normative element. Thus, within the group of each kind, whether we are talking about human beings, dogs, or trees, there will exist various examples of individuals that can be placed on a continuum or a scale that reflects which object is closer to or further from what it should become.[49] If this is true, then how do we know what the scale is for each different kind? The answer lies in understanding the Good of each kind, so I will now turn to that discussion.

The Good

Again, as I discussed earlier, Aristotle's account of the Good is contained in the *Nicomachean Ethics*.[50] The breadth and the depth of the topics he discusses in the document are astounding; unfortunately, after reading his work, if one is not careful, one may come away with the view that this work is disconnected from his views in the *Metaphysics*. Nothing could be further from the truth. Nevertheless, this is the question we are to explore now.

Aristotle begins this discussion with his commitment to the existence of the Good. He argues that whatever the Good truly is, most people believe that it is happiness (*eudaimonia*). And yet, although there is agreement about what the Good is, the issue of how to understand happiness is another matter. Some argue that it is pleasure, others argue that is tied to virtue or honor. Still others argue that it is study (or reflection) or in the making of money. Again, Aristotle rules out all but study (*theoria*).[51]

Next, he connects the Good to the human function. His argument, in short, is that the function of an object is the *same in kind* as the function of an object that is excellent. The implication, then, for humans is that the Good turns out to be living a life of not just reasoning but a life of *reasoning well* (*orthos logos*).[52]

But now the question is this: How do the *virtues* fit into this discussion? The notion of virtue is tied to the conception of the Good. In fact, as Aristotle points out, the virtues are (relative to) those character traits that promote the attainment of the good life, i.e., a life that reflects or exhibits the Good.[53] But how are we supposed to understand this point? Unfortunately, the exact narrative of this point is too complicated and too long for this text. Nevertheless, this much can be indicated. Like the Good, virtue is connected closely to our function. Indeed, as Aristotle makes clear, virtue makes a human being good by making him perform his function well.[54] But why? The reason is that when virtue is added to one's function (in terms of teaching and habituation), it contributes to the individual's ability to reflect the Good, or reason well. Let me make this point a little clearer.

According to Aristotle, when an individual is trained according to the standard that the Good provides, which includes training to calculate well (*logistikon*) about practical matters (*prakton*), he will be taught at least two different ways of reason.[55] (Again, a human will grow to reason, but without the proper training, i.e., without the virtues added to a natural ability to reason, a human being will not learn how to reason well in Aristotle's sense.) First, it causes a human being to find the "mean" or the middle of an action, if it admits one. That is, it causes him to find the middle ground between the excessive aspects of an action and the deficient aspects of an action.[56] Second, it causes him to keep the right relationship between feelings and reason.[57] The relationship spoken of here is one metaphorically related to that of a master and slave. Reason is master and one's feelings are to be trained to listen to *and* to agree with reason. Thus, adding virtue to one's function causes a human being to attain the Good and as a result become a good or virtuous person.

Although it may not be apparent, we are now in a position to connect Aristotle's metaphysical outlook to his virtue theory. The underlying line of thought, in brief, is as follows. As I discussed earlier, according to Aristotle, every living substance, whether plant, animal, or human, has an essence, which has been, in a sense, brought about by a universal kind. This essence does a number of things for us. Minimally, it provides us with a way of identifying, distinguishing, and counting objects.[58]

The most important concept is the following. The essence determines (or contains within it) the function of the object. But what exactly does this mean? There are two conclusions. First, associated with the function of an object is its distinctive natural goal or *telos*. By understanding the *telos* of a substance, we understand how it actually will act. For example, in the case of plants, the function is growth and nutrition. In the case of animals, the function is sense perception. And the same reasoning applies equally to humans. The function of a human is to live a life of reason and study. Second, by understanding the distinctive natural *telos* of a substance, we are provided, at the same time, a standard for evaluating its activity and development. This statement means that the function also acts as the basis for our understanding the Good for each substance because the Good of each is tied to its function.[59]

THE STOICS (344 B.C.–180 A.D.)

The last group of ancient Greeks to discuss are known as the Stoics. Although this movement is attributed to Zeno of Citium (333–261 B.C.), later members of the Stoa made significant contributions to the Stoic outlook. This has led to the consequence that there appears to be no single spokesperson who represents the official stance of the Stoics. There are, however, some common characteristics, which Diogenes Laertius and Joannes Stobaeus document, and it is their views from which I will heavily borrow.[60]

Although the Stoics present their viewpoint in a complex mixture of physics, logic and ethics,[61] my focus will be on the ethical aspect of their outlook. The reason is that the Stoics bring into sharp focus the notion of the law of nature. This is important because the law of nature becomes the foundation of human law in the Scholastic Period and even in the early Enlightenment period, as I shall discuss shortly.

Like Plato and Aristotle, the Good is happiness. The Good, though, is defined in a different way. Additionally, the virtues are the key center in ethics for the Stoics. Following closely to Plato instead of Aristotle, they emphasize four primary virtues: prudence, temperance, courage and justice.[62] These states are also relative to and determined by what they take to be the Good, which is defined as nature:

> The goal of all these virtues is to live consistently with nature. Each one enables a human being to achieve this [goal] in his own way; for [a human] has from nature inclinations to discover what is appropriate and to stabilized his impulses and to stand firm and to distribute [fairly]. And each of the virtues

> does what is consonant [with these inclinations] and does its own job, thus enabling a human being to live consistently with nature.[63]

This quote is important in many ways. First, it identifies the Good, which is *nature* (even though ambiguous). Next, reminiscent of Aristotle, this quote aligns itself with the emphasis on the agent-relativity of achieving the Good. This means that each human being must achieve this goal in his own way. Additionally, in the spirit of Aristotle's outlook, this text identifies a set of "natural inclinations" needed to "stabilize his impulses." Of course, this is tricky to spell out. Obviously, Aristotle describes humans as political animals. This means that Aristotle was convinced that humans have a natural inclination to live together, but beyond that, he is silent. The Stoics, at least from this quote, appear to be committed to a larger set of natural inclinations each corresponding to the primary virtues. This commits an error, which Aristotle makes clear, that we are not born with any natural inclination to be virtuous. The virtues must be habituated and taught from a very young age. Nevertheless, the Stoics open up a door that will not be closed until the late eighteen hundreds: The natural law doctrine is associated with a set of natural dispositions (something akin later to innate ideas), which act (to some authors) as the (partial) epistemic foundation for our knowledge of the natural law. Moreover, with the proper training of these dispositions, it is possible to train our desires or impulses. This is, of course, consistent with Plato and Aristotle because without the proper command over our desires, we cannot achieve the Good. Finally, with the proper training of our inclinations and the due command over our desires, we can hope to become virtuous and to live according to nature.

Still, the question remains: If Nature is the Good, what does it mean to live according to Nature? Fortunately, Stobaeus gives a nice summary of some of the different viewpoints taken by the Stoics: "Zeno defined the goal thus: 'living in agreement'. This means living according to a single and consonant rational principle since those who live in conflict are unhappy."[64] Zeno's followers modified his viewpoint and added their own interpretations:

> For Cleanthes, who first inherited [the leadership of] his school, added 'with nature' and defined it thus: 'the goal is living in agreement with nature'. Chrysippus wanted to make this clearer and expressed it in this way: 'to live according to experience of the things which happen by nature'. And Diogenes: 'to be reasonable in the selection and rejection of natural things'. And Archedemus: 'to live completing all the appropriate acts'. And Antipater: 'to live invariably selecting natural things and rejecting unnatural things'. He often defined it thus as well: 'invariably and unswervingly to do everything in one's power for the attainment of the principal natural things'.[65]

Except for Zeno and Archedemus' outlook, the Stoics mentioned, like Aristotle, are committed to an objective principle of morality found in nature. Unfortunately, it is not clear how to make the jump from nature to the primary four virtues: prudence, temperance, courage and justice. In fact, there is something counterintuitive about this position, and seriously so. Here is what I mean: What part of nature exemplifies the different virtues? I do not know if this question can be adequately answered.

This much can be clarified by Diogenes Laertius, living in agreement with nature means living according to virtue. This means that the world has been arranged by Zeus to harmonize with a set of predispositions found in the nature of human beings.[66] Humans, who use right reason, will live according to this objective law of nature, and consequently, will develop the four virtues, which represents a harmonization between the way the world is arranged (i.e., the Good) and the immanent dispositions found in human nature.[67] For example, if we suppose, as the Stoics do, that "prudence is the knowledge of which things are good and bad and neither [and] courage is knowledge of which things are to be chosen and avoided and neither,"[68] then following the good using right reason will develop the dispositions into the virtues. So, the gap between what nature is like and the four virtues rests on the foundation of the dispositions found in the minds (or souls) of humans. The virtues, it must be noted, are pursued for their own sake. That is, there is no fear or hope for any extrinsic considerations.

There are two more points to discuss, points which put the Stoics at odds with the Aristotelians. First, the Stoics take the view that individuals are either virtuous or vicious, *but not both.*[69] This is an interesting position to take. It indicates that unless an individual exhibits the four primary virtues, she is base. Given the impulse to see life in black-and-white terms, such a viewpoint seems plausible. But does not such a position seem counterintuitive, and seriously so? I think it does. Here is an explanation why.

Aristotle understands that it is possible to become virtuous despite the fact that he makes it virtually impossible for most people to do so.[70] Nevertheless, he argues that there are individuals struggling to be virtuous who do not qualify as base. For example, there are the continent (*enkrates*) and the incontinent (*akrates*) individuals. In the simplest of terms, the former are individuals whose appetites struggle with doing the right thing. Nevertheless, because the individual has control over his appetites, they eventually "listen" to the instruction of reason. The latter individuals are different. His appetites not only struggle with doing the right thing, the individual eventually gives in to the appetites, and commits a base action.[71] Fortunately, for the latter individual, there is a sense of shame that follows which sets up a form of cognitive dissonance. So, while there are individuals who struggle to follow right reason and who are not virtuous in the narrow sense of the term, they are not vicious. On the contrary, according to Aristotle, only the intemperate (*akolasia*) individual is vicious in the narrow sense of the term. For example, while every incontinent is prone to regret, the intemperate feels no sense of shame or regret.[72]

The second point follows on the heels of the last point. Unlike the Aristotelians, the Stoics imply that it is possible for any individual, at any stage of moral development, to become virtuous. There are three points to mention. First, according to Aristotle, the preconditions for virtue, especially the conditions that we do not control, make it virtually impossible for anyone to become virtuous.[73] The same conditions are missing and virtually irrelevant in the viewpoint of the Stoics. Second, according to Aristotle, although there are intemperate individuals in Aristotle's outlook, individuals described as "incurable," and incapable of being incontinent, let alone virtuous, the texts of the Stoics imply that no such individual exists. In other words, there is hope for even the worst individual. Such a view, of course, anticipates the New Testament authors who, in the light of free will, will argue that the worst sinner, while alive, always has the opportunity to change his ways. Third, such a view represents a puzzle. If it is possible to become virtuous, then this seems to imply that as I practice to become virtuous, i.e., making moral progress to become a better person, I am still considered a base or vicious person until I become virtuous. Such a view sounds morally odd and counterintuitive. Why is this so?

The reason for this bifurcation is elusive. On the one hand, such a position sounds like a false dilemma: either you are morally perfect or you are not. In fact, that is the view attributed to the Stoics. If the Stoic view is a false dilemma, which it may turn out to be, why did they not consider other alternatives (as Aristotle did) between being virtuous and vicious? On the other hand, why did they think that, *contra* Aristotle, becoming morally perfect is attainable during one's lifetime? Both questions raise the fascination of the inscrutable.

Of the former question, I can only speculate. Perhaps there is an element of Zeus' participation in this discussion, which predates the early Christian church. That is, in the New Testament documents, there is a tendency to bifurcate people into the saved and unsaved (or damned if one follows Calvinism). The split is explained by the *ordo salutis* or the order of salvation. On this view, especially in Protestant doctrine, salvation is a gift of God. In other words, no one can capture a saving faith of grace without God saving him or her first.[74] Such a doctrine may explain (even if this is not true) why the Stoics argue such a doctrine. Perhaps there is redeeming feature implemented by Zeus. Although the evidence is extremely sketchy, and I am reluctant to attribute any view to characterize the Stoa, Cleanthes writes the following: "Lead me, O Zeus, and you O Fate, to whatever place you have assigned me; I shall follow without reluctance, and if I am not willing to because I have become a bad man, nevertheless I will follow."[75] Perhaps,

Cleanthes is suggesting such a viewpoint assigned to Zeus. It is unclear to me if this is really the case. Nevertheless, the Christian New Testament seems to echo such a bifurcation between the good and evil.

The other point of perfection is inscrutable. As far as I can tell, the (majority of) Stoics argue that moral perfection is attainable during our lifetime. *Contra* Aristotle, this perfection is also attainable apart from the *polis*.[76] Although I am uncertain of this, perhaps what the Stoics mean is a kind of spiritual perfection, viz., a kind of judgment pronounced by Zeus. In other words, if Zeus participates in our moral development, perhaps our initiation is due to Zeus' influence, and once initiated, declared spiritually perfect.

CONCLUSION

To sum up this chapter. In order to understand the development of natural law later in the works of Aquinas, Grotius, and the Enlightenment authors, it is important to understand the viewpoints of (at least) Plato, Aristotle, and the Stoics. The main reason is that the metaphysical underpinnings, or what I call the metaphysical machinery of the truth-making conditions for the law of nature, is brought forward for a short period. All that being said, as the new science ideal with its emphasis on the atom emerges, the very same metaphysical machinery is rejected. As a result, what we see later is a deep reliance on the new science ideal in the legal community.

NOTES

1. *Plato: Complete Works*, ed. John M. Cooper, trans. G. M. A. Grube (Indianapolis and Cambridge: Hackett Publishing Company, 1997). Unless otherwise indicated, the references and quotes to Plato and his dialogues are from the Cooper edition. My reference to a passage within the Platonic corpus will use the traditional Stephanus numbers and letters found in the margins of Plato's text.

2. Plato discusses his view of universals throughout his dialogues. The initial use of the notion of universal, e.g., *eidos* and *idea*, in the early dialogues (e.g., *Euthyphro*), referred to characteristics that similar things shared. So, as Grube makes clear, the later technical sense of the transcendental nature of *eidos* did not emerge until the later dialogues. G. M. A. Grube, *Plato's Thought* (Indianapolis, IN: Hackett Publishing Co., Inc., 1980), 9; 292. The later transcendental nature of *eidos* is apparent in several places. Transcendental universals are specifically discussed in the *Phaedo* in his discussion of the nature of the soul. Plato, *Phaedo*, 100b–107a. Another obvious section occurs in the *Parmenides*. Plato, *Parmendes*, 130c. This section discusses the relationship between the forms and particulars. The discussion is quite long and convoluted. Another dialogue dedicated to a discussion of the forms is in *Philebus*. Although the discussion is mainly directed at the role of pleasure and knowledge as part of the good life, i.e., there are many different varieties of each, there is unity behind each which resolves the question of which should be pursued for its own sake. Plato, *Philebus*, 13e. See also Terrance Irwin, *Plato Ethics* (Oxford University Press, 1995), 318–338. Irwin discusses the same passages.

Of course, Plato's unrivaled discussion occurs in the *Republic*. Part of the context for the discussion concerns the education the guardians of Plato's Republic will receive. Their education must be directed toward understanding the Form of the Good. The Myth of the Sun is the first discussion. It is described by Plato as the "offspring of the Good" because it points to what the Form of the Good is like: "What the good itself is in the intelligible realm, in relation to understanding and intelligible things, the sun is in the visible realm, in relation to sight and visible things." Plato, *Republic*, 508c. Directly after this, the analogy is explained: When the sun illuminates objects in the world, we see clearly. Additionally, when night approaches, our vision turns shadowy. In the same way, when our soul focuses on something illuminated by truth and what is, it becomes perfectly understandable. Unfortunately, when we focus on the objects not illuminated by truth, our beliefs become very vague and perfectly unconvincing. Ibid., 508de. In the end, Plato writes: "So, what gives truth to the things known and the power to know to the knower is the Form of the Good. And though it is the cause of knowledge and truth, it is also an object of knowledge." Ibid., 508e. cf. Grube, *Plato's Thought*, 23–24.

The Divided Line is the next analogy and an offspring of the Form of the Good. There are four conditions in the soul corresponding to the four subsections of the line: The first half of the line concerns the cognitive states concerned with the particulars. The first part of the line (and the lowest cognitive state) is designated as the imagination (*eikasia*) which points to shadows or images of particular things. Ibid., 509e. Grube adds that this is where Plato might also place the products of fine arts. Grube, *Plato's Thought*, 25 and 27. The second part is our awareness of the objects themselves and our concomitant beliefs (*pistis*) about them. Plato, *Republic*, 510a. Although the first half of the line is dedicated to the world of appearances, the second half of the line is dedicated to the world of the forms and reality. The third part of the line focus on our ability to generate hypothesis about the common characteristics from the assemblages of images of particular objects. Although our cognitive state of thought (*dianoia*) gives us ideas of the (lower) forms of the objects in the first half of the line, we are no closer to the idea of the (higher) forms or the Form of the Good. The lower half of the higher section still uses images of the realities of the highest level. Grube explains that, at this level, the mathematician may use the images of triangle to study geometry. Unfortunately, to study only the images of triangles misses the mathematical reality in which geometrical figures have their being in. Grube, *Plato's Thought*, 25. The highest level of knowledge is the understanding or intelligence (*noesis*). According to Plato, reaching this level gives us "the unhypothetical first principle of everything." Such knowledge, if attainable, gives us a complete knowledge of the (lower) forms without anything visible at all. Plato, *Republic*, 511b.

The last analogy is Plato's vision of the Cave. It is the most famous allegory of the three. Ibid., 514a–518c. The Cave combines both the Sun and the Line analogies. Unfortunately, it is too complex to discuss in detail. Nevertheless, this much can be stated with evidential import. As the Divided Line makes clear, the Cave analogy represents two different cognitive states of awareness, i.e., the cognitive states associated with appearances and knowledge. The former is represented by the visions within the cave, viz., images and beliefs. The latter discloses the intellectual awareness of the realm of the lower forms and the higher form especially when the prisoner of the cave emerges and perceives reality for the first time. Unlike the shadows of the cave, the world outside of the cave is illuminated by the sun. Ultimately, the prisoner comes to understand the Form of the Good and the source of all knowledge. For an excellent discussion of all three myths, see Irwin, *Plato's Ethics*, 271–280.

3. Michael J. Loux, *Metaphysics: A Contemporary Introduction*, 2nd ed. (London and New York: Routledge, 1998), 23. Plato illustrates this view in the *Phaedo*. For example, Socrates begins his defense of the nature of the soul by assuming that universals exist. cf. Grube, *Plato's Thought*, 293. There is, for example, a Beautiful, a Good, and a Great. Plato, *Phaedo*, 100b. To explain what this means, Socrates develops the universal idea of the Beautiful. Ibid., 100c. So, the question he poses to Cebes is this: Why are things in the world beautiful? One might think that the answer has to do only with the color or shape. Ibid. However, Socrates makes clear (and Cebes agrees) that things are beautiful because they "share" in the Beautiful. Or, in other words, "all beautiful things are beautiful by the Beautiful." Plato, *Phaedo*, 100d. Thus, on the assumption that there are spatially disconnected beautiful things, they are all beautiful (at the same time) because they all share in the very same universal form of the Beautiful. The same doctrine is also brought up by Plato in *Philebus*, 15b,c. For problems associated with the

multiple location of universals, see D. M. Armstrong, *Universals: An Opinionated Introduction* (Boulder, CO: Westview Press, 1989), 98–99.

4. Mentioning different types of universals is important to note because the empiricists use the same terms in the Enlightenment period even though the same terms lack the meanings supplied by Plato and Aristotle. Part of the Enlightenment project included coopting the same terms used by the Scholastics and recast them from a purely empirical viewpoint.

5. Loux, *Metaphysics*, 23.

6. My example is not too farfetched. For example, as Grube points out, there are forms, which correspond to all general predicates. Not only that, but there is a form of Evil and even a form of Bed in Plato's dialogues. Grube, *Plato's Thought*, 30.

7. Loux, *Methaphysics*, 23.

8. Ibid., 23–24. cf. Plato, *Parmenides*, 129c. The Greek term in the *Parmenides* is *genos*. See note 6, 363.

9. Ibid., 27.

10. Plato, *Phaedo*, 96a–105c. Plato's specific discussion for the deathlessness and the indestructability of the soul begins 105d and ends roughly at 107a.

11. Ibid., 96a–97b.

12. Ibid., 100b.

13. Ibid., 100c. The specific text in question reads: "And that it is through Bigness that big things are big and the bigger are bigger, and that smaller things are made smaller by Smallness?—Yes."

14. According to Armstrong, states of affairs (from a metaphysical realist viewpoint), sometimes referred to facts, pick out particulars which exhibit monadic or polyadic universals, and so forth. In particular, as Armstrong makes clear, states of affairs bear a relationship to statements by acting as the truth-making conditions for statements. See Armstrong, *Universals: An Opinionated Introduction*, 88–89. Loux also adds that states of affairs refer to particulars (or situations) which necessarily obtain or fail to obtain. In fact, Platonists will insist that states of affairs exists eternally or necessarily. Loux, *Metaphysics*, 166–67.

15. Plato, *Phaedo*, 103b–105c. This doctrine is also defended by F. C. White, "The Compresence of Opposites in *Phaedo* 102," *The Classical Quarterly* 27, no. 2 (1977): 303–311. The doctrine that concrete things are the bearers of contrary opposities is also discussed in *Parmenides*, 129a–135c.

16. Plato's argument for his view of the soul is a response to Cebes' hypothesis that the soul eventually wears out. Plato, *Phaedo*, 87a–88b). Cebes argues that although the soul is strong enough to survive the death of many bodies, it is still possible that the soul is damage by its many births, and eventually destroyed in one of the deaths. Thus, unless we can prove that the soul is immortal, a man about to die must fear for his soul, and thus anyone who faces death with confidence is foolish.

17. Plato, *Phaedo*, 102e.

18. Ibid.

19. Ibid., 104c: "What I want to make clear is this: not only do those opposites not admit each other, but this is also true of those things which, while not being opposite to each other yet always contain the opposites, and it seems that these do not admit the Form which is opposite to that which is in them; when it approaches them, they either perish or give way."

20. See White's discussion of the same point: White, "The Compresence of Opposites in *Phaedo* 102," 305.

21. I will discuss the issue of the process momentarily which occurs in the *Phaedo*, 70d–71e. White, "The Compresence of Opposites in *Phaedo* 102," 309.

22. Patricia Curd, "Knowledge and Unity in Heraclitus," *Monist: An International Quarterly Journal of General Philosophical Inquiry* 74, no. 4 (October 1991): 537.

23. Ibid., 538.

24. Ibid., 538–39.

25. Plato, *Phaedo*, 71b. This point is not brought up at all in White's article quoted above.

26. Loux, *Metaphysics*, 22.

27. Gilbert Harman, "Ethics and Observation," in *Essays on Moral Realism*, ed. Geoffrey Sayre-McCord (Ithaca and London: Cornell University Press), 119–124 and Nicholas L. Stur-

geon, "Moral Explanations," in *Essays on Moral Realism*, ed. Georffrey Sayre-McCord (Ithaca and London: Cornell University Press), 229–255. Harman's viewpoint (i.e., his causal explanation to the best explanation) denies any realist explanation for virtue claims about individuals. Whereas, Sturgeon's outlook (i.e., his hypothetical explanation to the best explanation) argues that the character traits similar to Plato (and even Aristotle) will support a deep account of character traits needed to defend an account of moral realism. Against the existence of character traits, see Gilbert Harman, "The Nonexistence of Character Traits," *Proceedings of the Aristotelian Society* 100 (2000): 223–226. See also Gilbert Harman, "Skepticism about Character Traits," *Journal of Ethics* 13 (2009): 235–242. Later, Harman's arguments will underscore my skepticism toward natural law. For an excellent discussion of this debate and its relevance to the topic of this text, see Brian Leiter, *Naturalizing Jurisprudence* (Oxford University Press, 2007), 203–224.

28. Loux, *Metaphysics*, 26.

29. The latter claim underscores the debate between Harman and Sturgeon. If John R. is truly courageous, then, from Plato's point of view, because courage is a kind of knowledge, he will exhibit certain features explainable only by the presence of the virtue of courage. For example, the courageous person will stand steadfast at what is appropriate. See Grube, *Plato's Thought*, 217–18. The similarity between the Harman-Sturgeon debate partially turns on the role of the moral relevance of the character in the account of the explanation of our moral observations and moral beliefs. See Sturgeon's assessment of this issue: Sturgeon, "Moral Explanations," 245.

30. Loux, *Metaphysics*, 26.

31. Unless indicated otherwise, all the references to Aristotle will be from the *Complete Works of Aristotle: The Revised Oxford Translation*, ed. by Jonathan Barnes, 2 vols. Bollingen Series. (Princeton, NJ: Princeton University Press, 1984). References to Aristotle's text will employ the Bekker notation which consists of a page number, a column letter, and a line number found in the margins.

32. Aristotle, *Metaphysics*, 1039b20–27.

33. The following discussion is taken from Loux, *Metaphysics*, 123–138.

34. Armstrong, *Universals*, 62.

35. Loux, *Metaphysics*, 127. Italics in the text.

36. Ibid., 128.

37. Armstrong, *Universals*, 60. Armstrong also makes two interesting claims about Aristotle and John Locke that should be noted. First, he labels Aristotle and the Scholastics that followed what he calls the "substance-attribute view," which is close if not identical to Loux's discussion of the substratum theory. Against this background, as we shall see momentarily, Aristotle's view, what Loux calls "Aristotelian Substances" is a little more complex. Also, Armstrong also describes Locke in the same terms: "Locke definitely held a substance-attribute view of particulars." Armstrong, *Universals*, 64. Armstrong is mistaken. If Locke's viewpoint fits one of these viewpoints, it would be the bundle theory. This is because substances, according to Locke, are merely the cluster of atoms in motion which he calls the primary qualities of substances. See John Locke, *An Essay Concerning Human Understanding*, ed. Peter H. Nidditch (Clarendon Press, Oxford, 1975), II.viii.10. (References to Locke's *Essay* will indicate book, chapter and paragraph.) The primary qualities constitute the bulk, figure, texture and motion of substances. The textures and motions of the primary qualities of substances produce in us the secondary qualities, which we believe are concomitant with substances. The texture and motions produce in us the qualities of colors, sounds, tastes, and so forth. Ibid., II.viii.10. At the same time, as Locke makes clear, the secondary qualities, which are relative to our minds, do not resemble the primary qualities. Ibid., II.viii.15. Additionally, later on in the *Essay*, Locke incorporates the notion of essence used by the Scholastics and redefines it to be the real constitution of corporeal things that all the second qualities depend on. Ibid., III.iii.17–18. For an in-depth discussion of Locke's essences, see Samuel Zinaich, Jr., *Locke's Moral Revolution: from Natural Law to Moral Relativism* (Landham, MD: University Press of America, Inc., 2006), 85–103.

38. Loux, *Metaphysics*, 128.

39. Ibid., 124; cf. Aristotle, *Metaphysics*, 1031a28–1032a11.

40. Loux, *Metaphysics*, 124.
41. Aristotle, *Nicomachean Ethics*, 1098a1–5.
42. Loux, 126; cf. Aristotle, *Metaphysics*, 1029b15–1030b14.
43. Ibid., 130.
44. Aristotle, *Metaphysics*, 1035b30–1036a10.
45. Aristotle, *Physics,* 194b15–195a5. The four causes in Aristotle are the matter, formal, efficient, and final. The matter is what the object is made out of. The formal cause is the definition, account or *logos* of the object. This is spelled out in two ways. For example, as to the creation of artifacts like houses, the matter is the wood and the formal cause is the account (in this case, the blue prints) which the carpenter may follow. Concerning organic beings, the formal cause is the recipe of the organic being. As a kind of proto-DNA theory, it possesses the preferred and successive steps to mold the matter into what it will become. The next cause is the efficient cause. In the case of the house, the carpenter (following the formal cause) creates the house out of wood. In the case of organic beings, it is the internal, moving force of the being which (following the formal cause) molds the matter to become what it will become. Finally, the final cause (the *telos*) is the finished outcome of the process of the object to become what it is supposed to become. In the case of the stack of wood, relative to the formal cause the carpenter follows, we expect a (finished) house. We expect, in the case of an organic being, what it is supposed to become. So, if the formal cause reflects the definition of a cat, we expect a cat to emerge, and so forth.
46. Loux, *Metaphysics*, 130; cf. Aristotle, *Metaphysics*, 1029b11–16.
47. Aristotle, *Metaphysics*, 983a30–31 and 1013a22.
48. Ibid., 983a25–35 and 1013a22.
49. It should be noted that the formal cause of an organic being will develop in a straightforward manner with the result that there will be no question of the identity of the species. Later, however, Locke challenges this assumption by making clear that if this is true, then there should not be any question what species an organic being belongs to. Unfortunately, Locke makes clear that the "frequent Production of Monsters" in all species of animals, including the human species, contradicts this claim. Locke, *An Essay Concerning Human Understanding*, III.iii.17.
50. Aristotle, *Nicomachean Ethics*, 1097a15–1099b10.
51. Ibid., 1095b15–1096a10. Terrance Irwin makes clear that *theoria* is used here to refer to contemplative study. *Theoria* points to that part of happiness which guides the intellect or that part of the soul (*psuche*) which possesses reason (*logos*). See Terence Irwin, ed., Aristotle, *Nicomachean Ethics*, 2nd ed., ed. and trans. Terrance Irwin (Indianapolis and Cambridge: Hackett Publishing Company, Inc., 1999), 349. Later in Book X of the *Nicomachean Ethics*, Aristotle identifies the other aspect of happiness, viz., prudence (*phronesis*). Aristotle, *Nicomachean Ethics*, 1178a10–20. *Theoria* is part of the scientific part (*epistamonikon*) of the soul that studies things that do not change. The objects revealed by the scientific part exist by necessity (*anagkas*). Additionally, Aristotle argues that these objects must also be everlasting (*aidion*). Finally, if these objects are everlasting, then they are also uncreated (*agenata*) and indestructible (*aftharta*). Ibid., 1139b 20–25. *Phronesis* is part of the mind dedicated to the study of things that change. Aristotle calls this part the rational calculating part (*logistikon*). Ibid., 1139a10–15. *Phronesis* studies how to live well. It is concerned with not only actions but also feelings.
52. Aristotle, *Nicomachean Ethics*, 1098a5–25. There is a controversy surrounding the meaning of the term "*orthos logos*" or what is typically translated as "right reason." The problem focuses on the meaning of the ancient Greek term "*logos*." Jessica Moss explains that: "*Logos* is a word of notoriously many meanings. Its entry in LSJ has ten major headings and more than sixty translations." Jessica Moss, "Right Reason in Plato and Aristotle: On the Meaning of *Logos*," *Phronesis* 59 (2014): 182. In the contexts at which "*orthos logos*" is used, the traditional interpretation is applied to the status of that faculty which determines which actions and states (*heksis*) are virtuous. In Aristotle's *Nicomachean Ethics*, right reason finds the mean or the middle of an action or feeling, a middle between the excess and deficient. Moss argues that interpreting right reason as that superior part of our *psyche* (soul) which not only distinguishes us from animals, but also supplies the vital element to achieve virtue and *phrone-*

sis, misses deeply what both Plato and Aristotle mean. Ibid., 184–86. Rather, a better interpretation, one that captures what Plato meant by virtue and *phronesis*, and one which Aristotle agrees with, states that "the use of *logos* to denote something which, when grasped, transforms an inferior epistemic state into a superior one." Ibid., 187. What this means is that *orthos logos* "transforms both Platonic and Aristotelian inferior epistemic states like experience into *techné, epistémé,* or other forms of wisdom, is not a rule, proportion, ratio, or form, nor is it Reason itself; instead, it is a particular kind of deliverance of Reason." Ibid., 188. This particular kind of deliverance is *orthos logos*. So, in the case of virtue or *phronesis*, only individuals equipped with right reason may be considered virtuous or *phonetic*. Otherwise, individuals not disposed will only exhibit an inferior form of virtue, a proto form of virtue, and so forth. Thus, instead of focusing on the notion of reason, the focus should be on "correct practical syllogism: an account which prescribes the right action for the right reason. *Logos* in ethical contexts should he translated as 'account.'" Ibid.

Moss makes a satisfactory case for her viewpoint. Additionally, her point is well taken: Pinning down what *orthos logos* means remains a central focus into the Modern era, even when the notion of right reason becomes divorced from the metaphysical machinery it is connected to. It remains to be seen whether Aquinas and Grotius appreciate the subtle meaning Moss exegetes from the texts of Plato and Aristotle. Finally, even though the Enlightenment scholars I discuss reflect a nominalist outlook, right reason figures prominently in their viewpoints as well.

53. Aristotle, *Nicomachean Ethics*, 1098a5–25.

54. Aristotle, *Metaphysics*, 1098a16–17.

55. Training is also needed to for the scientific part (*epistamonikon*) as well. Such training, if it can be attained, will lead to a different sort of wisdom, viz., to scientific knowledge (*episteme*). So, adding virtue to this part of mind is not the same virtue needed to reason well about practical matters. The latter leads to practical wisdom or prudence (*phronesis*).

56. Aristotle, *Nicomachean Ethics*, 1106b17–1107a9. There are a number of words in the ancient Greek dedicated to the notion of the mean or the middle. In general the concepts are arranged around the notions of space or time. For example, the meaning of *mesogaios* points to the middle or inland space of a country or to the heart of the country. *Mesodme* refers to the bays or compartments between the pillars that support a roof. Additionally, *mesolabes* refers to a column being supported in the middle. Moreover, *mesopages* conveys how a soldier drove his spear in up to the middle, and although *mesos* basic meaning is middle, it is used to signify the middle of a shield. In other places, *mesos* stands for the judge between two opponents in an athletic context. Finally, *mesopotamios* refers to a land between two rivers. On the other hand, *mesembria* and *mesembrinos* both refer to the midday or noon. Additionally, *mesonuktios* denotes the middle of the night or midnight. Moreover, *mesouranema* means mid-heaven or mid-air, and finally, *mesoo* is used to indicate the midsummer. H. G. Liddell and Robert Scott, *An Intermediate Greek-English Lexicon*, 7th ed. (Oxford University Press, 1999). Originally published in 1889.

The word of choice for Aristotle's discussion of the mean is *mesos*. To illustrate his use of the term for virtue, he also begins by talking about the conventional usage of the term. He uses an arithmetical example: "If, for instance, ten are many and two are few, we take six as the intermediate in the object, since it exceeds [two] and is exceeded [by ten] by equal amount, [four]. This is what is intermediate by numerical proportion." Aristotle, *Nicomachean Ethics*, 1106a34–1106b1.

57. Aristotle, *Nicomachean Ethics*, 1139a22–26.

58. Loux, *Metaphysics*, 130.

59. My discussion of Aristotle is limited to the relationship between Aristotle's moral views in the *Nicomachean Ethics* and his views in the *Physics* and *Metaphysics*. Perhaps one noticeable absence in this discussion pertains to Aristotle's *Politics*. My decision not to include the *Politics* into this discussion is merely a matter of focus. So, while Aristotle's discussion within the *Politics* is enlightening, my focus is limited primarily to the metaphysical machinery needed to make clear the proto-scientific method Aristotle developed and which was utilized in the modern period. Much of the scientific community of the modern period relied, more or less, on many of the assumptions Aristotle defended. This is particularly clear in the minds of the

Scholastics (in particular Aquinas) and, as I will try to show in chapter 3, a source of tension for members of the new scientific community who rejected the metaphysical realism of Aristotle and, instead, embraced nominalism and the atom. Nevertheless, in the same vein of this text, Charles Covell reminds us of two things. First, the notion of distributive justice concomitant in the *Politics*, becomes part of the foundation in the modern period for the rule of law. Second, the state plays an integral part in the moral development of its human constituents. See Charles Covell, *The Defense of Natural Law* (New York: St. Martin's Press, Inc., 1992), 5–6.

60. *The Stoics Reader: Selected Writings and Testimonia*, trans. Brad Inwood and Lloyd P. Gerson (Indianapolis and Cambridge: Hackett Publishing Co., Inc., 2008). References to the Stoics' views will cite the text and paragraph.

61. Julia Annas, "Ethics in Stoic Philosophy," *Phronesis* 52 (2007): 58.

62. The Stoics also added to the discussion of the virtues that not only are their primary virtues but there are also subordinate virtues as well. The subordinate virtues are states needed to develop the primary virtues. Their value is not merely instrumental; rather, the subordinate virtues have extrinsic value because they lead directly to the primary virtues. Stobaeus reproduces a lengthy discussion about the subordinate virtues. *The Stoics Reader: Selected Writings and Testimonia*, 102.5b2. I mention this because the distinction between primary and subordinate virtues is not clearly articulated in either the works of Plato or Aristotle. For example, from Plato's point of view, the training of the rational part of the soul, as Irwin makes clear, is the process of turning the soul to the Form of the Good. This is illustrated, in particularly, by the Myth of the Cave. See Terrance Irwin, *Plato's Ethics*, 301. Like Plato, Aristotle values the role education plays to become virtuous. With that being said, Aristotle's approach is more direct. An individual is taught to be virtuous by habituating virtuous actions. Later, for example, the distinction developed by the Stoics is brought forward by Aquinas and others. Aquinas discusses the "perfecting" virtues as subordinate virtues. See Thomas Aquinas, *Basic Writings of Saint Thomas Aquinas,* ed. Anton C. Pegis, trans. Laurence Shapcote, (Indianapolis and Cambridge: Hackett Publishing Co., 1997), vol. 2, XI, Q. 61, Art. 5. References to Aquinas will refer to the volume, Chapter, Question, and Article.

63. *The Stoics Reader: Selected Writings and Testimonia*, 102.5b3.

64. Ibid., 102.6a.

65. Ibid. Cleanthes of Assos 331–232 B.C. He was the immediate successor of Zeno, and led the Stoic school from 263–232 B.C. The successor of Cleanthes was Chrysippus of Soli (c.280–207 B.C.). Diogenes of Babylon (c. 240–152 B.C.) was a student of Chrysippus. Archedemus of Tarsus (second century B.C.) started a school of Stoicism in Babylon. Antipater of Tarsus (second century B.C.) succeeded Diogenes of Babylon as head of the school in Babylon.

66. In her article, of the same topic, Annas writes: "Living according to virtue is living according to my nature, which is explicated by showing how it fits into the nature of the universe as a whole. Deferring in my reasonings to the will of Zeus as that is revealed in the ordered universe makes my life 'flow' well, as is achieved only by the virtuous." Annas, "Ethics in Stoic Philosophy," 76. I should note that Annas' agenda is different than mine. Her article attacks a foundational approach to the Stoic philosophy, and instead, is dedicated to defending an integrated relationship between the three parts of Stoic philosophy—logic, physics, ethics. The relationship is (partially) demonstrated in a description of the law of nature. Although Annas' topic is extremely interesting, the purpose of my analysis is tangential to her article. With this in mind, her article illuminates the Stoic's law of nature, which for my purposes, will underscore the importance the Stoic view later in the Scholastic period and the Enlightenment era.

67. This point is also developed by Phillip Mitsis. He attacks the view that the Stoics developed and defended a view of moral particularism. Against the view that the Stoics'develop merely a dispositional (internalist) account of virtue, Mitsis makes a case that the Stoics, in some ways similar to Aquinas, develops a set of law-like rules to guide behavior, externalist rules in some sense, traceable back to Zeus' commands. See Phillip Mitsis, "The Stoics and Aquinas on Virtue and Natural Law," (*The Studia Philonica Annual* 15, 2003): 37.

68. *The Stoics Reader: Selected Writings and Testimonia*, 101.92.

69. Ibid., 101.127 and 102.11g.

70. Aristotle, *Nicomachean Ethics*, 1106b15–35.

71. Ibid., 1145b10–15.
72. Ibid., 1150b30–1151a 25.
73. Ibid., 1099b1–10.
74. For example, see Ephesians 2:8–10.
75. *The Stoics Reader: Selected Writings and Testimonia*, 29. Another hymn dedicated to Zeus comes very close to a predestination viewpoint. As Stobaeus records: "For thus you [Zeus] have fitted together all good things with the bad, so that there is one eternal rational principle for them all—and it is this which the wicked flee from and neglect, ill-fated, since they always long for the possession of good things and do not see the common law of god, nor do they hear it; and if they obeyed it sensibly they would have a good life." *The Stoics Reader: Selected Writings and Testimonia*, 28. Such an outlook is reminiscent of the doctrines of the New Testament scriptures and the later interpretations of Calvin and Luther.
76. There is the need to qualify this point. For example, Diogenes Laertius alludes to the variety of the Stoics' views including one passage that stipulates that the virtuous man will not live in solitude because the virtuous man is made for living in a community. *The Stoics Reader: Selected Writings and Testimonia*, 101.123. Still, it is not clear whether the Stoics have in mind Aristotle's point, viz., the necessity of the *polis* to teach and learn virtue.

Chapter Two

The Scholastic Period (1265–1625)

INTRODUCTION

The Scholastic Period lasted roughly three hundred and sixty years. This text will not discuss the Medieval period between the last Stoic, Marcus Aurelius (120–180 AD), and the beginning of the Scholastic Period starting roughly at 1265 AD. No implications about the lack of philosophical worthiness should be assumed. On the contrary, the predicament is that the purpose of this text is designed to discuss the (relevant) contributions of (what I take to be) the most notable figures in the history of the law of nature. In this case, the views of Thomas Aquinas (1224–1274) and Hugo Grotius (1583–1645) are profoundly significant. This narrow approach is not without its justification. Contemporary legal theory, especially discussions aimed at the question of the justification of natural law, rarely, if ever, find relevance in the discussions in medieval scholarship.[1] Having said that, it is worth making brief note of the context which influenced the intellectual presuppositions of Aquinas and Grotius. The growth of Christianity is part of that context.

Again, a deep historical analysis of the rise of Christianity is a discussion that is far beyond the scope of this text. Nevertheless, it is of no little moment that the texts of the Gospels (including the Pauline Epistles) exerted an immense influence on the minds of scholars, emperors, monarchs, and commoners alike, not only in Western Europe but also in North Africa. In Western Europe, Christianity took on two versions: Catholicism initially and later Protestantism. In North Africa, numerous versions of the Eastern Orthodox Church emerged. Of course, the central figure that, in some ways, bridges the early church (Western as well as Eastern) with the central theological figures later including Martin Luther (1483–1546), John Calvin (1509–1564), and so forth, is Bishop Augustine of Hippo (354–430 AD). Both the Catholic and Protestant camps claim an intellectual debt to Augustine's writings. This is not surprising because Augustine successfully combines the viewpoints of Plato, Aristotle, and the Stoics with early church doctrine.[2] Unquestionably, Augustine's influence grips like steel bands the minds of both Aquinas, an Italian Catholic, and Grotius, a Dutch Protestant. However, before I discuss the contributions both scholars make to the doctrine of the law of nature, the Scholastic movement deserves recognition.

It is natural to think that Aquinas is, for all intents and purposes, the ideal representative of the Scholastic movement. There is no doubt that this is true. In fact, because of Aquinas' immense influence and prolific publications, it is not unreasonable to say he personifies the Scholastic movement itself.[3] Unfortunately, this claim overlooks something important. There are many other scholars who were part of the movement, but who were overshadowed by Aquinas' legacy.[4] If this is the case, then what is significant about the Scholastic period? This assessment will be brief.

In simple terms, the Scholastic period reflects a focus on the perennial topics in philosophy and theology. Following the ubiquitous focus of the topics in Aristotle's corpus, the Schoolmen of the Scholastic tradition concentrate in part on the following issues:

> a natural dualism of God and creature, mind and matter, thoughts and thing, as against monism and pantheism; it defends a moderate realism, as against the ultrarealism, nominalism, and conceptualism, in the problem of the universals; it is spiritualistic and not materialistic, experimental and not aprioristic, objectivistic and not subjectivistic; in sense-perception it is presentational and not agnostic or representational or idealistic; concerning intellectual knowledge it defends a moderate rationalism, as against sensism, positivism, and innatism; it is common-sense knowledge critically examined and philosophically vindicated.[5]

Although the details of Bittle's description of Scholasticism remain too detailed to hash out, one aspect implied in her description, viz., that Scholasticism is objectivistic and not subjectivistic, is the focus on natural law. In fact, as Heinrich A. Rommen makes clear, when "Scholasticism, approached its peak, the natural-law doctrine attained it most masterly expression."[6] Of course, and at least for the purposes of this text, such expressions of natural law are consummate in the minds of Thomas Aquinas and Hugo Grotius. I will begin with the former.

THOMAS AQUINAS (1224–1274)

To accurately capture Thomas Aquinas' viewpoint in this text, even a monograph dedicated entirely to his view, may be difficult to accomplish . Nevertheless, I spell out (some of) his fine discriminations in a chary manner. So, for the agenda of a text like this, I begin with his different views of law. Aquinas identifies four different kinds of laws: eternal law, divine law, natural law, and human law.[7] I will begin with eternal law and move forward.[8] In particular, I accentuate the importance of Aquinas's viewpoint in the doctrine of natural law.

Of eternal law, Aquinas states that it is a type of Divine wisdom that guides all actions and movements.[9] The notion of eternal law employed by Aquinas immediately raises the question of God's relationship to eternal law. This was also the same question Augustine pondered against the backdrop of his Neo-Platonism, especially after he became a Christian. As I understand this issue, there are three possible positions to take. First, eternal laws, laws akin to Plato's Universals, exist alongside and are co-eternal with God. Next, eternal laws are coextensive with God's mind. Finally, eternal laws are laws, in some sense, created by God. Augustine rejected the first and third positions. The first, because it would place God below the exemplars contained in eternal laws. The third, because it would suggest that the eternal laws have no deeper source than God's beliefs, desires, or preferences. Ultimately, Augustine embraced the second position: "Now, where would we think that these reasons are, if not in the mind of the Creator? For He did not look to anything placed outside Himself as a model for the construction of what he created."[10] Aquinas follows suit: "Consequently, the Divine intellect is true in itself; and its type is truth itself."[11] Such a position avoids making God's mind subjugated to eternal laws and the subjective idealism (theological voluntarism) of the third position.

Although eternal laws are coextensive with God's mind, there is still the issue of what we are to make of these laws. Following Rommen, there are three aspects to underscore about the eternal law.[12] The first feature of the eternal law includes "the laws of the natural sciences."[13] The second facet includes Aquinas' commitment to Aristotle's teleology.[14] And finally, eternal law serves as the foundation of "the laws of theoretical and practical reason."[15] The latter, of course, points to Aquinas' notion of natural law, a concept which has its roots in Aristotle's unformulated idea of natural justice and in the haziness of the natural law of the Stoics.

Understanding the law of nature as Aquinas discusses it is terribly complicated.[16] It is a combination of Aristotle's teleology, (perhaps) the Stoic's notion of natural law, and Aquinas' own brand of Christianity.[17] As I discussed earlier (see chapter 1), Aristotle's teleology revolves around the ideas that all (well-formed) humans possess a formal cause, which directs our development toward a final cause, i.e., our human function (to reason) and to our good (to reason well). Aquinas' version of natural law, while similar to the Stoics, goes beyond the Stoics with Aquinas' commitment to Christianity. Here is what I mean.

As I noted above, eternal law brings with it the possibility of a natural morality, one apart from the *supra*natural morality contained in the Old and New Testaments, specifically, divine law. This natural morality is made real by the fact that God places certain inclinations in us (See my discussion of the Stoics in chapter 1), which reflect the precepts of the natural law. There are basically four.[18] The first one states that "good is to be done and promoted, and evil is to be avoided."[19] The second one is the inclination toward the preservation of human life, and any obstacles inconsistent with this inclination.[20] The third is an inclination we share with the animals, which includes the desire for "sexual intercourse [and] the education of offspring, and so forth."[21] The last inclination is "to know the truth about God, and to live in society."[22]

After touching on the origin and content of natural law, I will briefly discuss the importance of natural law. There are three points to underscore. Natural law is significant because it prompts us to remember our duties to God and to one another. The go-to passage in the New Testament is Romans 1: 18–32.[23] To summarize this passage, it is important to note the author's indication that God has placed in the human mind a knowledge of Himself and other precepts of morality. Such knowledge includes the wrongness of "unrighteousness, sexual immorality,[24] wickedness, covetousness, maliciousness . . . envy, murder, strife, deceit, [and] evil mindedness."[25] Again, although such actions are wrong, the long-term problem concerns the kind of character such actions habitually create. For example, the text of Romans describes such individuals as "backbiters, haters of God, violent, proud, boasters, inventors of evil things, disobedient to parents, undiscerning, untrustworthy, unloving, unforgiving, [and] unmerciful."

The second reason why natural law is important is that it becomes the basis of a natural account of virtue. Such an account follows Aristotle closely, including the role of habituation, as well as the role and problem that pleasure and pain play in character development. The final reason is that natural law becomes the foundation for human law, which I will discuss next.

Human law is, of course, about the laws *humans* make for themselves. Such a point seems rather innocuous. However, it is not. In the simplest of terms, given the fact that human rules vary from culture to culture, there is a strong tendency to think that human rules have no objective foundation. Instead, rules reflect *merely* the beliefs, desires, and preferences of the legislator, or, in certain contexts, the beliefs, etc., of the majority of the citizens of the culture. While this may be true, as we will soon see, especially when the Enlightenment emerges, from Aquinas' perspective, such a viewpoint is mistaken, and seriously so. Following Augustine again, Aquinas argues that if a human law is not justified by the law of nature, "it is no longer a law but a perversion of a law."[26] But what does this mean or imply?

There are two points to make clear. Suppose there is a culture, which has a legal system in place. Additionally, let us assume that the legal system reflects, or is consistent with, the ends of a legitimate democracy. This implies that the rules of this culture reflect the beliefs and preferences of the majority of the citizens of that culture. Moreover, there is a just system to enforce those rules. Finally, let us suppose that there is a rule in place, which reflects the beliefs and desires of the majority of its citizens, but this rule is not consistent, or cannot be traced back to one of the laws of nature. Let us take a serious example recently explored in our own culture, e.g., the United States Supreme Court's recent decision to legalize gay and lesbian marriages. How would an individual from a natural law account respond? Here is how the argument might proceed:

1. If gay and lesbian marriages are just, then gay and lesbian marriages are consistent with the law of nature.
2. Gay and lesbian marriages are not consistent with the law of nature.
3. *Therefore*, Gay and lesbian marriages are unjust.

Of course, of the two premises, line 2 will be the focus. So, why might it be true? It is true, at least for the sake of argument, because it is inconsistent with the third natural law, viz., the desire for "sexual intercourse [and] the education of offspring, and so forth." Again, such a point may not be that obvious, because it mentions only the desire for sexual intercourse. When combined with the Christian prohibition against gay and lesbian sexual intercourse in Romans 1: 18–32, then line 2 can be thought to be true.

With that in mind, the natural law theorist following Aquinas and even Augustine will take the next step. If such a human law, legalizing gay and lesbian marriages, is not a legitimate human law at all, then there is no requirement to obey it:

4. If gay and lesbian marriages are unjust, then any human law which endorses gay and lesbian marriage is not a just human law and does not have to be obeyed.
5. Gay and lesbian marriages are unjust.
6. *Therefore*, any human law which endorses gay and lesbian marriage is not a just human law and does not have to be obeyed.

Unlike the first argument above, instead of the second premise above (line 2), the first premise (line 4) is the quarrelsome line. Are there any reasons to think it is true? Maybe it is analytic? Not on the surface of things.

That is, it does not seem to follow that if an action is unjust, it automatically follows that any law based on it is no law at all and does not have to be obeyed. So, if the antecedent and consequent are not conceptually connected, then there must be, at least, a middle term to connect the antecedent and consequent. What could that middle term be? Honestly, I'm not sure how to connect the two, and it may take too much time to do so.[27] Nevertheless, what needs to be emphasized is that the conclusion of the second argument underscores the conviction that any human law which cannot be justified by the law of nature is not a just human law and it does not have to be followed.

The second point follows on the heels of the first point. Like Aristotle, Aquinas understands the need for precise human laws. He makes clear that without the placement of proper human laws, the citizens within a community will not be able to arrive at the perfection of virtue. Again, like Aristotle, this implies that human law will function in two ways: First, it will point the way to encourage the young as well as the old to develop their natural dispositions toward virtue. Second, it is designed to keep in check those individuals who are depraved. So, the human law restrains the evil one might contemplate doing.[28] Mary M. Keys complains that the latter, negative narrative, overshadows the former point just articulated.[29] To counter this point, Keys teases out several passages from the *Summa Theologica* to show that human law is also necessary for positive moral development for the training for mature human virtue.[30] The same point is made in Book X of Aristotle's *Nicomachean Ethics*. Although more could be said about Aquinas' viewpoint, it is time to move on to discuss Grotius.

HUGO GROTIUS (1583–1645)

Hugo Grotius is considered the father of modern natural law.[31] Given Aquinas' influence, such a viewpoint seems puzzling. On the one hand, it may mean merely that his account of the law of nature is closer to or a part of the modern era, i.e., a time period between the 1600s and 1700s. On the other hand, to be designated as the "father" of the modern natural law appears to indicate his contribution to the doctrine deserves significant attention because it is the first and foremost consideration given to the law of nature. Of course, that cannot be true. So what is so significant about Grotius?

Apparently, Grotius' significance points to the fact that he was the first to apply natural law and positive law to international law, especially how it applies to the rules of war.[32] Moreover, as Rommen makes clear: "He may be said to have marked the transition from the metaphysical to the rationalist natural law."[33] Both points appear to give the special status Rommen claims Grotius has. For my purposes, the real reason for such an appellation, points to Grotius' view that natural law would exist even if God did not exist. Thus, as Schneewind indicates, disconnecting natural law from a religious point of view makes it possible to skirt the religious controversies associated with the law of nature.[34] I will turn to Grotius' view of natural law and to the (at times, imperceptible) changes he introduces. To understand his view of the law of nature, three questions need to be addressed. First, what is the law of nature and its source? Second, what is the force or obligatory status of the law of nature? Finally, what are the boundaries of the law of nature?

So, what is the law of nature and what is its source? Grotius initially defines the law of nature early on in Volume I of his text: "NATURAL RIGHT *is the Rule and Dictate of Right Reason, shewing the Moral Deformity or Moral Necessity there is in any Act, according to its Suitableness or Unsuitableness to a reasonable Nature*, and consequently, that such an Act is either forbid or commanded by GOD, the Author of Nature."[35] There are four elements to note. The first noticeable part is the term "natural right." At first glance, this definition seems geared toward spelling out something altogether different than natural law, explicitly, what a natural right means instead of natural law. Grotius' explanation of his definition indicates that what he has in mind is the law of nature. In fact, in the section prior to the quote above, Grotius makes clear that his third sense of right means the same thing as law.[36] So, in this case, "natural right," means natural law.

Next, the law of nature is the dictate of right reason. This feature speaks to what the law of nature means and its source. The law of nature is identified with the dictates of right reason, or the decrees which spell out the content of the law of nature. Thus, the source of the laws of nature is a part of the mind of each individual. Grotius acknowledges that right reason is an immanent characteristic which all humanity possess. In other words, the laws of nature originate from and are expressible by means of right reason.[37]

Another important note is needed. Our capacity of right reason gives us the benefit of not just being able to single out actions which are right or wrong. It does more than that. Right reason gives an insight into why actions are right or wrong. For example, on Grotius' viewpoint, an action is wrong, say, murder, because it possess a moral deformity, a deformity which is part of the order of the universe.[38] So, our capacity of right reason gives us the ability to not only recognize wrong actions, but to also define what makes them wrong.

Finally, the subordinate clause at the end of the definition brings with it an ambiguity often associated with Grotius' law of nature. To be exact, then, what is God's relationship to the law of nature? To partially resolve this curiosity, on the one hand, right reason gives us the ability to recognize the deformity or the necessity of an action which is part of the moral order of the universe. On the other hand, while humanity has the ability to recognize this order, Grotius makes clear that the recognition of the wrongness of an action does not put us under the necessity of avoiding wrong actions. In other words, even though right reason picks out, so to speak, actions, which are intrinsically wrong or right, there is no internal, necessary connection between our understanding not to murder and our motivation not to murder. So, the motivation to obey the decrees of the law of nature must come from a command of God.[39]

Second, what is the force or obligatory status of the law of nature? There are two points of interest. First, this question raises the issue of what sort of actions are right, wrong, or permitted. Grotius initially focuses on the relativity of certain rules because of the context. So, there are moral issues that are not a part of the dictates of right reason until the context makes them relevant. For example, Grotius appeals to the introduction of private property. The decrees of right reason do not dictate ahead of time any conclusions about the introduction of property or whether there are intrinsic decrees about property. In fact, the invention of private property, so to speak, is left up to our liberty to act as we see fit.[40] Nevertheless, as Grotius makes clear, unless otherwise dictated, once *private* property is introduced, natural law informs us that it is wrong to take away forcibly a man's private property.[41]

The second aspect of this question involves the subclass of actions directly identifiable as the dictates of the law of nature. According to Grotius, this subclass of action are unalterable. In fact, of these actions Grotius makes clear that God cannot change the precepts of the law of nature.[42] To do so would give God the ability to make a contradiction true which is not possible.[43]

Although this may sound suspicious to some individuals (especially of a Christian voluntarist stripe), it sounds very much like theological intellectualism, which becomes a competing viewpoint prominent in the modern era. Minimally, this means that the natural law is co-eternal with God. Grotius confirms this point and writes: "For Instance then, as God himself cannot effect, that twice two should not be four; so neither can he, that what is intrinsically Evil should not be Evil."[44] Of course, although one may be tempted to speculate that Grotius is aligned with theological intellectualism, there may be a position which is consistent with the quote above. Perhaps God will not—*not that He cannot*—break his own decrees. So, in other words, if God ordains that murder is wrong, He promises and covenants not to break that rule Himself. This is a version of theological voluntarism which implies that the laws of logic, morality, and so forth, are created by God, which He—*Himself*—promises to follow. Such a viewpoint, as we shall see, becomes prominent in the Christian community during the Enlightenment period.[45]

Unfortunately, this viewpoint does not seem to fit well with the following quote from Grotius. Of the metaphysical status of the natural law: "*And indeed, all we have now said would take place, though we should even grant, what without the greatest Wickedness cannot be granted, that there is no*

God, or that he takes no Care of human Affairs."[46] Such a quote puts Grotius squarely in the camp of theological intellectualism.

Finally, what are the boundaries of the law of nature? This question, unfortunately, is ambiguous and encompasses two separate but related issues. The boundaries addressed here apply to whether the law of nature applies to animals. At the same time, they apply to the boundaries between the law of nature, the divine voluntary law, and human positive law. The answer to the former question remains unmistakable. The latter, not so much. I will begin with the former topic.

The application of the law of nature, at first glance, may appear to apply to animals. This is so because we share several instincts including self-preservation and the protection of offspring. Nevertheless, while there is a causal law of nature which guides the behavior of animals, the moral natural law applies only to humanity.[47] The reason is familiar and has its origin in Plato and Aristotle. Whereas humanity is guided by right reason, animals are guided by instinct. Thus, even though we share many instinctual-like behaviors with animals, the notions of justice, equity, and so forth, apply only to humanity.[48]

The boundaries between animals and humanity rest upon the bright line of reason. This means, the question now explores a different boundary. It involves the boundary between the law of nature, the divine voluntary law, and human law. Following Grotius, I will begin with the human law.

Concerning the specifics of the human, Grotius stipulates that human law is divided into three (rather obscure) aspects: "a *Civil*, a *less extensive Right*, or a *more extensive Right than the Civil.*"[49] The civil law, as Grotius makes clear, belongs to the State. Following Aristotle, the civil law is necessary to guarantee the rights of individuals afforded by society and to make its members self-sufficient.[50] These laws, however, are indifferent because they are not founded on the constitution of our nature or, what amounts to, the law of nature. They represent rules which are relative to a specific context.[51] The less extensive right, although not derived from the civil law, points to the laws between parent and child, masters and servants, and so forth.[52] Although they are not derived from the civil authority, many of the laws derive their authorization from the civil authority. The last law, which is the more extensive right, applies to the right of nations, rights which all nations have and which are shared in common.[53] The last right is primarily the focus of Grotius' text, in particular, the laws that apply to war and peace. Grotius makes clear that the law of nations are, in reality, the same as the law of nature. If there is a difference between the customs of countries, the sole reason consists in the different applications open to the law of nature.[54]

After briefly spelling out Grotius' view of human law, it is now required to discuss the divine law. The divine law, which Grotius calls the "*Divine voluntary law*," is derived *only* from the will of God.[55] This is important to note because Grotius draws a sharp line between the rules created by God and the precepts of the law of nature. Again, to highlight the difference, Grotius qualifies this view in the following manner (answering the question posed to Euthyphro by Socrates). The laws that God creates are just laws, not because they are intrinsically just. On the contrary, what laws God wills are just laws because God wills them.[56] Grotius also explains that the divine law was revealed three times: after the creation of man, after the flood, and during the time of Christ. Such stories are recognizable to anyone with a remote idea of Christianity.

The question remains, then, concerning the relationship between all three laws. I have alluded to this point briefly. In summary, this much can be made clear: The precepts of the law of nature are intrinsically right or wrong (implying that even God must follow them). In fact, the laws of nature exist co-extensively with God. The divine laws originate in the mind of God. God's laws reflect primarily His own beliefs, desires, or preferences. They are not instrinsically right or wrong. Humans are nevertheless, like the laws of nature, required to follow these laws. Although the laws generated by humans reflect a contextual awareness of their concerns and projects (unlike the divine rules), they reflect in some sense, the law of nature because of our imminent capacity of right reason. Nevertheless, divine laws and human laws do not command or forbid actions which are in themselves right or wrong. Such a distinction raises an interesting point. Although we expect human laws to vary from culture to culture, and to change as the context of a culture changes, the same expectation does not seem to apply to the divine law, even so such an expectation is mistaken. The divine law, based primarily on beliefs, preferences or desires of God, may change from time to time (as long as they are consistent with the law of nature) as God may see fit. Such changes are most obvious when the rules of the Old Testament are compared to the New Testament.

There are two other issues, related to the analysis above, that require attention. First, what, if any, does the role of habituation play in this complicated story? And second, what is the justification, if any, for human positive law?

Although Grotius' discussion of the importance of habituation is rather scant, a topic central in the writings of Aristotle, much of what he discusses seems to imply the importance of habituation. Nevertheless, with such a limited account, where does our motivation originate to follow the law of nature? Richard Tuck raises an interesting answer to this question—our primary motivation comes from a superior:

> The Fitness or Unfitness, which may be termed the *natural Morality* of Actions, is indeed a Reason for acting, or not acting; but then it is not such a Reason as imposes an indispensable Necessity, which is implied in the Idea of

> an *Obligation*. This Necessity can come only from a *superior*, that is, from some intelligent Being existing without us, who has a Power of restraining our Liberty, and prescribing Rules for our Conduct.[57]

Although such a viewpoint may seem, at first glance, harmless, we shall see that it points to a more modern outlook of moral motivation. Here is what I mean. The prevailing outlook concerning moral motivation was dominated by Aristotle (see chapter 1). Aristotle argued that through a process of intense habituation an individual can become an individual who naturally does what is morally appropriate without the threat of external compulsion by the civil legislator. Of course, no one can attain this kind of moral maturity without living in a culture ruled by a legislator who is committed to making his subjects virtuous. Others, as Aristotle makes clear, including the continent and the incontinent, need the rules provided by legislation (including the threats of disobedience) to help them do the right things (even though they know what is the right thing to do). Aware of this, Grotius drives a wedge between the moral dispositions provided by right reason and the motivation to follow those dispositions.[58] There is no longer the possibility of an individual who does not need the guidance of civil legislation. Eventually, as we shall see in the next section, once the dispositions of the law of nature are completely precluded, the civil authority becomes the most immediate source of moral, legal, and unfortunately, in some contexts, religious motivation.[59]

The last topic, barely hinted at earlier, concerns the justification of civil laws. Grotius makes clear that the foundation of the civil law is the natural law: "XVI. *Again, since the fulfilling of Covenants belongs to the Law of Nature, (for it was necessary there should be some Means of obliging men among themselves, and we cannot conceive any other more conformable to Nature) from this very Foundation Civil Laws were derived.*"[60] What does this mean? It means that we have a tendency to create civil laws that resemble the law of nature. Although this is a bit flimsy, there is a sense in which this is true. The reason is that, as I made clear earlier, Grotius argues that humanity possesses the capacity of right reason. This means that we are inclined to create rules to govern ourselves, and under the best conditions, those rules will reflect the law of nature which originates in our capacity of right reason. I think this is what Grotius means in the following passage: "*for the Mother of Natural Law is human Nature itself, which, though even the Necessity of our Circumstances should not require it, would of itself create in us a mutual Desire of Society: And the Mother of Civil Law is that very Obligation which arises from Consent, which deriving its Force from the Law of Nature, Nature may be called as it were, the Great Grandmother of this Law also.*[61]

If this is the case, then why do cultures make civil laws inconsistent with the law of nature? The problem is this. We find the law of nature in the civil laws of nations which are cultivated correctly, but: "*That Law which is called the Law of Nature, is unchangeable, in the Opinion of all Men who are of a right and sound Mind: But if it does not appear so to Men of weak and disturbed Judgements, it argues nothing to the Purpose; for we all allow Honey to be sweet, tho' it may taste otherwise to a sick Person.*"[62]

Thus, Grotius, following in some respects the lead of Aquinas, opens up the opportunity to critique the warrant of civil laws. Civil law, under ideal conditions, will reflect right reason deriving their warrant from the same.

CONCLUSION

To sum up, so far the story of this text is focused on two periods of the history of ideas. Although, I admit that my efforts do not give the topics the justice they deserve, what I have tried to show is that (at least from a Western civilization point of view), there is a consistent thread of ideas which are connected, a thread which shows how the thirteenth- and seventeenth-century scholars, Aquinas and Grotius, came to understand themselves and the world. But, what may be missed by a cursory understanding of the same history, is how much Aquinas and Grotius relied on the ancient Greeks. In fact, what I think is the case, is that most people who read, for example, Aquinas or even Grotius, do not appreciate two things: the intellectual debt they owe to the scholars who came before them, and *especially* the metaphysical machinery that is needed to justify their beliefs. Certainly, as I will try to show, the Moderns understood this all too clearly. Thus, this text has stressed the need to understand this latter point with the upmost urgency. So, later in chapters 5 and 6 of this text, when scholars, say, Finnis or Dworkin, mention and employ the natural law to warrant legal statements, it should be understood that just mentioning the natural law will not provide the truth-making conditions of legal statements, or settle hard cases. To take such a position requires serious attention. In other words, it requires that the truth-making conditions must also be articulated. As I intend to show, *such conditions are not forthcoming*. It is now time to make our move into the Enlightenment period.

NOTES

1. One notable scholar not typically mentioned is the great, English Franciscan, William of Ockham (1285–1349). Ockham rejected the immanent nature of natural law. Instead, he brought to the forefront an early account of theological voluntarism. See Covell, *The Defense of Natural Law*, 8.

2. Heinrich A. Rommen, *The Natural Law: A Study in Legal and Social History and Philosophy*, trans., Thomas R. Hanley (Indianapolis, IN: Liberty Fund, 1998), 33–34. This point is also discussed at length by James Bissett Pratt, "The Ethics of St. Augustine," *International Journal of Ethics* 13, no. 2 (January, 1903). This article is (still) valuable because of the

way Pratt shows how Augustine's platonic views bear upon the formation of his Christian ethics.

3. Charles Covell makes the same assessment of Aquinas' influence. Covell, *The Defense of Natural Law*, 7.

4. Rommen mentions and briefly discusses three such individuals: St. Anselm of Canterbury (1033–1109), Alexander of Hales (d. 1245) and Duns Scotus (d. 1308). Rommen, *The Natural Law: A Study in Legal and Social History and Philosophy*, 37–39, 51–53. To this list we may also add the Spanish Jesuit Priests, Luis de Molina (1535–1600) and Francisco Suarez (1548–1617).

5. Celestine N. Bittle, *Reality and the Mind: Epistemology* (Milwaukee: Bruce Publishing Co., 1936), 146. Bittle's reference was brought to my attention by Heinrich A. Rommen's text, *The Natural Law: A Study in Legal and Social History and Philosophy*, 34.

6. Rommen, *The Natural Law: A Study in Legal and Social History and Philosophy*, 34.

7. Aquinas, *Basic Writings of Saint Thomas Aquinas*, vol. 2, XIII, Q. 93.

8. I will only mention the divine law very briefly. My focus will be on the other three laws.

9. Aquinas, *Basic Writings of Saint Thomas Aquinas*, vol. 2, XIII, Q. 93, Art. 1.

10. Augustine, *The Essential Augustine*, 2nd ed., ed. Vernon J. Bourke (Indianapolis, IN: Hackett Publishing Co., 1974), 62–63. See also Rommen, *The Natural Law: A Study in Legal and Social History and Philosophy*, 33.

11. Aquinas, *Basic Writings of Saint Thomas Aquinas*, vol. 2, XIII, Q. 93, Art. 1. To speak of the existence of eternal or necessary truths coextensive with the mind of God still remains a puzzle. In fact, the great Benedict de Spinoza also appreciates this problem. Spinoza puts the issue in this way. What do we mean when we say that the nature of a triangle is eternally contained in the mind of God? This means, minimally, two things: God has the idea of a triangle and God understands the nature of a triangle. Even so, it means something more specific, and in particular, it points to a position, which Spinoza rejects. The necessity attributed to a triangle by the mind of God (or the divine nature) depends on the nature of the triangle and not on the necessity of the mind of God. Benedictus de Spinoza, *The Theological-Political Tractate* in *Spinoza: Complete works,* ed. Michael L. Morgan and trans. Samuel Shirley (Indianapolis and Cambridge: Hackett Publishing Co., Inc., 2002), 430.

12. Rommen, *The Natural Law: A Study in Legal and Social History and Philosophy*, 40.

13. Ibid.

14. Ibid.

15. Ibid., 40–41.

16. Aquinas, *Basic Writings of Saint Thomas Aquinas*, vol. 2, XIII, Q. 94.

17. Covell, *The Defense of the Natural Law*, 7.

18. Aquinas, *Basic Writings of Saint Thomas Aquinas*, vol. 2, XIII, Q. 94, Art. 2.

19. Ibid. Aquinas comments that this is the "first precept of law" and that all the other natural laws are based on this one. So, there are reasons to think it is not a natural law. The other natural laws are also presented in their order of importance. Three points seem relevant. First, it is not clear whether Aquinas is advocating a foundational relationship between the first precept of law and the other natural laws. In any case, it is not clear to me that his first precept of law has the epistemic warrant to qualify as a properly basic belief. Second, instead of a properly basic belief, the first precept appears to function like the universal premise in a (Aristotelian) practical syllogism. So, as Aquinas makes clear, when our "practical reason" apprehends something good or evil, we conclude it should be done or avoided. Perhaps what he has is mind is *synderesis*. In scholastic moral philosophy, *synderesis* is the natural capacity or disposition of the practical reason to apprehend intuitively the universal first principles of human action. In this case, then, we have one belief that is a universal and one belief about a particular, namely, an act apprehended as good or bad. The conclusion is not to be affirmed, but to be acted upon (or avoided). See Aristotle, *Nicomachean Ethics*, 1147a 25–30. Finally, the order of importance of the laws of nature is puzzling. For example, if we suppose that self-preservation is the most important natural law, it seems apparent that, under abnormal conditions, a parent will protect the life of her child by sacrificing her own life. This is not always clearly the case. Likewise, the accounts of soldiers sacrificing their lives for their comrades spells trouble for Aquinas. Both examples seem contrary to the order Aquinas takes for granted.

Added to this is Aristotle's point that, in terms of its moral significance, the community is prior in moral importance than the individual. This also seems to push the order Aquinas wants to maintain to the side. cf. John Finnis, *Natural Law and Natural Rights* (Oxford: Clarendon Press, 1980), 94. Finnis takes issue with the same passage. cf. Covell, *The Defense of the Natural law*, 6.

20. Aquinas, *Basic Writings of Saint Thomas Aquinas*, vol. 2, XIII, Q. 94, Art. 2.

21. Ibid.

22. Ibid.

23. The New Testament quotations are from the *New King James Version* (Thomas Nelson, Inc., 1982).

24. This includes not only premarital sex, but also adultery, gay, and lesbian sexual relations.

25. It is interesting to note at this point that many of the Enlightenment scholars, for example, John Locke, *ignore* this passage when he denies the existence of innate ideas in the first book of the *Essay Concerning Human Understanding*. I will return to this point later.

26. Aquinas, *Basic Writings of Saint Thomas Aquinas,* vol. 2, XIII, Q. 95, Art. 2.

27. The justification of line 4 may proceed as a pure hypothetical syllogism: 1. If gay and lesbian marriages are unjust, then no legal system has the legitimate authority to authorize gay and lesbian marriages. 2. If no legal system has the legitimate authority to authorize gay and lesbian marriages, then any human law, which endorses gay and lesbian marriages, is not a just human law, and does not have to be obeyed. Therefore, if gay and lesbian marriages are unjust, then any human law, which endorses gay and lesbian marriage, is not a just human law, and does not have to be obeyed. As arguments go, the justification for line 4 looks sound. Of course, both premises benefit from the assumption that the authority of a legal system and its rules derive their warrant from an independent notion of morality and justice. Thus, if the legal positivists are correct (which I agree they ultimately are about this issue), and law and morality suffer the inevitable consequences of being separated, then both premises are false, and the conclusion is not worthy of belief.

28. Aquinas, *Basic Writings of Saint Thomas Aquinas,* vol. 2, XIII, Q. 95, Art. 1.

29. Mary M. Keys, "Aquinas's Two Pedagogies: A Reconstruction of the Relation between Law and Moral Virtue," *American Journal of Political Science* 45, no. 3 (July 2001): 520.

30. Ibid., 522–525.

31. Rommen, *The Natural Law: A Study in Legal and Social History and Philosophy*, 62. In this text, I will use the three volume set published by Liberty Fund: Hugo Grotius, *The Rights of War and Peace*, ed. Richard Tuck, 3 vols. (Indianapolis, IN: Liberty Fund, 2005). Original work published in 1625. References to the main text will refer to the volume, chapter, section, and paragraph. I also quote the *Prelimary Discourse* at the beginning of Grotius' text. References to the *Preliminary Discourse* will refer to volume and paragraph.

32. Rommen, *The Natural Law: A Study in Legal and Social History and Philosophy*, 62–65. This is especially apparent because Grotius begins his pioneering discussion in volume 1 emphasizing the focus of war and peace. See, for example, Grotius, *Preliminary Discourse*, I.ii. and the later discussion at I.1.i–v.

33. Ibid., 62.

34. J. B. Schneewind, ed., *Moral Philosophy: from Montaigne to Kant*, ed. J. B. Schneewind (Cambridge University Press, 2003), 88. This same point is emphasized by Knud Haakonssen. He adds that "Grotius's separation of natural law from the Christian religion is underlined in several ways. For instance, he firmly denies that natural law can be identified with either the Old or the New Testament." Knud Haakonssen, *Natural Law and Moral Philosophy: From Grotius to the Scottish Enlightenment* (Cambridge University Press, 1996), 29.

35. Grotius, *The Rights of War and Peace*, I.1.x.§1. The italics, and so forth, are in the text.

36. For example, see I.1.ix. See also the extended discussion of natural law: I.1.x.§2–7.

37. I.1.x.note 1.

38. I.1.x.note 3.

39. I.1.x.§2. See also, I.1.x.note 3.

40. I.1.x.note 4.

41. I.1.x.§4.

42. I.1.x.§5.
43. I.1.x.note 14.
44. I.1.x.§5. It is interesting to note that in Grotius' *Commentary on the Law of Prize and Booty*, he defends a version of theological voluntarism. For example, Grotius writes: "What God has shown to be His Will, that is law. This axiom points directly to the cause of law, and is rightly laid down as the primary principle." Hugo Grotius, *Commentary on the Law of Prize and Booty*, ed. Martine Julia van Ittersum (Indianapolis, IN: Liberty Fund, 2006), 19. Additionally, of the law of nature, Grotius writes: "The Will of God is revealed, not only through oracles and supernatural portents, but above all in the very design of the Creator; for it is from this last source that the law of nature is derived." Ibid., 20. Grotius never published this text. In fact, it remained unknown until it was discovered among his personal papers auctioned off in 1846. It was later published in 1868. Martine Julia van Ittersum, ed., "Note on the Text," in ed. Martine Julia van Ittersum, *Commentary on the Law of Prize and Booty*, xxiii. It is unclear why he changed his mind.
45. On this point, John Colman writes that theistic voluntarism can be expressed by three different but related theses. So, to make clear what this doctrine means, let us ask why, for example, God forbids murder? The first answer is simply that murder is wrong because God forbids it. In fact, He might have willed otherwise and made murder permissible. As far as God's will is unconditioned by the rules he creates, Colman writes: "no reason can be assigned as to why these precept are as they are, for God might have willed them quite otherwise. Thus the only possible answer to the question why say, murder is wrong is that it is so because God forbids murder." John Colman, *John Locke's Moral Philoso*phy (Edinburgh: Edinburgh University Press, 1983), 33. The second version is similar. Even though God is above the rules he creates, "Reasons may be given for the moral precepts binding mankind, but God can on particular occasions suspend these precepts." Ibid. The last version is more complicated. Unlike the first two versions, although mysterious from our point of view, God's will is conditioned by reasons He enlists to create moral rules for our lives. Thus, as Colman makes clear, "what God wills, whether it be the general precepts of morality or particular commands, may appear arbitrary and unjust; but this is only an appearance due to the feebleness of human understanding." Ibid.
46. Grotius, *The Rights of War and Peace*, I.xi. This is a quote from *The Preliminary Discourse*. The italics are in the text. Concerning this point, Grotius writes in a footnote (on the same page): "That the Maxims of the Law of Nature are not merely arbitrary Rules, but are founded on the Nature of Things; on the very Constitution of Man, from which certain Relations result, between such and such Actions, and the State of a reasonable and sociable Creature." I.xi.note 1.
47. I.1.xi.§1.
48. I.1xi.§1–2. See also footnotes: I.1.xi.notes 2–9.
49. I.1.xiv. Italics are in the text.
50. Ibid.
51. I.1.xiv.note 1.
52. I.1.xiv.
53. Ibid.
54. I.1.xiv.note 3.
55. I.1.xv.
56. Ibid. Of course, Socrates' answer was just the opposite.
57. Richard Tuck, ed., Hugo Grotius, *The Rights of War and Peace*, ed. Richard Tuck, 3 vols. (Indianapolis, IN: Liberty Fund, 2005), 1:151n3.
58. Haakonssen suggests that Grotius understands that while we have the ability to understand what is good and bad via the natural law, it is not until God forbids such actions that we are under an obligation to follow them. Haakonssen, *Natural Law and Moral Philosophy*, 27.
59. This point is also underscored by Martin Harvey. In the briefest terms, Harvey develops the thesis that (foreshadowing Hobbes' political absolutism) Grotius develops his own version of "moral pessimism." This means that the motivational gap between duty and human self-interest must be supplied by the sovereign's sword. Martin Harvey, "Grotius and Hobbes," *British Journal for the History of Philosophy* 14, no. 1 (2006): 36. This is so primarily because,

as Harvey argues, Grotius rejects the teleological conception of political society. Rather, Grotius paves the way for Hobbes to conceive of political society as "an artefact brought into existence for predominantly secular and prudential reasons." Ibid., 33. Although I recognize and (partially) defend the "moral pessimism" Harvey attributes to Grotius, I do not give adequate attention to Harvey's claim that Grotius' moral pessimism explains the genesis of Hobbes' political absolutism. Nevertheless, it is a thesis worth further investigation.

60. Grotius, *The Rights of War and Peace*, I.xvi. This is a quote from *The Preliminary Discourse*. Italics are in the text. Additionally, Grotius writes in a footnote: "So that the *Civil Laws*, though no kind of Law is in itself more arbitrary, is at the Bottom no more than an Extension of Natural Law, a Consequence of that inviolable Law of Nature, *that everyone is obliged to a religious Performance of his Promise*." I.xvi.note 1. Italics are in the text.

61. I.xvii. This is a quote from *The Preliminary Discourse*. Italics are in the text.

62. I.1.xii. Italics are in text.

Chapter Three

The Enlightenment: Hobbes, Pufendorf, Locke, and Hume

INTRODUCTION

To fully appreciate the age of Enlightenment requires a keen historical, political, economic, and philosophically discerning insight. It is a complex time period and hardly a pool of transparent clearness to wade through, and in such a short text as this, easy to oversimplify. Nevertheless, for the purposes of this text, there are (at least) three notable features of the Enlightenment period to underscore: First, a dominate note points to the dispute associated with political collectivism. Second, a profoundly significant change in the ideal of science. Finally, the nearly incomprehensible rise of individualism. An orientation toward these topic illuminates the importance of natural law, and ultimately, to its demise.

Part of the history of ideas up to about the 1700s involves the tension created by the ruthless attempts to protect and justify political collectivism. This is a discussion about the historical context that philosophers normally ignore. And yet, without understanding the political collectivism that dominated most cultures, especially the brand found in Great Britain, much of the intellectual and emotional energy spent by the writers discussed below may fall on deaf ears.

So, now, the question is this: What is political collectivism? Of course, political collectivism is one version of collectivism. As a political theory, collectivism stresses the priority of group goals over individual goals and the importance of cohesion with social groups (within the collective). Surviving aspects of collectivism may be found in contemporary institutions like fire and police stations. Political collectivism is often an aspect associated with societies organized around a monarchy (or a centralized form of government). Part of the collectivism includes (caste) social ranks, ranks which determined one's identity and function within a monarchy. Great Britain, during the 1600 and 1700s provides us with a near infallible indication of such a political collective. In fact, Britain's context is quite unusual and, in many ways, explains why there was an absorbing (violent) passion with this topic in the sixteen hundreds. A short description may help thin the copse hiding the significance of England's Stuart Crown.

When the reign of Queen Elizabeth I (1533–1603) came to an end,[1] the King of Scotland, James the VI, became the King of Scotland, Ireland and England.[2] Audacious rumors abounded about his character (fueled primarily by the Puritans from the country), even in the light of his authorization of a new translation of the Christian bible, *The King James Version*, that he was bisexual or gay, and his court was sexually decadent.[3] This view was also aggravated by King James' role in the Overbury Affair.[4] With these scant issues in place, another issue emerged, which made Britain's political collectivism an unbearable raging fever to some, viz., King James' insistence on the divine right of kings.

King James VI and I, as well as his son, Charles I (1600–1649),[5] insisted that the origin of their political authority came directly from God. In fact, as some argue, the Kings and Queens of England were direct descendants of Adam and Eve, the first King and Queen of the earth.[6] The claim is that the King is *only* accountable to God, not to Parliament, the House of Lords, or to any commoners in England. Such a viewpoint was a standing menace to the members of Parliament. Ultimately, the reputation of the Stuart Crown and the unwarrantable insistence on the divine right of Kings, added fuel to the flame of the crisis of the English civil war between the Royals, those Catholics who supported the Crown, and the largely Protestant members of the Parliament. As we shall see soon, the social contract theory emerged as a counter to the divine right of kings. The social contract theory made explicit the dictum of the origin of civil communities and the origin of political authority of the government. In short, both originate from the consent of the members of the civil community. I will now turn to discuss the impact the changing ideal of science concomitant with the Enlightenment period.

To speak of the *changing* ideal of science during the Enlightenment era is to indicate the dynamic quality of the scientific enterprise among the members of the scientific community.[7] This is not to imply that the scientific method, which is the foundation of our current scientific community, was the same as the one during the Enlightenment. That would be an erroneous impression. On the contrary, what we see is that the scientific communities (in the loosest sense of the term) were largely dominated by two groups, the "chymists'"or "spagyrists" and the "peripatetics."[8] I will begin with the former.

According to Peter Alexander, the spagyrists were medical chemists who had the theoretical aim of giving accounts of illness and health in chemical terms and the very practical aim of discovering chemical cures for illnesses.[9] According to the spagyrists, the ultimate products of analysis were chemical principles. Most spagyrists held "that there were three principles, salt, sulphur and mercury, called the 'tria prima.'"[10] Alexander adds: "The favoured method for the investigation of the composition of substances was 'analysis by fire' seen as the breaking up of those substances into their constituents by heat, usually by exposure to naked flames."[11]

Contra the spagyrists, Alexander writes: "The Aristotelian elements, earth, water, air and fire were the focus of the peripatetics. They considered the elements to be unanalysable components, in various combinations, of observable bodies and substances whose observable qualities could be explained in terms of properties attributed to these elements."[12] Alexander marks the difference between these two groups in terms of spagyrists' focus on experimentation and the peripatetics' focus on theorizing. Unfortunately, as Alexander makes clear, many scientists grew weary of this division, primarily because it appeared to their own scientific intuitions, that no real scientific advancements were being achieved. Why that is the case, I cannot discuss now; Nevertheless, Alexander states that this criticism was especially in the forefront of Sir Robert Boyle's (1627–1691) mind. Here is what he means.

Boyle stresses that the peripatetics rely heavily on books while the chemists bank on laboratories. So, the peripatetics' strong point is that they mine the wealth of reasoning, general theories and consistency while their weak point is that they were quite content to neglect experiments. With the chymists, it is the other way about; their strong suit lies in their experimentation. Theorizing is of small consequence.

Thus, as Alexander explains, Boyle's understanding of the Peripatitics and the Chymists is two-edged: What emerges is that "what he admires about the peripatitics is their *attitude* to theorizing and that what he admires about the chymists is their *attitude* toward experimentation; it is evident that he thinks little of the content of the theories of both groups."[13] As a consequence, Alexander explains that Boyle understood "how little they understand what they mean by their own explanatory concepts."[14]

With these criticisms in mind, Boyle takes the notion of theorizing from the peripatitics and the experimentation from the chymists, and contra both groups and their reliance on Aristotle's metaphysics and physics, reintroduces the notion of the atom.[15] Of course, although the atom was discussed earlier by Pierre Gassendi (1592–1655), Boyle takes the notion of the atom to explanatory lengths not seen before. In fact, Boyle introduced ingenious experiments (with testable predictions), that showed, with few theoretical assumptions about atoms, his explanations were more compelling than the chymists and the peripatitics elucidations about the world.[16] So, although the changing ideal of science saw its birth in the mind of individuals like Gassendi, it was not until Boyle applied his scientific genius to the issues that the changing ideal of science based on the atom became established. I will now move on to the issue of individualism.

Oddly, the points above contribute *partially* to the rise of individualism (a point I want to mention but I cannot discuss at the length the topic deserves). As the term indicates, individualism is the socio-politico-economic doctrine that focuses on the importance of the individual. In fact, the focus of individualism, contra political collectivism, is on the individual as the most important constituent of a common wealth and not the government or the monarchy.[17] If that is the case, then how does a culture dominated by monarchies, especially Great Britain, break the chains of political collectivism and move toward individualism? The explanation is (partly) a combination of the rise of atomism within the scientific community and the doctrine of the Social Contract Theory, which was an alternative response to the political collectivism. To make this a little clearer, I will now turn to several authors who were influential in this area.

THOMAS HOBBES (1588–1679)

Our discussion begins with the modern period's most infamous author, Thomas Hobbes. Known by many of his contemporaries as the "Monster of Malmesbury," he was a prolific author, scientist, and philosopher. His best-known work, even in the minds of contemporary scholars, is the *Leviathan*.[18] This work exemplifies an attempt to defend a version of the social contract theory described briefly above. There are four points to discuss: 1. What portrayal accurately captures what humans are like and does this representation precisely depict what humans are like in the state of nature? 2. Historically speaking, what does Hobbes take to be origins of the formation of a civil society? 3. What kind of government does he advance and what is the foundation of the political authority of that government? 4. What view of the law of nature, if any, does Hobbes develop?

Of humans in general, Hobbes writes: "So that in the nature of man we find three principal causes of quarrel: first, competition; secondly, diffidence; thirdly, glory."[19] Each point will be briefly examined. Competition among humans is the result of the perceived equality each individual assumes about himself in terms of his own physical strength and strength of mind.[20] The perceived equality, cashed out (at times) as a strict form of psychological egoism,[21] gives rise to each individual's feeling of diffidence toward each other. This means that, minimally, each individual will be willing, in certain circumstances, to kill another in order to get what he wants especially when it comes to living safely.[22] The last feature of human nature points to the vital necessity that humans have to be respected and to reject all signs of disrespect.[23]

With such a nonplussed and gloomy view of human nature in mind (regardless of whether humans are rational or irrational by nature),[24] Hobbes makes his political philosophy clear, beginning with the state of nature which is a (hypothetical) time prior to the existence of a civil society. Briefly, the state of nature is a time "without a common power to keep them all in awe."[25] This is a common feature among social contract theorists. Unique to Hobbes, though, is that the state of nature is a time of never ending war, Hobbes writes:

> Every man is enemy to every man, the same is consequent to the time wherein men live without other security than what their own strength and their own invention shall furnish them withal. In such a condition there is no place for industry, because the fruit thereof is uncertain, and consequently, no culture of the earth, no navigation, nor use of the commodities that may be imported by sea, no commodious building, no instruments of moving and removing such things as require much force, no knowledge of the face of the earth, no account of time, no arts, no letters, no society, and which is worst of all, continual fear and danger of violent death, and the life of man, solitary, poor, nasty, brutish and short.[26]

Although such a view of human nature may disturb our intuitions about what humans are like, the following quotation may raise even greater suspicions about Hobbes' viewpoint:

> To this war of every man against every man, this also is consequent: that nothing can be unjust. The notions of right and wrong, justice and injustice have there no place. Where there is no common power, there is no law; where no law, no injustice. Force and fraud are in war the two cardinal virtues. Justice and injustice are none of the faculties neither of the body, nor mind.[27]

Such a claim is controversial because Hobbes asserts that (perhaps apart from our intuitions) nothing is right or wrong prior to the formation of a civil society. Rather what dominates the moral landscape is the doctrine of eliminative naturalism.[28] No doubt, Hobbes has his arrows aimed at the scholastic tradition (including Plato and Aristotle), and in particular, at the truth-making conditions which warrant the *cross-cultural* and *trans-historical* significance of moral precepts. For Hobbes, these views are without a vestige of truth. Law and morality only emerge and are relevant when a civil society is formed. So, why is this the case? I will turn to the issue now.

This second issue is now relevant: Why do civil societies form? The answer to this question forms the first pillar of the social contract theory, more specifically, why do individuals in the state of nature, *a perfect state of freedom*, create a civil society? Hobbes writes the following: "The passions that incline men to peace are fear of death, desire of such things as are necessary to commodious living, and a hope by their industry to obtain them. And reason suggesteth convenient articles of peace, upon which men may be drawn to agreement. These articles are they which otherwise are called the Laws of Nature."[29]

Even though the state of nature is a perfect state of freedom, the continual threat of death overrides and motivates the individuals (in cooperative groups)[30] in the state of nature to come to some sort of agreement to form a civil society.[31] The quotation above also mentions that such an agreement must be mediated by creating a set of rules in order to cooperate with one another. Hobbes calls these rules the Laws of Nature.[32] Before I discuss this point, it is necessary to discuss the second pillar of Hobbes' brand of the social contract theory, that is to say, the origin of political authority.

Naturally, as the individuals move from the state of nature to form a civil society, they will need a political authority to enforce the rules and laws the citizens agree to follow. Although, from a historical point of view, there were different forms of governments open to him, e.g., an aristocracy, an oligarchy, a democracy, and so forth, he had a very clear conviction (given his view of human nature) that the only form of government suitable will be a *monarchy*. But there is an important caveat—the monarch will possess *absolute and arbitrary power*, which was perfectly evident to the majority of contemporary monarchs including the Stuart Crown.[33] In any case, such an extreme form of government seems unintuitive, and utterly so. Why would anyone agree to give up all their liberty to such an individual? No doubt, such a set up seems like a disguised version of the state of nature. Here is the answer: Given what humans are like, this is the only way to keep order in society.

Finally, although I touched briefly on this point, it is of prime importance to consider Hobbes' view of the law of nature. Historically speaking, when scholars of the early Modern period of philosophy, turned to the law of nature, they referred to a set of moral precepts that existed independently of the minds of humans, and even in Grotius' case, independent of the mind of God, and to a set of corresponding dispositions in the soul or mind of humans.[34] However, Hobbes' view is not cut out of the same cloth. In contemporary terms, scholars tend to describe Hobbes as an ethical subjectivist.[35] This means two things. First, he is an ethical idealist, which means that the truth-conditions of ethical claims are in virtue of someone or other's mind. Second, in Hobbes' viewpoint, the moral claims, or the laws of nature, are true or false relative to the desires, preferences, or goals of the *monarch*. In other words, whatever the monarch decides is moral becomes what is moral including what is immoral. No doubt, such a viewpoint seems extreme, and it was certainly too extreme when he published the *Leviathan*.[36] Nevertheless, although his view of a monarchy is eventually rejected by the academic community, his view of moral idealism is embraced by many scholars even to this day.

Even though Hobbes may be accurately described as an ethical subjectivist, what role does the law of nature play in his outlook? Hobbes offers several convenient articles of peace, which he calls the laws of nature. Let us begin with what he takes to be a law of nature: "a precept, or general rule found out by reason, by which a man is forbidden to do that which is destructive of his life, or taketh away the means of preserving the same, and to omit that by which he thinks it may best be preserved."[37] Such an article of peace, limited initially to one's own self-preservation, only makes sense under the contractual process of moving out of the state of nature. That said, there is the question whether the Monarch must follow the articles of peace.[38] A destructive dilemma looms on the horizon.

Hobbes argues that the Monarch is not accountable to anyone except God.[39] This implies that the Monarch is not required to follow the articles of peace. But if this is true, then the Monarch has the liberty right to ignore the articles of peace, which initially were the foundation of leaving the state of nature. Again, one can only imagine what desperate conditions a Monarch with supreme power could create—one reminiscent of the state of nature. This I take to be the first horn of the dilemma.

The other horn is this: If the Monarch *must* follow the articles of peace, then the Monarch does not have supreme authority. So, given Hobbes' view of the authority, either the door is open to a return to something akin to the state of nature in civil society or the Monarch does not have supreme power.

Although Hobbes' standpoint is faced with serious objections, his writings still command attention. At least for the purposes of this text, Hobbes represents the Enlightenment abandonment of the traditional approach to the law of nature and human positive law. Instead, his work makes clear where we end up after we embrace nominalism. Such conclusions, as I will try to demonstrate, are common among the scholars who align themselves to the post-Aristotelianism which is beginning to take root in the minds of the philosophical and scientific community.

SAMUEL PUFENDORF (1632–1688)

Although Hobbes was the most infamous philosopher during the middle to late seventeenth century, the most widely read (and, in contemporary terms, relatively unknown scholar) is the German philosopher, Samuel Pufendorf. He is known, in certain circles, for his text *The Whole Duty of Man, According to the Law of Nature,* published in 1673.[40] In fact, it was a compact version of his magnum opus, *On the Law of Nature and Nations*, published in

1672.[41] According to J. B. Schneewind, both works were widely read and very popular.[42] Indeed, as Schneewind makes clear, "the Duty of Man, in Latin or in modern languages, became the textbook with which students in much of Europe and in many of the *American colonies* studied natural law until well into the eighteenth century."[43] In this section, I will discuss Pufendorf's view of natural law and the foundation of (human) positive law.

Pufendorf portrays himself as the founder of modern natural law and the successor of Hugo Grotius. The former makes sense, as I shall make clear shortly, but the latter raises doubts. For example, if we take "successor" in the broadest sense of the term, in particular, the "heir" or "replacement" of Grotius, we might expect Pufendorf to defend the doctrines Grotius espoused, e.g., theological intellectualism and metaphysical realism. But the fact is this: Pufendorf casts off both perspectives. Instead, Pufendorf endorses theological voluntarism and nominalism. I will begin with the latter viewpoint.

Again, in the simplest of terms, nominalism denies the existence of forms or universals. Rather, particulars provide us with all the resources we need for understanding the phenomena of attribute agreement, prediction, and abstract reference.[44] But if this is the case, then how does Pufendorf make sense of natural law, since he claims and was recognized to be the founder of modern natural law? Hopefully, the answer will be plain for everyone to see.

Pufendorf's notion of natural law follows on the heels of his discriminating insight of the nature and disposition of man:

> So then Man is an Animal very desirous of his own *Preservation*; of *himself* liable to many *Wants*; *unable* to Support himself without the Help of *other* of his Kind; and yet wonderfully fit in Society to promote a *common Good*: But then his is *malicious*, *insolent*, and easily *provok'd*, and not less *prone* to do Mischief to his Fellow than his is *capable* of effecting it.[45]

Thus, Pufendorf writes the following: "The Rules then of this Fellowship, which are the Laws of *Human Society*, whereby Men are directed how to render themselves useful Members thereof, and without which it falls to pieces, are called the *Laws of Nature*."[46]

As the quotations above indicate, it needs no great play of imagination to see the connection between human nature and the natural law. If we suppose that Pufendorf's viewpoint is correct, then what unambiguous natural laws follow from Pufendorf's notion of human nature and what validation, if any, do these moral laws warrant?

Pufendorf makes clear that there are three main headings under the natural law—laws needed for the sociability and survival of society: "the first of which gives us Directions how by the single Dictates of right Reason Man ought to behave himself towards *God*; the *second* contains our Duty towards *our selves*; and the *third* that towards *other Men*."[47] I will begin with the former.

The first absolute duty Pufendorf mentions is that no one should harm or damage one another or let no one injure another.[48] Pufendorf explains that this is the broadest and most necessary duty.[49] Although labeling this an absolute duty smacks of no exceptions—and it is unclear whether this is what Pufendorf means—there is nothing ambiguous about the requirement: "so as by this it is forbidden to take away, spoil, damage, or withdraw, in whole or in part, from our Use, whatsoever by a lawful Title we are possess'd of."[50] In addition to these requirements are the following, forbidden, perilous actions, viz., "Whence all those Actions are hereby made Crimes, by which any Wrong is done to others, as Murther, Wounding, Striking, Rapine, Theft, Fraud, Violence, whether practis'd directly or indirectly, mediately or immediately."[51]

The second aspect of our duties to others points to the natural equality among all men: "It follows that, among those *Duties which Men owe to each other*, this obtains the *second* Place, That *every Man esteem and treat another*, as naturally *equal to himself, or as one who is a Man as well as he*."[52] To this precept, Pufendorf makes a relevant qualification that respect is due regardless of their circumstances: "As on the other side the Niggardliness of *Nature* or *Fortune* cannot of themselves set any Man so low, as that he shall be in worse Condition, as to the Enjoyment of *Common Right*, than others."[53]

The last absolute precept, which is directed at the common sociability, is this: "Among the Duties of one Man towards another, which must be practis'd for the sake of *Common Society*, we put in the *third* places this, *That every Man ought to promote the Good of another, as far as convenitently he may*."[54] Such a requirement may be satisfied in, at least, two ways. First, we may promote the advantage of other people by simply cultivating our own lives in a way that may be useful to others.[55] Additionally, some, who are blessed with wealth or means, may act as a community's benefactor with the following qualifications: First, there is no requirement of the friend of humanity to give more than they are able, and second, the patron must allocate tangible and intangible goods according to the constraints of distributive justice.[56]

On top of the absolute duties, Pufendorf makes clear that there are conditional duties associated with contracts, promises and agreements: "With respect to this general Duty it is an Obligation of the *Law of Nature*, that *every Man keep his Word*, or fulfil his Promises and make good his Contracts."[57] What this means is familiar. Unlike the standing absolute duties discussed above,[58] while there is no requirement, per se, to make a promise or an agreement, to do so puts one under two different kinds of obligations. Here is the meaning. Unless, this agreement has legal ramifications, a typical non-legal breach of faith does not imply coercion: "I can only charge him with

Rudeness, *Cruelty* or *hard dealing*; but I cannot *compel* him to do me reason either by my own Power or by any superior Authority."[59]

With Pufendorf's notion of the law of nature in mind, the ultimate justification or warrant for the precepts of natural law must be noted. It is within this discussion that Pufendorf's commitment to nominalism comes to the surface.

The question of justification of moral statements was a central concern among the scholars of the seventeenth- and eighteenth-centuries. The growing skepticism toward the metaphysical realism defended by both Catholics and Protestants alike supplied part of the motivation.[60] Although the question of justification began to emerge prior to the Enlightenment period, one obvious representative of the turn away from metaphysical realism is brought forward as early as Thomas Hobbes. As I note earlier, Hobbes rejects metaphysical realism, embraces nominalism, and uses moral subjectivism, a version of moral idealism, as a justification for moral statements, and ultimately, the basis for moral authority and (contra Curley) moral obligation. Although Pufendorf does not follow Hobbes in this line of enquiry, he, nevertheless, rejects metaphysical realism, embraces nominalism, and defends a version of moral idealism. Such a perspective deserves attention.[61]

Before I begin, the following qualification is necessary. Even though Schneewind's edition contains only twelve pages from Pufendorf's eight-volume set of *The Law of Nature and of Nations*, it is still a complicated viewpoint to articulate. So, in an attempt to keep my own discussion manageable, I will be as brief as possible with the hope to spell out accurately Pufendorf's warrant of moral claims. It should also be noted that Pufendorf's position gets picked up and elaborated in more detail by John Locke eighteen years later in the *Essay Concerning Human Understanding*.[62]

Pufendorf's rejection of metaphysical realism, perhaps the kind articulated by Grotius and others of like kind, leaves behind the possibility of giving a deep account of moral justification. But what does this mean? In rough terms, this means that (hopefully without sounding anachronistic) in terms of the justification of a moral statement, say, for example, it is wrong to murder, one must trace, so to speak, back to a set of moral facts which make this statement true. Although this sounds simple (and in many ways it is simple), it is the status of the moral facts which are in question. In this case, following the metaphysical realists before him, the moral facts exist independently of the beliefs, desires, and preferences, of all rational beings, including God. Another way of putting this is to say that the moral facts are mind-independent. Pufendorf (including Locke and later Hume) rejects this approach. If this is so, what alternative approach, if any, is available to Pufendorf? This question is relevant because he speaks of the various precepts of the law of nature *as if* they have truth values.

The alternative approach available to Pufendorf—but, perhaps, not as clearly articulated as his position could be—traces the justification (somewhere) back to the beliefs, preferences, and desires of someone else's mind. Again, two positions are worth mentioning. In contemporary terms, the viewpoints in focus are subjectivism and intersubjectivism. As I tried to make clear, the former points to a position articulated by Hobbes. As the term *subjectivism* indicates, especially in Hobbes' outlook, the beliefs, desires and preferences stem from the monarch who has absolute power. So, on this view, whatever the monarch says is true, right, wrong, or otherwise, *is* true, right or wrong. Another popular position to take, one which took root during the reformation and later, (contra Hobbes) is to rely solely on the beliefs, preferences, and desires of the Christian God. This position is called theological voluntarism (see chapter 2, and in particular, John Colman) shared among (some) Catholics as well as Protestants alike. Of course, the important implication is obvious. Without a legitimate authority, one recognized for his (or her) wisdom, impartiality, and so forth, no moral statement may possess a truth value.

Intersubjectivism is the other viewpoint.[63] Contrary to subjectivism, the meaning of intersubjectivism may not be so noticeable, and unlike the focus of subjectivism, which concentrates on the desires, preferences, and beliefs of a single *individual*, the stress of *inter*subjectivism is placed on the desires, and on the conventions of a group, community, culture, or society. In the simplest of terms, the implication is that whatever the moral beliefs of a culture, and so forth, accepts, i.e., stems from or is consistent with its beliefs, desires, and preferences, acts as the justification for moral claims, and other such beliefs. This is, no doubt, a provocative claim to make for various reasons. For example, one problem points to the status and meaning of conventions. The other problem involves pointing to examples, which qualify as conventions. The former problem I will ignore for the purposes of this discussion. The other problem is not quite as hard to satisfy, although they may be controversial and some may not qualify as a moral issue. Here is what I mean. Recently, with the Supreme Court ruling on same-sex marriages, the traditional view of marriage, namely heterosexual marriages, was challenged. Although the ruling has not changed the prevalent viewpoint of the cultural institution of marriage, the accepted view of marriage, at least for our culture, is a heterosexual view of marriage. Therefore, although this is beginning to change, the moral claim, "Only heterosexual marriages are morally right," is true (regardless of the USSC ruling) relative to the cultural convention of our society. The same may also be said of claims associated with the issues of gun ownership and the Second Amendment, capital punishment and the Eighth Amendment, and so forth.

The question to address now is this: Where does Pufendorf fit into this discussion? Unfortunately, a clear answer is not forthcoming. The main reason is that the distinctions above are too specific to place Pufendorf into in order to make it plain for everyone. However, there is enough evidence in *The Law of Nature and of Nations* to cast an informing light upon Pufendorf's moral justification. Pufendorf's warrant for the normative status of moral claims falls (at least) within the moral idealism camp, and in particular, theological subjectivism. In other words, unlike Grotius, the moral justification (and moral authority) of the laws of nature, ultimately has its source in the beliefs, desires, and preferences in the mind of God.[64] Although this sounds like a misapprehension of Pufendorf, I plan to make this claim apparent.

There are two basic issues to discuss about Pufendorf's moral idealism (at least for the purposes for this text). The concepts of moral entities and moral ideas are the bright lines to understand Pufendorf's viewpoint. I will begin with the former.

There is a certain ambiguity associated with the concept of moral entity. It is used in two different ways, which are, nevertheless, consistent with one another. The main use of the term is fairly straightforward and clear.[65] A moral entity is a moral property attached, so to speak, to an action by which "the moral and actions of men are judged and tempered, so that they may attain a character and appearance different from the rude simplicity of dumb animals."[66] There are two issues here: what constitutes a moral property and what is their origin?

Typically, to speak of a moral property, at least at the time of Pufendorf's writing (as I pointed out earlier in chapter 1), is to point out a one-place or monadic universals. Such universals include colors, shapes, and virtues. What is interesting about these universals is that a virtue, or the color or the shape of an artifact, actually belongs to the object to which it is attached.[67] For example, as I explained earlier, to articulate the claim that "John R. is courageous," will be true (minimally) just in case it is true that John *possesses* the virtue of courage. So, the universal property of justice exists independently of the desires, preferences, or beliefs of any mind. There is another important point as well.

Although possessing the virtue of courage does not satisfy the perceptual requirements of the universal properties associated with colors or shapes, properties like the virtues are captured indirectly. What does this mean? While such a discussion is too long and difficult to pursue here, this much may be brought forward for inspection: A virtue indirectly explains the behavior of a person who possesses the virtue. This means two things. First, we expect an individual who possesses a virtue, say, courage, to act in a manner consistent with that virtue. That is, he will act courageously in the face of danger. Nevertheless, acting a certain way is only part of the story. The other part concerns the feelings and emotions of the individual said to be courageous. Namely, an individual who possesses the virtue of courage will feel pleasure in the face of danger or, at least, will not feel any fear.[68] Thus, as the discussion implies, if both conditions obtain (and other circumstances not mentioned), the possession of a virtue will be unavoidably recognizable (to the trained mind) and have an epistemic corroboration.

With these thoughts in mind, Pufendorf's position stands in stark contrast to the traditional view attributed to Plato, Aristotle, the Stoics, Aquinas, Grotius, and others not mentioned here:

> Now as the original way of producing physical entities is creation, so the way in which moral entities are produced can scarcely be better expressed than by the *imposition*. For they do not arise out of the intrinsic nature of the physical properties of things, but they are superadded, at the will of intelligent entities, to things already existent and physical complete . . . [and] come into existence only by the determination of their authors.[69]

Moral entities, or moral properties, are not a part of the physical properties of things.[70] On the contrary, God and even humans impose (or project) them on the actions, which they arbitrarily, in some sense, find problematic.[71] There are three issues to bring up before I move on to Locke.

First, whereas humans tend to arbitrarily pick actions for moral evaluation, Pufendorf qualifies this viewpoint: "Although moral entities owe their origin to imposition and are not necessary, they have not arisen in a loose and general manner, that scientific knowledge about them is on that account utterly uncertain."[72] So, as I understand this quote, three points are relevant. First, although he does not say why, some moral entities (moral claims) are created by the act of imposition, but not in an arbitrary manner. At first glance, we might be tempted to think that this applies primarily to humans only. Pufendorf's theological voluntarism points otherwise to God's choice of actions: His decisions about which actions are right, wrong, or permissible are also imposed, but (like the human act of imposition) not completely arbitrarily chosen. The best we may attempt at an answer is God's goodness.[73] Fortunately, later Locke attempts to clear the air of this ambiguous matter. Second, because moral entities are created by the desire and beliefs of both God and man, they are not necessary. What does he mean? Unfortunately, this is no small matter to leave unattended. Earlier, Pufendorf indicated that moral entities are not intrinsic to the nature of actions (a point Hume later endorses). Nevertheless, there is still not a happy consummation of this puzzle. Pufendorf's meaning of the relationship between what is necessary and what is intrinsic remains at a low visibility. Unfortunately, I cannot divest myself of the impression of the ambiguity associated with this point.

The third point speaks to the issue on which part of the thesis of this text rests upon. Pufendorf, like Hobbes, Locke, and Hume, understood, all too clearly, the faint relationship between moral justification and the new scientific ideal. Here is the issue. As Aristotle's physics and metaphysics lost its hegemonic position in the science community, it was (initially) unclear what sort of implications there would be for the concomitant discussion of moral theory (i.e., an *Arête* Theory). This is not so for Pufendorf. It was perfectly evident that the new scientific ideal was ill equipped to discuss the occult properties of substantial forms or universals. But there is another issue as well. Even if we assume that actions possess the intrinsic properties of rightness or wrongness, from a scientific point of view, they are explanatorily irrelevant. Later, from a contemporary point of view, any natural law justification, whether a deep account developed by Finnis or a superficial account employed by Ronald Dworkin, will also fall prey to the same critique the early moderns like Pufendorf began to understand and employ.[74]

Second, although (like Plato and Aristotle) universals possess an active force to produce physical motion or change in an individual, Pufendorf makes clear that the active force associated with moral entities is dissimilar: "The active force which lies in them does not consist in their ability directly to produce any physical motion or change in any thing. One source of force (viz., the threat of good and evil) of moral entities flows from God as man's creator. One source comes from men by their own inventions."[75] Such a qualification, as we shall see, will become the difference between a law which is authoritative and one which is not.

Finally, since the moral entities Pufendorf speaks about are imposed or superadded, their stability depends upon the minds of God or of humans:

> In conclusion, as moral entities owe their origin to *imposition*, so from this they obtain their stability, as well as their variations, and when it has ceased to operate, as it were, they simultaneously disappear, just as a shadow disappears the instant a light is extinguished. Moreover, those which are of divine impositions are removed again only at the divine pleasure. Those which have been established by the will of men are abolished again by the same, even though the physical substance of the person or things remain unchanged.[76]

Because this quote speaks for itself, I will now move on to discuss John Locke. As we shall see, Locke owes an intellectual debt to Pufendorf when it comes to the warrant of moral claims, including the doctrine of "superadded moral properties."

JOHN LOCKE (1632–1704)

It requires no extraordinary perception to discern Locke's influence in the history of ideas. In fact, some scholars have suggested that Locke was the progenitor of the Enlightenment period. This may be true, but if he is, we should not assume that the Enlightenment was started by him. Some scholars attribute the origins of the Enlightenment period in the works of René Descartes, and maybe even earlier. The point is that Locke's two major works, the *Essay Concerning Human Understanding* and the *Two Treatises of Government* (*Two Treatises*),[77] seem to capture, in a dramatic way, the turn toward personal autonomy concomitant in the Enlightenment era. In any case, like Hobbes, Locke advocates a version of the social contract theory. I will now turn to that discussion. First, I will discuss Locke's version of social contract theory including his view of the state of nature and his connected doctrine of the law of nature, and the form of government he endorses. After that, I will discuss his view of virtue. His analysis of virtue occurs in the *Essay* and it also involves the law of nature.

The state of nature is foremost on the mind of Locke in the *Second Treatise of Government.*[78] Again it is a time that is prior to the formation of a commonwealth or a civil society. There is no government, no legal system, no police force, no fire departments, and so forth. Nevertheless, *unlike* Hobbes, Locke argues that "though this be a *State of Liberty*, yet it is *not a State of License*."[79] Instead, as Locke makes clear: "The *State of Nature* has a Law of Nature to govern it, which obliges every one: And Reason, which is that Law, teaches all Mankind, who will but consult it, that being all equal and independent, no one ought to harm another in his Life, Health, Liberty, or Possessions."[80] This is an interesting twist. What does this quote mean?

It is unclear exactly what it means. Still, two points may help. First, contra Hobbes, the state of nature is not a perfect state of freedom. Nevertheless, Locke's state of nature closely resembles Hobbes' because there is no government or legal system in place. But, unlike Hobbes' work, even in the state of nature the law of nature retains a permanent significance. Thus, like the eternal verities, everyone is bound, everywhen, to follow the law of nature. Unfortunately, we are no closer to understanding what he means. Is this a Stoic account of the law of nature? Or does it reflect the accounts developed by Aquinas, Grotius, Pufendorf, or Hobbes? These are five different accounts of the law of nature. In fact, what is not generally known is that Locke actually defended a deep account of the law of nature (similar to Aquinas) which is dated 1660. He never published it. Eventually, it was discovered in 1947 by Wolfgang von Leyden and published in 1954. In that text, *Essays on the Law of Nature* (*Essays*),[81] Locke defends an account of the law of nature, which is very close to Thomas Aquinas' viewpoint.[82] So, what should we think? Is Locke's account of the law of nature in the *Essays* the same as his (albeit brief) account in the *Second Treatise*? This leads me to my second point.

Although Locke uses the term "law of nature" in the *Second Treatise*, there are doubts that Locke has anything in mind like his early account of the law of nature in the early *Essays*. Additionally, there are shadows of uncertainty that his view resembles the Stoics' view or even Aquinas' or Grotius' viewpoint. This is because, by 1690, when the *Two Treatises* were published,

Locke no longer accepted the kind of metaphysical machinery that is needed to defend those accounts. So, does this mean that Locke's view of natural law is more like Hobbes' or Pufendorf's account? That is, does Locke's account resemble the Hobbesian convenient article of peace, created by and consented to by the individuals moving out of the state of nature? Or is it more similar to Pufendorf's law of nature that is deduced from his descriptive account of the social character of humans? Although there are unvarnished differences between the two, there are some similarities as well. Let me explain.

Locke wrote the *Two Treatises* at the same time he was writing *An Essay Concerning Human Understanding*. The latter text is dedicated to defending a corpuscular (atomistic) account of the world. There is evidence that both texts are (logically) consistent, and because the *Essay* is a nominalist, corpuscular account of the world, the *Second Treatise* also assumes such an account is true.[83] Thus, according to Locke, if we use our reason correctly (even as Hobbes recommends), we will be able to figure out the moral importance of self-preservation and the preservation of others: "Every one as he is *bound to preserve himself*, and not to quit his Station willfully; so by the like reason when his own Preservation comes not in competition, ought he, as much as he can, *to preserve the rest of Mankind*."[84]

So, the issue before us, then, provokes a challenge to eliminate the misgivings I have raised against Locke's account of the law of nature in the *Second Treatise*. On the assumption that the *Second Treatise* is a constructive program developed against the backdrop of corpuscularism, then two points are relevant. First, this testifies to the fact that Locke's later account of the law of nature in the *Second Treatise* differs very widely from his early account of the law of nature in the *Essays*. Again, the reason is that the former account is affiliated with nominalism, which is also the guiding assumption of the *Essay*. Whereas, the *Essays* are consistent with and derived from the metaphysical realism discussed in chapter 1. Second, while Locke's view of the law of nature is decidedly different than Hobbes' convenient articles of peace, Locke shares Hobbes' nominalism. That said, it is doubtful that Locke shares the unsympathetic narrative of the human demeanor. What about Pufendorf? Certainly, Locke shares Pufendorf's nominalism. But what about Pufendorf's acute representation of the common nature (sociability) of humanity? Locke's version is not distinguished by the same sort of candor or insight found in Pufendorf. In fact, Locke's interpretation follows on the heels of the discussion in the *First Treatise* of the *Two Treatises*. Whereas Filmer argues that all people are not born free or equal,[85] Locke, after utterly repudiating Filmer's defense of the divine right of kings, simply maintains the reasonable assumption that all people are born free and equal. And, in the same vein as Pufendorf, deduces his version of the law of nature: "no one should harm another in his Life, Health, Liberty, or Possessions."[86]

The next question is this: What form of government does Locke advocate? Again, from his basic assumptions, Locke breaks with tradition and forges a new link in the chain of progress to freedom and equality. Like Hobbes, Locke argues that because the state of nature is harried by uncertainties, the members of the state of nature will (eventually) assent with one another in order to form a new, civil society. At the same time, Locke argues that the members of this new civil society will create and consent to a distinctive form of government. Instead of a monarchy, which he says is just a form of the state of nature, he advocates a form of government which has three branches: the legislative, the executive and the federative. The legislative branch creates laws "for the preserving the Community and the Members of it."[87] The executive branch enforces those rules.[88] The third branch, viz., the federative branch, is dedicated to "the Power of War and Peace, Leagues and Alliances, and all the Transactions, with all Persons and Communities without the Commonwealth."[89] What is the relationship between all three branches?

Of the three, the legislative possesses the most power.[90] The power the legislative contains, though, does not possess the lure of despotic power. Rather, it is a power guided by the law of nature[91] and the power it possesses is transferred to it by the consent of the members of the civil society.[92] Additionally, unlike a monarchy, Locke adds that the legislative branch is bound in the straightest bonds, and as a result, it is restricted in many ways, including the restriction of seizing privately owned property without the owner's consent.[93] Finally, because the members of the legislative are elected by the commonwealth, the legislative branch "*cannot transfer the Power of Making Laws* in any other hands."[94] Although I have not spent nearly enough time discussing these points, it is for the sake of time that I will now discuss Locke's view of virtue.

Locke's view of virtue is found primarily in the *Essay*. In an almost reassuring phrase, Locke (as Pufendorf did) claims that there are three different kinds of laws according to which people generally judge their actions (and it is here that we are introduced to the role virtue and vice play): "1. The *Divine* Law. 2. The *Civil* Law. 3. The Law of *Opinion* or *Reputation*, if I may so call it."[95] Additionally, attached to each law is a specific way of referring to the actions that conform or disagree with the law. Actions judged by the Divine law are called sins or duties, actions judged by the Civil law are called criminal or lawful, and finally, judged by the third law, the Law of opinion or reputation, actions are called either virtue or vices.[96]

Because the focus of this text is on Locke's notion of virtue, I will only briefly discuss the first two. Locke is unambiguous about the importance of the Divine law: "This is the only true touchstone of moral Rectitude; and by comparing them to this Law, it is, that Men judge of the most considerable Moral Good or Evil of their Actions."[97] The Civil law also plays an important role in the lives of a commonwealth. In subtle contrast to the Divine law, Locke points out that in a commonwealth nobody overlooks the Civil law, and it does not take any great play of imagination to understand why this is so. It has the power to "protect the Lives, Liberties, and Possessions, of those who live according to its Laws, and has power to take away Life, Liberty, or Goods, from him, who disobeys."[98]

Next, Locke turns to the topic of virtue and vice. It is important to note that in terms of the way he illustrates the ontological significance of the Divine law and prudential concerns associated with the Civil law, Locke spends most of his time discussing virtue and vice.

Although we should expect Locke to proceed in an open and aboveboard manner, he conflates (at least) three topics that should be discussed separately. Nevertheless, he weaves them together into a dizzying, swirling pool of ideas that would exasperate even the most patient among us.

Locke places his discussion of virtue and vice within his own views of the origins of political societies. As I mentioned earlier, even though men give up "to the publick the disposing of all their Force,"[99] there is still the need to coordinate the lives of the citizens of the commonwealth. The Law of opinion or reputation becomes a powerful tool to set a limit to the lives of each individual. And, the opinion of the community and the loss of reputation become the basis of virtue and vice: "yet they retain still the power of Thinking well or ill; approving or disapproving of the actions of those whom they live amongst, and converse with: And by this approbation and dislike they establish amongst themselves, what they will call *Vertue* and *Vice*."[100]

Despite the fact that the law of opinion is established in every commonwealth, we must not think that there is any convergence about what is approved or disapproved. It is tempting to believe this because of the prevailing attitude that virtue and vice refer to actions that in their own nature are right or wrong. Such a view Aristotle maintains. However, Locke makes clear that this is not so: "Vertue and vice are Names pretended, and supposed everywhere to stand for actions in their own nature right and wrong."[101] Rather, as the same passage indicates, the only convergence among the nations and different societies is this: "But yet, whatever is pretended, this is visible, that these Names, *Vertue* and *Vice*, in the particular instances of their application, through the several Nations and Societies of Men in the World, are constantly attributed only to such actions, as in each Country and Society are in reputation or discredit."

The third topic is really the most important one. The issue: If the convergence is limited to only the way the words 'virtue' and 'vice' are used and the names do not stand for actions in their own nature right and wrong, what is, if any, the standard for virtue and vice? Locke's answer is surprising. He makes clear that "the measure of what is every where called and esteemed *Vertue* and *Vice* [is] the Judgment, Maxims, or Fashions of that place."[102]

It is this last point that Locke attempts to underscore. To Locke, this point is utterly obvious. One has just to be remotely familiar with the customs of different cultures: "[T]hat this is the common *measure of Vertue and Vice*, will appear to any one, who considers, that though that passes for *Vice* in one Country, which is counted a *Vertue*, or at least not *Vice*, in another."[103]

Although different contexts give rise to different customs, Locke adds a qualifying point that customs have a tendency to converge because virtue and vice correspond to the rules of right and wrong because they are established by God. This may be true for similar cultures. But there is still, what Locke calls the "corruption of manners," where we see the divergence of virtue and vice (from our own perspective), the boundaries of the law of nature, which should be the rule of virtue and vice, are still preserved.[104] This is an interesting claim to make because not only does it make reference to the law of nature, it makes reference to the fact that the law of nature is the standard of virtue and vice. With this in mind, two puzzles are raised.

First, Peter Laslett correctly points out that "The Essay has no room for natural law."[105] Elsewhere it is argued at length to demonstrate that Laslett is correct because, given the kind of project the *Essay* represents, the text of the *Essay* rejects the essentialism of the *Essays* and the essentialism defended by the Scholastics (including substantial forms), in his treatment of good and evil, and his rejection of moral absolutism in favor of an early version of moral relativism.[106] So, the question remains, what is Locke trying to accomplish by adding this reference to natural law? One way to deal with this anomaly is to interpret it in the light of Locke's use of the law of nature in the *Second Treatise*. The law of nature, then, represents his similar approach to Pufendorf. This means that from a set of characteristics (seemingly) common to all humans, we may derive a set of obligations which guide human behavior. And in this case, Locke argues for a principle of harm, which he calls, for the lack of better term, the law of nature.

The second puzzle concerns Locke's notion of mixed modes.[107] Following Pufendorf, Locke develops the idea that a part of the set of complex ideas we possess are ideas, which are created by us to talk in specific ways about the world. For example, in contrast to our complex ideas of substances, which consist of our ideas about the (secondary qualities) objects in the world, our complex of mixed modes are ideas we create to correct the world. This means that mixed modes are, for the most part, put together by us to speak about moral, political, and legal ideas. And, although there is tendency to think our moral ideas, and so forth, satisfy the correspondence requirement our complex ideas of substances satisfy, mixed modes are projected onto the world. So, as Locke explains, whether our ideas of mixed modes are true or false, e.g., our ideas of justice, murder, gratitude, and so forth, unlike our ideas of substances, e.g., gold, man, horse, and the like, are not determined by reality. Rather, we tend to assess the truth of mixed modes against those we think are authorities.[108] So, there are two puzzles which we must face to interpret Locke in a coherent manner and which lend themselves to undermining any sort of deep account of the law of nature.

Before Locke turns to briefly talk about another aspect of his viewpoint of moral goodness and evil, he adds one more point about virtue and vice. His view of moral goodness requires that laws be attached to the expectation of reward or the threat of punishment. So, the question about the law of reputation is this: where is the prospect of reward or the threat of condemnation? This seemingly obscure issue is relevant because it indicates, as John Austin (attacking specifically this passage in Locke) later will take issue with in chapter 5, is the prospect that the law of opinion is not really a law at all. This is because, unlike the Divine law and the civil law, there is no prospect of reward or penalty. Again, Locke remarks that a cursory understanding of the history of mankind reveals that no one escapes the censure of the company he keeps including his club or his own society. In fact, in a statement reminiscent of the character of Hester Prynne (at least from our perspective), Locke writes: "He must be of a strange, and unusual Constitution, who can content himself, to live in constant Disgrace and Disrepute with his own particular Society."[109] It is now time to discuss our final author for this chapter, David Hume.

DAVID HUME (1711–1776)

David Hume represents an important turn away from natural law and any sort of foundation for virtue. In fact, Hume even rejects the social contract theory, which make sense because of the link between the two. In this last section, my focus will be to elaborate on the reasons why Hume rejects the social contract theory and, even though he discusses virtue, there appears to be no foundation to make any moral statement true. Finally, I will apply Hume's conclusions about morality to the notion of justice. I will begin with the former after one qualification.

Before I begin, ending this chapter in this way seems odd given the fact that Hume rejects what most of the earlier writers accepted as true. And yet, what this last section illustrates is an early attempt by Hume, and other philosophers not mentioned, to distance themselves from the doctrine of natural law, including any foundation of human law connected with morality. Although such a project is part of the Enlightenment, that is to say, the rejection of religious, political, and ethical authority, ultimately Hume's (perhaps too extreme) outlook opens the door for the introduction of the doctrine of positive law and its defense in the Romantic or Counter-Enlightenment Period. To begin this analysis, I will reproduce Hume's rejection of the social contract theory from an essay entitled "Of the Original Contract."[110]

To start, I will begin with what the social contract theory attempts to do. It attempts to establish two different claims: Civil societies start when the human race moves out the state of nature and individuals voluntarily consent with one another to form a commonwealth, *and* the authority of the government and its political leaders is derived from the consent of members of the commonwealth when they voluntarily consent to give up part of their liberty to the representatives of the government.[111] Hume rejects both viewpoints. But why? I will start with the former.

Hume attacks the first claim by arguing that there is no evidence for any culture of a document of consent.[112] Of course, he might be right—Hume was a first-rate historian. Additionally, even if there is such a consent, history indicates that the consent is really about the coercion and manipulation of the commoners by the early chieftains.[113] Moreover, the social contract theorist, that is, John Locke's version, not Hobbes',[114] argues that such consent also is found in the minds of each individual in each successive generation. Each individual promises to follow the articles of allegiance to the civil society to which his forefathers consented.[115] Again, Hume argues persuasively that such a position is mistaken because "we find, every where, princes, who claim their subjects as their property, and assert their independent right of sovereignty, from conquests or succession."[116] In fact, Hume makes clear that, after a certain amount of time, people tend to forget how the current government actually came into power. Hume remarks, "Obedience or subjection becomes so familiar, that most men never make any enquiry about its origin or cause."[117] Thus, in Hume's mind, the first claim is false.

What about the second claim? Social contract theorists argue that the authority of the government and its political leaders is derived from the consent of members of the commonwealth when they voluntarily give up part of their liberty to the government. Like the first claim, Hume rejects the second by making clear that "[A]lmost all the governments, which exist at present, or which there remains any record in story, have been founded originally, either on usurpation or conquest, or both, without any pretense of a fair consent, or voluntary subjection of the people."[118] Although Hume's historical evidence is very limited in his text, he tries to shore up his position by pointing out, at least from his contemporary point of view, he sees no evidence of either viewpoints: "[T]he face of the earth is continually changing, by the increase of small kingdoms into great empires, by the dissolution of great empires into smaller kingdoms, by the planting of colonies, by the migration of tribes. Is there any thing discoverable in all these events, but force and violence? Where is the mutual agreement or voluntary association so much talked of?"[119]

If the Social Contract Theory does not accurately capture the origin of governments or the origin of the government's authority, then what better explanation, if any, can he provide? I will summarize Hume's account. No matter in what manner a new government is started, the members of the society are apprehensive, and obedience is motivated by fear. Additionally, because the new government, prince, or otherwise, is aware of this fact, he will keep a watchful eye on any attempt to overthrow him. Eventually, however, if the new government survives, as time passes, the misgivings fade. In fact, the members of the seasoned society, consent to the authority of the government because, as Hume states: "they think, that, from long possession, he has acquired a title, independent of their choice or inclination."[120] What this (albeit brief) story indicates is that consent is not part of the formation of a new society and consent is not the foundation of the prince's authority.

It is unclear whether Hume's story is at least as plausible as the social contract theory. Nevertheless, there seems to be some plausibility to his view as long as the history of civilizations bears witness. In any case, I will move on to discuss Hume's view of morality and virtue.

Although Hume never really addresses the issue of the law of nature, his view of morality makes it impossible to defend such a view. The implication, of course, is that Hume has no interest whatsoever in the topic. Instead, Hume thoroughly is an empiricist and a nominalist and, as such, has no intention of giving any lip service to the notion of natural law such as Hobbes, Pufendorf, and Locke may have done. What, then, is it about his view of morality that eliminates natural law? To make this clear, I will begin with a distinction Hume makes between reason and sentiment, which is often thought to be the result of the is-ought distinction.[121]

Consider, for example, what Hume calls the crime of ingratitude. On the one hand, reason is concerned only with matters of fact or relations, and following Locke, Hume considers ingratitude to be a moral relation.[122] For example, to understand this, reason reveals to Hume that "I see first good-will and good-offices in one person; then ill-will and ill-will in the other."[123] Hume asks us, then, to reveal the crime present in ingratitude. This is a request for the moral wrongness of such an act: "first, where is that matter of fact, which we here call crime; point it out; determine the time of its existence; describe its essence or nature; explain the sense of faculty, to which it discovers itself."[124] Taunting us, so to speak, Hume remarks that we will never find the crime associated with this relation. So, where is the crime? "It resides in the mind of the person, who is ungrateful. He must, therefore, feel it, and be conscious of it. But nothing is there, except the passion of ill-will or absolute indifference."[125] Thus, the crime of ingratitude is not a fact perceived or revealed by reason; rather, such indifference excites the moral sentiment of blame in the mind of the victim. In the simplest of terms, morality is merely a matter of the formation of sentiments, or feelings, appropriate to one's own culture. This seemingly cements the is-ought distinction. If this is the case, then what is the role, if any, for the virtues? Let me turn to that answer.

Hume's answer is pretty clear: "The hypothesis which we embrace is plain. It maintains, that morality is determined by sentiment. It defines virtue to be *whatever mental action or quality gives to the spectator the pleasing sentiment of approbation*; and vice the contrary."[126] There are two qualifications. With such a seemingly simple explanation, one might wonder whether morality and virtue are even worthy of our attention. Ultimately, if virtue is important, then it must be a mental sentiment that is useful to ourselves, immediately agreeable to ourselves, and immediately agreeable to others.[127] Of course, what is useful or agreeable may vary from culture to culture. Nevertheless, even if we suppose that there is some convergence between cultures, this has no bearing on the universality of morality or virtue—there is no such thing.

The second qualification takes up the point above. Of course, Hume makes clear that without the warm feelings and sentiments toward what is virtuous, all men would be rendered indifferent to virtue and to its distinctions. However, like our sentiments of beauty, the moral sentiments we use to pronounce actions praiseworthy or blamable are themselves determined by an internal feeling, which Hume explains "nature has made universal in the whole species."[128] Such a claim opens the door for the role of reason. In fact, Hume reasons, that when we compare the two extreme moral positions, one which resembles a purely rational approach and the other which is purely subjective, "*reason* and *sentiment* concur in almost all moral determinations and conclusions."[129] Here is what I mean.

In his view, Hume understands that the standard of taste is also guided by the same two approaches dominant in moral discussions. On the one hand, the judgments in aesthetics are not the result of *a priori* reasoning nor are they merely just a matter of subjective taste. On the contrary, the possibility remains open to refine our aesthetic judgments about works of art. This is so because, like our feelings toward certain moral actions, we have internal sense or feeling toward the physical attributes of (visible) works of art or to the intangible propositions associated with the prose of literature or poetry. Thus, on the occasion that an individual fails to appreciate the beauty of a work of art, reason may be employed to adjust our sentiments to capture a proper sentiment of beauty.[130] This same approach also applies to morality. Thus, from our internal sense or universal feeling, if an individual fails to appreciate the virtuous worth of an individual's behavior, reason may be brought in to bear upon the discussion in order to adjust the individual's disapproval. The role of reason casts a shadow of doubt on an unqualified bifurcation between what is the case and what ought to be the case. Later this topic becomes a source of tension for some of the contemporary legal scholars who endorse natural law.

Although there is more to Hume's view of morality and virtue, it is important to move on to discuss his theory of justice.

Hume's account of justice is longer and much more complex. Upon reading his account of justice, Hume's discussion could not fail to delight a cultivated reader. So here is Hume's view of justice in capsule form: The virtue of justice depends entirely on the particular state and condition in which men are placed.[131] To illustrate his meaning, Hume describes several situations in which the virtue of justice does not apply, when the virtue of justice is suspended, and when it does apply. I will begin with the first of the three.

Hume invites us to imagine a possible world in which every one of man's needs and desires are satisfied:

> The perpetual clemency of the seasons renders useless all cloaths or covering: The raw herbage affords him the most delicious fare; the clear fountain, the richest beverage. No laborious occupation required: No tillage: No navigation. Music, poetry, and contemplation, form his sole business: Conversation, mirth, and friendship his sole amusement.[132]

Immediately after that Hume, draws out the implication the virtue of justice: "It seems evident, that, in such a happy state, every other social virtue would flourish, and receive tenfold increase; but the cautious, jealous virtue of justice would never once have been dreamed of."[133] Even in his own time, as Hume makes clear, such reasoning also applies to any object found in nature which is in a state of unlimited abundance, e.g., water and air.[134]

The next possible world that Hume imagines is one which is like his own world, but with one difference, viz., everyone possesses the virtue of benevolence: "Again; suppose, that . . . every man has the utmost tenderness for every man, and feels no more concern for his own interest than for that of his fellows."[135] Again, the obvious consequence for the virtue of justice, even in the presence of scarce resources, is that justice would not be needed, as Hume claims: "And the whole human race would form only one family; where all would lie in common, and be used freely, without regard to property; but cautiously too, with as entire regard to the necessities of each individual, as if our own interests were most intimately concerned."[136]

Although Hume recognizes that this world does not exist, he argues that there is an aspect of his world which comes close to his last point. Hume explains that we find such benevolence between married persons.[137] Again, where the ties between two people satisfy his example, we would expect that the virtue of justice would not be required.

The last examples Hume brings to our attention are different from the last two. It is not so much about examples where justice could never have place in the catalog of virtues as it is a reflection on (real-world) situations in which the virtue of justice is suspended. He describes five different situations. First, in the case of a shipwreck, the virtue of justice is suspended, because no one would consider it a crime to lay hold of someone else's property to survive in the water.[138] The second case describes a situation in which a city is cut off from all external resources during a war. As a result, the citizens of this imaginary city are perishing from hunger. In such a horrible situation, the virtue of justice is suspended because, even though no greater evils can be imagine in such a situation, "every man may now provide for himself by all the means, which prudence can dictate, or humanity permit."[139]

The next case is of special interest, and in my mind, the most controversial. Hume describes a virtuous man who falls in the hands of criminals, and who has no recourse to the civil authorities. What is this virtuous person supposed to do? Hume's answer is surprising:

> He, mean while, can have not other expedient than to arm himself, to whomever the sword he seizes, or the buckler, may belong: To make provision of all means of defence and security: And his particular regard to justice being no longer of USE to his own safety or that of others, he must consult the dictates of self-preservation alone, without concern for those who no longer merit his care and attention.[140]

This passage is surprising because even though he describes justice in *aretiac* terms, and a virtuous person as possessing the virtue of justice, he steps outside of the orthodox tradition of virtue by maintaining that a virtuous person is not required to maintain the virtue of justice (contra Aristotle) including the mean that regulates a virtuous person's actions in such a situation. Later, I will explain why such a position is consistent with Hume's justification of morality.

There are just two more examples. The first one is reminiscent of Locke's view of what should happen to a criminal in civil society. Like Locke, Hume argues that the "ordinary rules of justice are, with regard to him, suspended for a moment, and it becomes equitable to inflict on him, for the benefit of society, what, otherwise, he could not suffer without wrong or injury."[141] The last position concerns whether justice applies in war. Again, Hume's view point is cut out of the same cloth as Locke's standpoint. For example, Hume argues two points: First, Hume makes clear that war is a state in which the adherence to justice is suspended. Second, when a civilized nation goes to war with barbarians—a group of people presumably unconcerned with any rules in war—the same position applies: the civilized nation must also suspend the notion of justice.[142]

CONCLUSION

To sum up, it is the settled policy of this chapter to make clear some of the significant changes that took place in the justification and warrant of moral theory in the seventeenth- and eighteenth-centuries. To fulfil this purpose it is necessary to see clear and to think straight. My examination, with this purpose in mind, focused on four major scholars, who exerted enormous influence at the time of their writings and who also remain (for the most part) the focus in contemporary scholarship.

So the goal, then, of this chapter puts the question of moral warrant to the forefront. This focus is precipitated (partly) by the new scientific ideal which emerged and forced the discussion in a specific way: How do we talk meaningfully about ethics in a world dominated by the atom? In fact, there is a growing disposition to return to the Modern's discussion of moral justification in order to shed light on the discussion of contemporary metaethics. The same interest applies to myself as well, although my aim is slightly different. My interest in contemporary and modern metaethics is motivated by my suspicion that contemporary legal theory has largely failed to appreciate the enormous amount of intellectual energy spent by the Moderns on the topics of moral warrant and the justification of natural law and human positive law. Although my arrows are aimed primarily at the legal scholars who appeal, in one way or another, to the law of nature, the legal positivists also face serious problems. Against the former I will maintain that if any scholar, legal or otherwise, appeals to natural law in order to justify a hard legal case, they will be faced with an endless number of impatient delays to give their views warrant. Against the latter, I will argue that without some sort of standard, natural or otherwise, to guide judges' legal decisions, we must rely on their own moral vision of which legal statute is justified. Ultimately, my fear is that we will be forced to return to a Hobbesian outlook.

NOTES

1. She reigned from November 17, 1558 to March 24, 1603.

2. James VI and I was King of Scotland as James VI from July 24, 1567 and King of England and Ireland as James I from the union of the Scottish and English crowns on March 24, 1603 until his death on March 27, 1625.

3. Alastair Bellany, *The Politics of Court Scandal in Early Modern England: News Culture and the Overbury Affair, 1603–1660* (Cambridge, 2002): 7–8. Bellamy writes: "According to the country ideology, the court was wicked, extravagant, corrupt, promiscuous, homosexual, drunken, xenophile, diseased, sycophantic, tyrannical and popish. The country . . . was virtuous, thrifty, honest, chaste, heterosexual, sober, nationalist, healthy, outspoken, constitutional and Protestant leaning to Puritan." Ibid., 10.

4. Ibid., 21. The Overbury Affair is an incident which is as interesting as it is poignant. It took place roughly between 1612–1613 during the reign of James I. Thomas Overbury was a knighted gentleman and known for his accomplished intellect. Early on Overbury became friends with Robert Carr, who was a relatively unknown earl. Nevertheless, Carr caught the eye

of the King, James I, because of an accident where Carr broke his leg. Later, however, Carr was recruited by and joined forces with the Howard movement, which took power of most of the government. During this time, Carr met and fell in love with the married Frances Howard, Countess of Essex, daughter of the Earl of Suffolk. They began an affair, which Overbury opposed. Carr resisted Overbury's pleas to end the affair, and, roughly at the same time, Overbury wrote and published a poem called "The Wife." The poem spells out the virtues a man should demand from a women before he marries her. Francis Howard was convinced that the poem was about her and the affair she was having with Carr. After she petitioned for a divorce and proved her husband never consummated the marriage, she brought this poem to the attention to James I. In order to ameliorate the situation, James I offered Overbury a position overseas, which Overbury refused to accept. His refusal incensed James I, who arrested him and placed him in the tower of London on April 13, 1613. Overbury was found dead September 14, 1613. He was systematically poisoned for his opposition to the marriage of Carr and Francis Howard.

5. Charles I reigned from 1625 until his death in 1649, when he was executed.

6. See, for example, Sir Robert Filmer, *Patriarcha and Other Writings*, ed. Johann P. Sommerville (Cambridge University Press, 1991). Also see John Locke's attack of the Sir Robert Filmer's defense of the Divine Right of Kings in the first treatise of John Locke's *Two Treatises of Government*, 3rd ed., ed. Peter Laslett (Cambridge 1960). Original work published 1690.

7. As I will discuss shortly, the changing ideal of the science speaks specifically to the devaluation of and the eventual rejection of Aristotle's natural philosophy. Catherine Wilson makes clear that the change emerged because of a decided dissatisfaction with Aristotle's explanation of certain central issues including Aristotle's discussion of the soul. Although her article focuses primarily on this latter topic, what her article brings to light is the unexpected turn toward ancient materialism and ancient mechanics. In fact, her article, like other similar articles, locate part of the impetus of change in the works of the Jesuit Priest, Pierre Gassendi (1592–1655). In place of Aristotelian substances, Gassendi reclaimed the atom as the ultimate constituent of the nature of reality. Catherine Wilson, "Matter, Mortality, and the Changing Ideal of Science," in eds. T. Sorell et al., *Scientia in Early Modern Philosophy*, *Studies in History and Philosophy of Science* 24 (Springer Science+Business Media B.V., 2010): 35–51. Of course, as I will make clear, while Gassendi's efforts focused on the atom's placement in Catholic theology, it was not until individuals like Sir Robert Boyle who designed experiments to show why the atom is a better explanation for the way nature works.

8. Peter Alexander, *Ideas, Qualities and Corpuscles: Locke and Boyle on the External World* (Cambridge University Press, 1985), 15.

9. Ibid.

10. Ibid., 19.

11. Ibid., 20.

12. Ibid., 19.

13. Ibid., 23.

14. Ibid.

15. Boyle doesn't use the word "atom," per se. Instead, he uses the term "corpuscle." This is so because, after reading Aristotle so closely, he realized that atomism was associated with atheism and moral relativism in the mind of Aristotle—two doctrines he did not want to be associated with. Later, with the publication of Locke's *Essay Concerning Human Understanding*, he would realize all too clearly that Aristotle was right.

16. Robert Boyle, *Selected Philosophical Papers of Robert Boyle*, ed. M. A. Stewart (Indianapolis and Cambridge: Hackett Publishing Company, Inc., 1991).

17. For example, see Alexis de Tocqueville, *Democracy in America*, 4 vol., ed. Eduardo Nolla, trans. James T. Schleifer (Indianapolis, Liberty Fund, Inc., 2010). Original work published in 1835. One focus of his text is the rise of individualism in American culture. Tocqueville describes this change as a pervasive attitude of equality. In other words, unlike the attitudes of individuals in non-democratic countries governed by monarchies, Americans looked at each other, not from the unequal caste systems prevalent in the political collectives associated with monarchies, but as individuals playing, so to speak, on a level playing field. In

fact, Tocqueville is conscious of the importance of this point. In a later passage of his text, he contrasts the American attitude with the attitude found among cultures organized around Aristocratic institutions. The individuals in these cultures are organized into classes which are distinct, and for the most part, unchanging. Thus, from these fixed positions, each individual "sees above him a man whose protection he needs, and below he finds another whose help he can claim." Ibid., 883. Tocqueville makes clear that individuals in these cultures, then, are "almost always tied in a close way to something that is located outside of themselves, and they are often disposed to forget themselves." Ibid.

18. Thomas Hobbes, *Leviathan: with selected variants from the Latin edition of 1668*, ed. Edwin Curley (Indianapolis and Cambridge: Hackett Publishing Co., Inc., 1994). The original work was published in 1651. To quote Hobbes I will indicate part, chapter, and paragraph. Additionally, as evidence of the vigorous scholarship dedicated to the view of Hobbes, see Edwin Curley, "Reflections on Hobbes: Recent Work on his Moral and Political Philosophy," *Journal of Philosophical Research*, vol. 15 (1989–90): 169–250. Among other accolades, Hobbes clearly breaks tradition with the philosophical viewpoint of Plato and Aristotle. See Charles Covell, *The Defense of Natural Law*, 5.

19. Hobbes, *Leviathan*, I.xiii.6.

20. I.xiii.3.

21. Curley, "Reflections on Hobbes: Recent Work on his Moral and Political Philosophy," 171. According to Curley, psychological egoism, at least Hobbes' brand, is the view all voluntary action are motivated by self-interest (Ibid.). Curley later qualifies his view by stating that Hobbes probably was not a strict psychological egoist. Rather, following Greg Kavka, (regardless of Hobbes' own personal viewpoint) his text may be best described as a constructive program dedicated to "predominant egoism." So, such a view allows rare moments of altruism and even sacrifices in favor of family and close friends. Curley, "Reflections on Hobbes," 173.

22. Hobbes, *Leviathan*, I.xiii.4.

23. I.xiii.5.

24. Curley, "Reflections on Hobbes: Recent Work on his Moral and Political Philosophy," 171.

25. Hobbes, *Leviathan*, I.xiii.8.

26. I.xiii.9.

27. I.xiii.13.

28. Minimally, eliminative naturalism is the view that there are no ethical statements or no ethical properties or relations. The former view, as Robert B. Scott, Jr. makes clear, while hardly a version of moral naturalism, indicates an extreme form of emotivism attributed to A. J. Ayer in his text *Language, Truth, and Logic* (New York: Dover, 1952), 107. The latter view is defended by P. H. Nowell-Smith in his text *Ethics* (Middlesex, England: Penguin Books), 36–43, 48–60 and 64. See Robert B. Scott, Jr.'s discussion in his article "Five Types of Ethical Naturalism," *American Philosophical Quarterly* 17, no. 4 (October 1980): 269–70.

29. Hobbes, *Leviathan*, I.xiii.14.

30. Curley, "Reflections on Hobbes," 179. Although cooperation suggests, as Curley makes clear, that "people are naturally rational planners," it may be more consistent with the doctrine of "predominate egoism" to argue that, regardless of whether people are rational or not, they often have moments of (lucky?) lucidity. Ibid., 181.

31. Samuel Clark (1675–1729) offers an interesting criticism of Hobbes' reasons for why individuals decide to move from the state of nature to a civil society. Here is a summary of his objection. First, Clark summarizes Hobbes' viewpoint:

> All obligation of duty to God, arises merely from his absolute irresistible power; and all duty towards men, merely from positive compact. If we assume that this is true, then there is no natural difference in things themselves, no difference between good and evil, just and unjust. So, it stands to reason that, in the state of nature, before any compact be made, it is equally as good, just and reasonable, for one man to destroy the life of another, not only when it is necessary for his own preservation, but also arbitrarily and without any provocation at all, or any appearance of advantage to himself. Naturally, as Hobbes makes clear, staying in the state of

nature will lead ultimately to the destruction of mankind, which is an undeniably a great and insufferable evil. Thus, to prevent the destruction of mankind, Hobbes concludes that it is reasonable for men to enter into a certain compact to preserve one another.

Samuel Clark, *A Discourse of Natural Religion* in *Moral Philosophy from Montaigne to Kant*, ed. J. B. Schneewind (Cambridge University Press, 2003), 297.

Clarke's attack proceeds in this way: If the destruction of mankind by each other's hand, be such an evil, that, to prevent it, that men should enter into compacts to preserve each other, before any such compacts, then it was clearly unreasonable, that mankind should all destroy one another. But here is the rub: if it is unreasonable that mankind should destroy one another, then it was also unreasonable, *antecedent* to all compacts, that any one man should destroy another arbitrarily and without any provocation, or at any time when it was not absolutely and immediately necessary for the preservation of himself. Clark concludes that it is false that there is no natural difference in things themselves, no difference between good and evil, just and unjust. This also leads Clark to conclude that Hobbes moral subjectivism is also false. That is, it is false that all obligation of duty to God, arises merely from his absolute irresistible power; and all duty towards men, merely from positive compact. Ibid., 297–99. cf. Lon L. Fuller, *The Law in Quest of Itself*, 14–38. Fuller also presents a significant critique of Hobbes. It includes the very famous distinction between the considerate sovereign and inconsiderate sovereign. Ibid., 34–38.

32. Formally, Hobbes defines a law of nature as "a precept, or general rule, found out by reason, by which a man is forbidden to do, that, which is destructive of his life or taketh away the means of preserving the same, and to omit that which he thinketh it may be best preserved." Hobbes, *Leviathan*, I.xiv.3.

33. Of course, this should have satisfied those in favor of the Stuart monarchs, but it did not—Hobbes rejected the doctrine of the divine right of kings.

34. Martin Harvey spells out the traditional understanding of the law of nature by (among other things) comparing the law of nature defended by Grotius and the version Hobbes sets out in the *Leviathan*. Harvey, "Grotius and Hobbes," 39–44.

35. Geoffrey Sayre-McCord, ed., "Introduction: The Many Moral Realism," in *Essays on Moral Realism*, ed. Geoffrey Sayre-McCord (Ithaca and London: Cornell University Press, 1988), 16–18. Although Curley does not articulate this point in precisely the same way, he attributes to Hobbes a metaethical theory that is "highly subjectivistic." Curley, "Reflections on Hobbes," 187.

36. For an excellent discussion of the hysteria surrounding the publication of the *Leviathan*, see Samuel I. Mintz, *The Hunting of Leviathan* (Cambridge University Press, 1962).

37. Hobbes, *Leviathan*, xiv, 3.

38. Curley underscores this point by making clear that the law of nature in the *Leviathan* amounts to a set of hypothetical imperatives, and so they are not moral imperatives. Curley, "Reflections on Hobbes," 188. Unfortunately, Curley argues that because the law of natures are not moral imperatives, "strictly speaking, Hobbes has no theory of moral obligation, and hence . . . no moral philosophy." Ibid. This is a mistake because Hobbes clearly articulates a version of moral subjectivism described earlier. Of Hobbes, Fuller maintains, also, that the sovereign Monarch must also obey the law of nature as well. In fact, Fuller places Hobbes together with Pufendorf and Grotius as champions of natural law. Fuller, *The Law in Quest of Itself*, 22–23. I will show that such a view does not conform exactly to the truth of matter.

39. Hobbes, *Leviathan*, II.xxiii.6.

40. Samuel Pufendorf, *The Whole Duty of Man, According to the Law of Nature*, ed. Ian Hunter and David Saunder, trans. David Saunder (Indianapolis, IN: Liberty Fund, Inc., 2003). Originally published in 1673. References to Pufendorf's text will be indicated by book, chapter, and paragraph.

41. Samuel Pufendorf, *On the Law of Nature and Nations*, in J. B. Schneewind, *Moral Philosophy from Montaigne to Kant* (Cambridge University Press, 2003). The excerpt in Schneewind's edition comes from Samuel Pufendorf, *On the Law of Nature and Nations,* trans. C. H. Oldfather and W. A. Oldfather (Oxford: Oxford University Press, 1934). Originally

published in 1672. References to Purfendorf's text will be indicated by simply the page number in Schneewind's anthology.

42. Schneewind, *Moral Philosophy from Montaigne to Kant*, 156.

43. Ibid. Italics are mine.

44. Michael Loux, *Introduction to Metaphysics*, 22, 25, 31.

45. Purfendorf, *The Whole Duty of Man, According to the Law of Nature*, 1.III.vii. Italics are in text.

46. Ibid. Italics are in text.

47. 1.III.xiii. Italics are in text.

48. 1.VI.ii–iii. Italics are in text.

49. Ibid. Italics are in text.

50. 1.VI.iii. Italics are in text.

51. Ibid. Italics are in text.

52. 1.VII.i. Italics are in text.

53. 1.VII.ii. Italics are in text.

54. 1.VIII.i. Italics are in text.

55. 1.VIII.ii. Italics are in text.

56. 1.VIII.v. Italics are in text.

57. 1.IX.iii. Italics are in text.

58. Although Pufendorf does not use the term "standing absolute duties," the text implies something similar later to what Immanuel Kant calls perfect and imperfect duties. The late Tom Regan, a deontologist as well, spells out the concept in terms of unacquired and acquired duties. The idea is familiar. The former prima facie duties point to obligations we always possess relative to other rational individuals. The latter prima facie duties direct our attention to obligations we voluntarily acquire by means of informed consent.

59. Purfendorf, *The Whole Duty of Man, According to the Law of Nature*, 1.IX.iv. Italics are in text.

60. John Locke brings this issue to a head, as we will see in the next section.

61. The following discussion is from the partial text of Pufendorf's *The Law of Nature and of Nations* reproduced in Schneewind, *Moral Philosophy from Montaigne to Kant*, 170–182. See complete reference above.

62. See, e.g., Locke's *Essay*, Book II and Book III.

63. Geoffrey Sayre-McCord, ed., "Introduction: The Many Moral Realism," 18–19.

64. This is an important point. Here is what I mean. Stephen Darwall contrasts this source of moral obligation between Suarez, Grotius and Pufendorf. Stephen Darwall, "Pufendorf on Morality, Sociability, and Moral Powers," *Journal of the History of Philosophy* 50, no. 2 (April 2012). Darwall makes clear that Pufendorf advances a theological voluntarism. Ibid., 214. So, on this view, using a distinction made by the early moderns, the formal and efficient cause of the moral obligation of the law of nature, the former points to the source or origin of the *content* of the natural law and the latter, the source of moral *authority*. For Pufendorf, the formal and efficient cause of the law of nature resides in the mind and authority of God. But how does Pufendorf fair toward Grotius and Suarez? On my view, Grotius argues that the source of the former is a moral reality similar to the Platonic forms. The latter source is God. Darwall adds that, for Grotius, "sociability enters somehow into natural law's foundations, whereas, for Pufendorf, natural law can be grounded only in God's superior authority." Ibid., 215. Darwall is correct. The sociability he makes reference to may be explained by Grotius' emphasis on the capacity of right reason. Although right reason is not the foundation of the law of nature, i.e., it is not the formal cause, it is a reflection, so to speak, of the law of nature. This means that under ideal conditions, including individuals properly cultivated, a natural sort of sociability will obtain between the members of a civil society. With this in mind, of Suarez, Darwall writes: "Pufendorf does not hold, as Suarez did, that God's authority is necessary only for moral *obligation*, with our rational (and social) nature being sufficient to ground natural rightness and wrongness, as on the Thomist classical natural law view." Ibid., 215. So, according to Suarez, the formal cause is the rational nature of humanity, and the efficient cause is God's authority. Schneewind underscores the same point and states that Suarez attempted to bridge the gap

between theological intellectualism and theological voluntarism. Schneewind, *Moral Philosophy from Montaigne to Kant*, 68.

65. I will not discuss the other meaning of moral entity Pufendorf mentions.
66. Samuel Pufendorf, *The Law of Nature and of Nations*, 170–171.
67. Hume also understood the issue in the same way, as I will make clear soon.
68. Aristotle, *Nicomachean Ethics*, 1115b 15–20, 1116a 10–15, and 1117a 30.
69. Pufendorf, *The Law of Nature and of Nations*, 171.
70. See Darwall, "Pufendorf on Morality, Sociability, and Moral Powers," 218.
71. Simon Blackburn revived the phenomena Pufendorf (and later Locke) describes as our propensity to impose moral properties onto the character of individuals whose behavior we find morally applaudable or suspicious. Blackburn labels this propensity as projectivism. Roughly this means that, under certain conditions, we project onto some aspect of the world what we take to be an objective property. In the case of morality, we project what we take to be an objective, moral property onto an action we may find inconsistent with our moral code. Simon Blackburn, "Supervenience Revisited," in *Essays on Moral Realism*, ed. Geoffrey Sayre-McCord, 72–73.
72. Pufendorf, *The Law of Nature and of Nations*, 175.
73. Darwall, "Pufendorf on Morality, Sociability, and Moral Powers," 220. Darwall draws in Hobbes' analogy between ethical evaluations and our experience of color. Like the projection of color onto an object (which it does not possess), we also do the same with ethical properties. We shall see the same doctrine in Locke as well.
74. As we shall see, the same issues are brought up by Hans Kelsen. See Hans Kelsen, "Absolutism and Relativism in Philosophy and Politics," *American Political Science Review* 42, no. 5 (1948): 906–914.
75. Pufendorf, *The Law of Nature and of Nations*, 171.
76. Ibid., 174.
77. John Locke, *Two Treatises of Government*, ed. Peter Laslett (Cambridge, 1993). Original work published in 1690. I will quote the text of the *Two Treatises* by referring to the *First Treatise* or *Second Treatise* (I or II), chapter, and paragraph.
78. *Treatises*, II.ii.
79. II.ii,§6. Italics are in the text.
80. Ibid. Italics are in the text.
81. John Locke, *Essays on the Law of Nature, Together with Transcripts of Locke's Shorthand in his Journal of 1676*, ed. W. von Leyden (Oxford: Clarendon Press, 1965). Original work published 1954.
82. Samuel Zinaich, "John Locke's Moral Revolution: from Natural Law to Moral Relativism." *The Locke Newsletter* 31 (2000), pp. 79–114. (Journal now known as *Locke Studies*). cf. Samuel Zinaich, "The Internal Coherency of Locke's Moral Views in the *Questions Concerning the Law of Nature*." *Interpretation: A Journal of Political Philosophy* 29, no. 1. (Fall 2001), pp. 55–73. In the second article mentioned, I attack the view that Locke's *Essays* do not present a coherent view of the law of nature. The accusation of incoherence is thought to be by design and not by mistake. Locke is following Leo Strauss' esoteric approach to the history of philosophy. I demonstrate that Strauss' "secrete message" approach does not apply to Locke's discussion in the *Essays*.
83. Samuel Zinaich, Jr., *Locke's Moral Revolution: from Natural Law to Moral Relativism*, 153–180.
84. Locke, *Treatises*, II.ii.§6.
85. Filmer, *Patriarha and Other Writings*, 3. Locke summarized Filmer's argument in this way: Because the only legitimate form of government is a monarch, it follows that no man is born free. Locke, *Treatises*, I.i.§3.
86. Locke, *Treatises*, II.ii.§6.
87. II.xii.§143.
88. II.xii.§144.
89. II.xii.§146.
90. II.xii.§150.
91. II.xi.§135.

92. II.xi.§136.
93. II.xi.§138.
94. II.xi.§140. Italics are in the text.
95. Locke, *An Essay Concerning Human Understand*, II. xxviii. 7. It is important to note a change in Locke's thinking. Ordinarily, in a discussion dedicated to the defense of the law of nature, we would expect the three sources of law to be the Divine law, the Civil law, and the light of nature. For example, see Samuel Pufendorf's discussion in *The Whole Duty of Man, According to the Law of Nature*, 16. The light of nature refers to the common ability among well-formed humans to discover the various precepts of the law of nature.
96. Locke, *An Essay Concerning Human Understanding*, II.xxviii.7.
97. II.xxviii.8.
98. II.xxviii.9.
99. II.xxviii.10.
100. Ibid.
101. Ibid.
102. Ibid.
103. II. xxviii. 11.
104. Ibid.
105. Peter Laslett, ed. in John Locke, *Two Treatises of Government*, ed. Peter Laslett (Cambridge University Press, 1988), 81.
106. Zinaich, *Locke's Moral Revolution: from Natural Law to Moral Relativism*, 2006, 136.
107. Locke, *Essay Concerning Human Understanding*, II.xxii.
108. II.xxx.4 and II.xxxii.11.
109. II.xxviii.12.
110. David Hume, "Of the Original Contract," *Essays: Moral, Political and Literary*, Eugene F. Miller, ed. (Indianapolis: Liberty Fund, 1985).
111. To this is added that the members of each successive generation, upon the age of consent, or full maturity, makes the same promise even if it is only a tacit consent. Ibid., 469. Hume rejects this viewpoint by simply pointing out that this just is not the case. To those who claim power to rule see their subjects, for all intents and purposes, as property. Ibid., 474–477. That said, Hume qualifies this view by pointing out that explicit or tacit consent does apply to those who immigrate to other foreign countries. Ibid., 476.
112. Hume, "Of the Original Contract," 468.
113. Ibid.
114. Hobbes argued that the original contract was a hypothetic thought experiment. Locke, argues, that such a contract does have place in history. Not only that but he also argues that a state of nature exists between sovereign countries. This point is argued effectively in Richard H Cox, *Locke on War and Peace* (Oxford: Clarendon Press, 1960).
115. Hume, "Of the Original Contract," 469.
116. Ibid., 470.
117. Ibid.
118. Ibid., 471.
119. Ibid.
120. Ibid., 474.
121. This topic is important to bring up because much of contemporary legal positivism turns on the legitimacy of the is-ought distinction or the fact-value gap. Although I should add that, for the most part, Hume's is-ought distinction is misunderstood by many contemporary legal theorists.
122. David Hume, *An Enquiry Concerning the Principle of Morals*, ed. J. B. Schneewind, (Indianapolis and Cambridge: Hackett Publishing Company, 1983), Appendix 1.i. Original work published in 1751. To reference the main text of *Hume's Enquiry*, I will reference section and part. Additionally, when needed for clarification, I will add page number. To reference the appendix of the *Enquiry*, I will indicate the appendix number and section. I may add page number when needed.
123. Hume, *An Enquiry Concerning the Principle of Morals*, appendix 1.i.
124. Ibid.

125. Ibid.

126. Ibid. Italics are in the text. It is tempting to describe Hume's moral viewpoint as a version of error theory. On this view, while error theorists give moral statements a cognitivist interpretation (and, therefore, they are about facts), there are no reasons to think that moral statements (e.g., person-centered *arête* claims, or otherwise) are true. See Geoffrey Sayre-McCord's discussion "Introduction: The Many Moral Realism," 10. Despite the plausibility of this view (contra J. L. Mackie's view about Hume), I will try to show that Hume's viewpoint resists such an interpretation. cf. J. L. Mackie, "The Subjectivity of Values," in ed. Geoffrey Sayre-McCord, *Essays on Moral Realism*, 99, 106, 111–12, 114.

127. Hume gives a vivid portrayal of what benevolent people are like and examples of individuals who satisfy the requirements. In a discussion reminiscent of Samuel Richardson's description of Pamela Andrews in *Pamela: or, Virtue Awarded* (1740) not only does the benevolent person contribute to the happiness of society, he takes care of his parents, he concerns himself for his family, his friends, his domestics and dependents. Hume, *An Enquiry Concerning the Principle of Morals*, II.ii. Additionally, he contributes to the poor in terms of food and clothing.

128. Hume, *An Enquiry Concerning the Principles of Morals*, I, 15. The following discussion is normally ignored by scholars who desire to interpret Hume purely as a subjectivist.

129. Ibid. The following discussion reveals something important about Hume's moral view. That is, if it is possible that the *arête* claim we make can be mistaken, then Hume can maintain that there are appropriate truth-making conditions that make some moral statements true.

130. Here it is useful to mention Hume's alliance with Pufendorf's and Locke's doctrine of the world-correcting aspect of moral judgments. In this case, Hume follows both the Pufendorf and Locke views that we impose or project moral attributes onto the character of individuals. cf. David Hume, *A Treatise of Human Nature*, 2nd ed. (Oxford University Press, 1978), I.iii.14. For a treatment of Hume's contribution to this discussion, see John McDowell, "Values and Secondary Qualities," in ed. Geoffrey Sayre-McCord, *Essays on Moral Realism*, 175–76.

131. Hume, *An Enquiry Concerning the Principles of Morals*, III.i.

132. Ibid.

133. Ibid.

134. Ibid.

135. Ibid.

136. Ibid., 22.

137. Ibid.

138. Ibid.

139. Ibid., 23.

140. Ibid.

141. Ibid.

142. Ibid.

Chapter Four

The Counter-Enlightenment Period and Romanticism (1770–1870)

INTRODUCTION

Ending with Hume in the last section is important because he represents the inevitable demise of the value of reason, the importance of the social contract theory, the foundational function of the law of nature for human law, and a deep account of virtue theory. In its place, there is an emphasis on the scientific outlook of empiricism, which focuses only on tangible facts, nominalism and the rejection of universals and immanent essences, the replacement of virtue theory with moral idealism including subjectivism and intersubjectivism, the replacement of political collectivism with individualism, and the value of passion over reason. These latter viewpoints represent the focus of the Counter-Enlightenment period and Romanticism. No doubt, such changes affected the outlook of the view of politics, economics, art, music, parenting, slarery, marriage, and so forth. Unfortunately, although I wish I had time to do so, I cannot discuss these issues. Instead, for the purposes of this text, I will focus on the foundation of human law. There is no doubt that such an outlook as legal positivism, which concerns the foundation of human law, would step up to fill the void. The significance of this point is brought out by Rommen:

> Positivism . . . is the consequence of the doctrine of the primacy of the will with respect to the intellect in both theology and human psychology. Besides, *voluntas* here means more than mere will: it denotes passion, irrational appetite, and so on. Positivism signifies the renouncing of all efforts to know the essences of things (nominalism), the repudiation of the metaphysics of hier-

archized being and value. Accordingly, it is also found in the same conceptual pattern in the thinking of the nineteenth and twentieth centuries, even though it is concealed under different names.[1]

Rommen's quote certainly captures some of the contributing factors supporting the rise of legal positivism.[2] In fact, like myself, Rommen even attributes the turn to positivism to Hume's early philosophical influence. Additionally, he also points to the contribution made by the utilitarians, who emerge during the romantic period and, in particular, the progenitor of (early) contemporary consequentialism, Jeremy Bentham (1748–1832).[3] While there is no doubt about Bentham's influence, two other scholars (both utilitarians themselves) exert a significant influence as well (at least in Great Britain and America): the legal scholar John Austin (1790–1859), and the philosopher John Stuart Mill (1806–1873). In this section I will discuss the viewpoint of all three scholars, starting with Bentham. After that, I will discuss the views of Austin and Mill in that order.[4]

JEREMY BENTHAM (1748–1832)

Bentham is most notably known for his brand of utilitarianism.[5] In fact, it may be safe to say that, under his direction, utilitarianism regained a foothold as a viable moral theory. Of course, what this means is simply that his brand of utilitarianism—mental state hedonism—was generally looked upon with a jaundiced eye by scholars throughout history. Nonetheless, using his version of utilitarianism, Bentham made great strides in the improvement of the political, legal, and judicial systems in Great Britain. In this section, I begin with Bentham's version of utilitarianism. After that, I elaborate his attack of natural law and natural rights.

Bentham's utilitarianism, an action-based moral theory, is a version of consequentialism. This means that the focus of his moral theory is only on the outcome of the actions, and not just that, the outcomes must be maximized or as close to it as possible. So, if an action is morally right or wrong, it will be right or wrong relative to the maximization of the outcomes of the action or the maximization of the consequences of the action.[6] This raises the question of what kind of consequences we are talking about.

Like his godson, John Stuart Mill, Bentham was a mental state hedonist. This means two things. First, the normative status of an action is chosen, among the many alternatives available, by the kind of mental state it produces in the minds of everyone involved.[7] Such a viewpoint may be difficult to determine because such a decision often amounts to a prediction about the future. Nevertheless, the problems with such a view may be ameliorated when an action is chosen which is known, historically speaking, to maximize the best consequences. Additionally, because of his commitment to empiricism, it may be possible, if there is time, to consult the appropriate scientific disciplines relevant to the context. Second, Bentham is also a hedonist, not one committed to the primacy value of reason.[8] This means that the mental states he focuses on are the actions which produce the mental states of pleasure, and the ones to avoid produce the mental states of pain. This view, while embraced by Epicurus, was rejected by Aristotle. I will underscore this point.

Bentham, like Plato, Aristotle, the Stoics, Aquinas, Grotius, and others not mentioned, were teleologists.[9] Although this much is true, Bentham develops his own version of teleology that takes the mental-state of pleasure to be the Good or which, with other like-minded individuals, he calls happiness.[10] Thus, whatever action brings about the Good is right and those actions which miss the mark are considered, all things being equal, wrong. Thus, the notions of right and wrong are relative to the Good. Nevertheless, there is a worry about this viewpoint. Which pleasures does Bentham have in mind? Certainly, there are pleasures which people enjoy but our moral intuitions condemn, e.g., the pleasures of rape, pedophilia, necrophilia, murder, torture, and so forth. So what kind of pleasures does Bentham have in mind? Bentham's response to this is twofold. First, he makes no distinction between the experiences of pleasure. In other words, the feeling of pleasure is just the feeling of pleasure whether it is the feeling of pedophilia or the feeling of being in love.[11] So, such a point sounds like Bentham was not aware of the fact that pleasures toward certain actions possess a different normative status. That is, we condemn the pleasures of pedophilia, but we don't condemn the pleasures associated with beneficence. It is clear that he is aware of the difference, but how does he deal with this issue? Here is how he addresses it.

There are seven points to consider when considering the normative status of a pleasure: the pleasure's intensity, duration, certainty or uncertainty, its remoteness, fecundity, purity, and its extent.[12] The last three criteria appear to be relevant to this issue.[13] The fecundity points to the potential of pleasure produced by the initial pleasure. Does pleasure follow pleasure? Does pain follow pain? The purity points to the chance of whether the pleasure will lead to pain or whether the pain will lead to pleasure. Finally, the extent points to the individuals affected by the action. Naturally, under normal conditions, a person convicted of assault, for example, may not feel pleasure after the assault—fecundity; the pleasure was followed by pain because of guilt or incarceration—the purity; and to all those involved—the extent—the pain of those affected by the action.[14] Thus, using these criteria, we may be able to make a distinction between the pleasures that should be pursued and those that should be avoided. Unfortunately, many scholars were not convinced that Bentham's position would work. It is not until Mill makes a startling distinction between pleasures that mental state hedonism is believed to or is considered to have a chance to work. Mill's discussion will have to wait. I will now move on to Bentham's diatribe against the natural law and the social contract theory.

In August 1789, the *Declaration of the Rights of Man and of the Citizen* was passed by France's National Constituent Assembly. It was written largely by Thomas Jefferson. It spells out in a number of articles what rights all individuals have in virtue of the law of nature. Bentham publishes and publicly attacks this declaration in a little known work (from a contemporary viewpoint) called "Anarchical Fallacies: being an examination of the Declaration of Rights issued during the French Revolution."[15]

The portion of his writing, most relevant to this text (and certainly, reminiscent of Locke), is his attack of Article II, which states "The end in view of every political association is the preservation of the natural and imprescriptible rights of men. These rights are liberty, property, security, and resistance to oppression."[16] Bentham's attack comes in two steps. He first attacks natural rights and natural law, and then the Social Contract Theory. I'll begin with the former.

Bentham's attack is not grounded so much on arguments as it is simply a denial of natural law.[17] Bentham writes that natural rights simply do not exist: "There are no such things as natural right—no such things as rights anterior to the establishment of government—no such things as natural rights opposed to, in contradistinction to, legal."[18] Of course, it is interesting to note that, like Hume, Bentham has Locke's view of natural law in mind, not Hobbes'. Only Locke mentions that the law of nature exists prior to the establishment of a government and a legal system.

After this denial, Bentham remarks that there is clear and empirical evidence about how men live without a government. He speaks at length about the "savages of New South Wales."[19] There are no laws, no government, no rights, no property, no legal security. Such a point lends itself against Locke. Moreover, his denial of natural rights doesn't end there:

> [T]hat which has no existence cannot be destroyed—that which cannot be destroyed cannot require anything to preserve it from destruction. *Natural rights* is simple nonsense: natural and imprescriptible rights, rhetorical nonsense,—nonsense upon stilts. But this rhetorical nonsense ends in the old strain of mischievous nonsense: for immediately a list of these pretended natural rights is given, and those are so expressed as to present to view legal right. And of these rights, whatever they are, there is not, it seems, any one of which any government can, upon any occasion whatever, abrogate the smallest particle.[20]

Again, there is no argument here, no reasons given to reject natural law and natural rights. Nevertheless, with such a rejection, Bentham claims that there is no foundation for a legal right.

This brings us to consider Bentham's position about the warrant of legal claims. Does Bentham embrace legal positivism? The answer is yes.[21] In fact, Bentham is treated, as Schauer indicates, as the founding father of legal positivism.[22] To understand Bentham's view of legal positivism, it is necessary to spell out, as Schauer makes clear, three versions of positivism because Bentham's view draws from all three versions.[23] Briefly, the three versions of positivism are conceptual positivism, normative positivism, and decisional positivism. Conceptual positivism is described as the view that "morality is not a necessary condition of legality in all possible legal systems in all possible worlds."[24] Rather, the nature of law is an indispensable constituent of a stable political community, which represents the command or prohibitions of the recognized legislative body of the community.[25] This is what I take to be the central core of positivism.[26] Normative positivism (attributed to Jeremy Waldron) is the view that "those who hold this position believe positivism is chosen by a society rather than just emerging, and offer reasons why it is better for some purpose other than descriptive accuracy for a theorist to choose positivism over its alternatives."[27] In its briefest terms, the last version eschews common law, limits judicial discretion, and restricts the array of acceptable social sources as conventional legal sources.[28]

Although Schauer makes clear that all three versions may be found in Bentham's texts, Bentham clearly articulates conceptual positivism.[29] There are good reasons for this claim. Contrary to what Schauer argues, normative and decisional positivism do not reflect the central idea of legal positivism. They may be true claims, but they do not capture what positivism means, per se. Rather, both reflect the contexts at which conceptual positivism is applied. Here is what I mean. If we begin with the conceptual gap between law and morality, then it is natural to wonder where positivism might emerge (including why one version is better than another) and the possible constraints it might dictate for the legal system in place.

Another important point to underscore is Bentham's view of the social contract theory: "[T]he origination of governments from a contract is a pure fiction, or in other words, a falsehood. It never has been known to be true in any instance; the allegation of it does mischief, by involving the subject in error and confusion, and is neither necessary nor useful to any good purpose."[30] Such a denial is interesting. Fortunately, unlike his first point, Bentham attempts to give us reasons why this is true. Like Hume, Bentham appeals to history. He remarks that, except for a few exceptions, history teaches us that all governments are formed by force. As a consequence, legal laws and contracts only make sense within the establishment of a government.

The same topic is also discussed in Bentham's "A Fragment on Government."[31] With his arrows aimed at Blackstone's defense of the original contract as the legitimate source of society, he credits Hume with demolishing the social contract theory.[32] Additionally, confirming Hume's insistence that there is no historical evidence for the original contract, Bentham's cross-examination of individuals who supported the (Lockean) original contract admitted that it was a fiction.[33] This led, of course, to Bentham's claim that society is itself a basic fact, an artifact, if you will. This means that, as Paola Rudan comments, society "is not entirely produced through the establishment of government, nor is it conceivable as a 'state of nature.'"[34] Such an outlook also has designs upon the notions of freedom and equality as well.

Conceiving society as an artifact also led Bentham to readdress the status of individuals within society. As Locke maintains against Filmer that all people are born free and equal, Bentham argues that such equality is another fiction to be unearthed.[35] Rudan points out the same conclusion.[36] Bentham makes clear the obvious fact that when we are born (until the age of consent), we are subject to the authority of our parents. Additionally, we are subject to different authorities even after the subjugation of our parents.[37]

While the foregoing points seem disconnected in some respects, Bentham ties them together in the following manner. It is natural to think that many of Bentham's intuitions about the origin of political and legal authority stem from the insights of Thomas Hobbes and John Locke. That said, Bentham's viewpoint, while sharing some of their assumptions, ultimately found most of their views useless. For example, while he shares Hobbes' view (contra Locke) that law is a command of the sovereign (not an absolute authority like Hobbes, but one modified by convention[38]), he rejects the defense of the origin of civil society and origin of political authority argued by Hobbes and Locke. Opposing Hobbes and Locke, there is no social contract from which humanity moved from a state of nature to a civil society, and certainly no evidence that the authority of government rests upon the foundation of public consent. Moreover, Bentham makes clear his rejection of the notion that all people are born free and equal. As a result, Bentham rejects the appeal to natural rights and natural law as limits to social and political authoritarianism. Such a view, while absent in Hobbes, rests firmly in the mind of Locke's discussion of the moral limits within the state of nature, and ultimately, the moral limits and separation of powers within a commonwealth.

Still, what seems to be missing is how Benthan's utilitarianism fits into this discussion. Toward the end of the *Fragment*, Bentham writes: "the greatest happiness principle is the character of the standard of right and wrong in the field of morality in general, and of Government in particular."[39] This statement creates a tension between Bentham's logical positivism and the principle of utility as the standard for government. How can he maintain both views consistently? Moreover, prior to this, to make things seemingly worse, Bentham makes clear that the principle of utility is the only and proper defensible end of government.[40] How do we weave both views into a coherent viewpoint? Perhaps this interpretation will work.

Bentham can maintain both views because both perspectives speak to different aspects of the source of government authority. On the one hand, Bentham's logical positivism speaks to the antecedent source of law which is located in the supreme authority to make laws.[41] On the other hand, to argue that utility is the defensible end of government is to insist on two things. First (contra the fictional social contract theory), the principle of utility secures the legitimacy of authority of the state over the individual. Second, the principle of utility gives the state a normative direction to address the collective social welfare of its citizens.[42]

While I would like to spend more time developing Bentham's viewpoint, I will move on to talk about John Austin.

JOHN AUSTIN (1790–1859)

Following upon the heels of Bentham is the legal scholar John Austin (1790–1859), who, like many scholars and artists, received little scholarly attention until after his death, Austin's life, prior to his death, reveals the most unhappy: "he had very few clients, he was unable to attract many students, and he wrote relatively little."[43] In fact, his wife, Sarah Austin, who was better known than her husband was before he died, described his life "as one of 'unbroken disappointment and failure.'"[44] Fortunately, after Austin's death, Sarah "dedicated the final eight years of her life to the arduous task of editing her husband's lectures and papers on jurisprudence."[45] The implication is that Austin's work may have grown dim and dissipated without her efforts. Sarah's efforts transformed "Austin from a minor figure into a dominant force in nineteenth-century British jurisprudent."[46]

Austin's life may be accurately characterized as melancholic, however the question of why anyone should read Austin still remains an open one. For my purposes, two reasons stand out: Austin's relationship to Bentham, and Austin's discussion of positive law. Because the latter is by far the most important issue, the bulk of my comments are dedicated to this subject. Until then, I will briefly spell out his relation to Bentham.

There is no doubt that Bentham and Austin were friends and neighbors,[47] but such a point is as uninteresting as it is innocuous. The interesting point, at least for our purposes, is the influence Bentham had over Austin's viewpoint. Like Bentham, Austin defends a version of utilitarianism. While he articulates the Principle of Utility in Lectures 2–4, his comments (unlike those of Bentham and Mill) are not deeply linked to the chain of the development of the concept of utility, per se.[48] Rather, Austin employs the concept of Utility to justify the distinctions between and the foundations of natural and positive law. I will turn to that discussion now.

Leaping into the dark is not always a prudent strategy when explicating an author like Austin, yet I am afraid there is no other way to shed light upon his viewpoint without doing so. Thus, robbed (for the most part) of tranquility, I will begin with the following quotation:

> [N]ow without a clear apprehension of the hypothesis of utility, of the pure hypothesis of a moral sense, and of the modified or mixed hypothesis which is compounded of the others, the distinction of positive law into *natural* and *positive*, with the various derivative distinctions which rest upon that main one, are utterly unintelligible. Assuming the hypothesis of utility, or assuming the pure hypothesis of a moral sense, the distinction of positive law into *natural* and *positive* is senseless.[49]

At least two important issues deserve attention. These are Austin's notion of positive law (and the distinctions it implies), and Austin's reference to what he calls the modified or mixed hypothesis. I will begin with Austin's view of positive law.

Austin's primary focus in the *Lectures* is on the nature of positive law. In its strictest sense, "Every positive law, or every law simply and strictly so called, is set by a sovereign person, or a sovereign body of persons, to a member or members of the independent political society wherein that person or body is sovereign or supreme."[50]

Initially, Austin divides his strict sense of positive law (*jus civile*) into the categories of *law natural* (*jus gentium*) and *law positive* (*jus civile*).[51] The former are crimes considered wrong in themselves, e.g., violent crimes. The latter are crimes that are not necessarily wrong in themselves. While they may be illegal, e.g., jaywalking, there is nothing inherently wrong or evil about these acts. He assures us that, in some respects, all laws, whether proper or improper, fit taxonomically under one or the other grouping. Austin recognizes that there are three principal classes of laws (reminiscent of Pufendorf and Locke): the law of God, laws created by men as political superiors, and rules of positive morality.[52] The meaning of the first two types of laws are obvious. The third, not so much. There are two relevant points. First, the rules of positive morality are created by men for other men to follow. That said, the framers of these rules are not political superiors. Second, although moral rules are closely analogous to the proper laws mentioned in the first two classes, they are merely human opinions or sentiments."[53] With these distinctions in mind, if I had to guess, the laws of God belong to the *law natural* category, and the other two belong to the *law positive*.

Next I will focus on Austin's "intermediate hypothesis." After this, I will attempt to offer an explanation as to why he claims that the distinctions he made about law including the three categories, discussed above, will not make sense without his intermediate hypothesis. I will now try to give a plain explanation of Austin's intermediate hypothesis.

In the simplest of terms, the intermediate hypothesis consists of two theses: the hypothesis of utility and the hypothesis of a moral sense.[54] I will begin with the former first. What does Austin mean by the hypothesis of utility? To understand this topic, there are three points to make. First, like Bentham and other utilitarians, Austin advocates consequentialism. Minimally, this means that there is an emphasis placed on the outcome of actions. Second, depending upon the Good, an action will be identified as right, wrong, or permissible relative to the Good. This simply means that if the consequences of an action tend to or produce good outcomes, the action is right and thus permissible. This means that the action is obligatory (and a moral requirement) or it is an optional act, an action that is neither obligatory nor wrong to do. Otherwise, it is wrong.

Of course, it is natural to wonder about what kind of utilitarian Austin is. In other words, what does he take the Good to be? As far as I can tell, Austin does not identify the Good for us. Nevertheless, if this is so, then what kind of problem, if any, does this create for Austin? Perhaps someone could object that, without some conception of the Good, we have no idea what acts or rules it will justify. Thus, Austin must give us something specific to avoid this objection. But does he?

Austin's summary of the theory of utility alleviates part of this problem. In the simplest of terms, Austin states that, on the occasion that revelation gives us no indication what to do, we are to consult the probable effects our action will have on the general happiness, presumably, for everyone related to the issue.[55] Although the term "general happiness" get us a little closer, we are still left in the dark. My guess, given his relationship to Bentham, Austin follows a mental-state hedonism as well.

So, in terms of the identification of our *proper moral conduct*, there are two subsets to determine what we should do—the law of God and the principle of utility. That said, there is one other source which Austin discusses—the hypothesis of a moral sense.

As Austin indicated above, the intermediate hypothesis is the combination of the hypothesis of utility (which I briefly elaborated) *and* the hypothesis of a moral sense.[56] The question now is this: What is the hypothesis of a moral sense? Although Austin rehearses what he does not mean by the hypothesis of a moral sense, a discussion too lengthy for the purpose of this examination, Austin states that the moral sense also reveals, like the principle of utility, what God's commands do not explicitly make clear. So, like the principle of utility, the moral sense reveals a part of what we are required and forbidden to do. Still, a question remains: What is the moral sense?

Austin's explication of a moral sense turns on a thought experiment about a feral, human savage. Here is the story. A human savage stumbles accidentally upon a hunter carrying a deer he killed. This is the first time the human savage has ever seen another human. Perhaps unseemly hastened by the pain of hunger, the savage attacks the hunter in order to steal the deer and although the hunter fights back, the savage gains the advantage by seizing a stone and hits the hunter in the head. According to the hypothesis, we expect the savage to feel remorse and compassion after he recognizes what he did to the hunter. Austin makes clear that we might explain his reaction as some sort of moral sentiment. But this is not the case at all. Our feral individual will be affected with self-condemnation or remorse in the same way an individual raised in a civil society will feel after committing a murder.[57]

The story of the savage continues, but with a twist. The savage encounters another hunter who has recently killed a deer. Again, the savage hits the hunter over the head, presumably killing him. But, in this case, the savage's action is a matter of self-defense, and not one motivated by greed or envy.[58]

Without laboring too hard to anticipate Austin's response, he writes:

> Now here, according to the hypothesis, he is *not* affected with remorse. The sufferings of the dying man move him, perhaps, to compassion: but his conscience (as the phrase goes) is tranquil. He feels as you would feel, after a justifiable homicide: after you had shot a highwayman in defense of your goods and your life: or after you had killed another under any combination of circumstances, which, agreeably to your notions of utility, would render killing innocuous, or, agreeably to the current morality of your age and country, would render the killing of another a just or lawful action.[59]

So, as the thought experiment goes, the story assumes that there is a human who survives in the wilderness without the help of any other human. In fact, the importance of Austin's tale turns on the imperative that the savage has not had any contact with another human. Nevertheless, because the savage is human, Austin's intuitions anticipate some sort of response to the interaction he has with the first humans the savage has ever encountered. At first glance, some sort of reaction makes sense, but the question for Austin still remains: Why does the savage react emotionally the way he does? At least to me, it seems equally plausible that the savage could have reacted in a variety of ways, ways we may not be able to anticipate or ways we might expect from an individual living so close to the environment, with an instinctual reaction of self-preservation.

Of course, if we shift our focus from the savage to an individual raised in a political (civilized) economy, Austin argues that both responses we attributed to the non-savage may be best explained by education or the perception of utility. In fact, no appeal to the instincts of the civilized individual is needed. Unfortunately, as Austin makes clear, neither options just mentioned will explain the savage's reaction. So, it seems we are left with an explanation that involves an instinct. But is this Austin's viewpoint? The answer is yes and no. No, because, as far as I can tell, Austin does not specifically attribute the savage's reaction to just pure animal instinct, and yes, because Austin does attribute the savage's reaction to an innate practical principle.[60]

Austin invokes the notion of a moral sense, a doctrine rejected, for the most part, by the (secular) academic community; however, he is also aware of the drawback of this position and makes two qualifications. First, Austin rehearses two arguments in favor of the existence of the moral sentiments and rejects the minor premise of each argument: If the moral sentiments exist, then the judgments we announce will be immediate and involuntary. Again, if the moral sentiments exist, all men should react in precisely the same way.[61] Unfortunately, in the first place, there is no evidence of such feelings, and in the second case, it is clear there is no cross-cultural or trans-historical convergence of moral viewpoints. The best we can say, is that there is some convergence of a small set of actions; otherwise, the majority differ.[62]

This leads to the second qualification that speaks in favor of a small set of moral sentiments, which we find innate and basic: "[T]he difference, supposed by the hypothesis, between the feelings of the savage must therefore, be ascribed to a *moral sense* or to *innate practical principles.* Or (speaking in homelier but plainer language) he would regard the actions with different sentiments, *we know not why.*"[63] Unfortunately, although such a claim is honest (and even reminiscent of Descartes' answer to the problem of evil), ultimately it is dissatisfying.

The last issue for this section concerns why Austin argues that without the mixed hypothesis, "the distinction of positive law into *natural* and *positive* . . . are utterly unintelligible. Assuming the hypothesis of utility, or assuming the pure hypothesis of a moral sense, the distinction of positive law into *natural* and *positive* is senseless."[64] To be sure, this claim holds the interest with a good grasp. Unfortunately, Austin leaves us with little or nothing to suppose why this is true. Now, while it may be tempting to explore the various interpretations of what Austin means, for the purpose of this text, I will simply spell out what I think he means, and then move on to talk about John Stuart Mill.

The closest thing to a justification follows on the heels on the passage above:

> In other words, if the modified or mixed hypothesis be founded in truth, positive human rules fall into two parcels—1. Positive human rules which obtain with all mankind; and the conformity of which to Divine commands is, therefore, indicated by the moral sense, and 2. Positive human rules which do not obtain universally; and the conformity of which to Divine commands is, therefore, not indicated by that infallible guide.[65]

Again, although this by no means resembles a solid underpinning for the claim above, what it does indicate is the logical nature between the truth of the mixed hypothesis and the logical conclusion that positive human law may be broken down into two further categories. Assuming that this interpretation is accurate, Austin argues that if the mixed hypothesis is true, then positive law can be broken down into *law natural* and *law positive*. That said, why should we think this is true and why is it even relevant?

The answer to the latter question Austin gives is that without the truth of mixed hypothesis, we will not be able to meaningfully make a distinction between two different kinds of crimes, e.g., crimes which are wrong in themselves (*mala in Se*) and crimes which are not inherently wrong (*mala quia Prohibita*). Undeniably, both categories are important. To make such a distinction captures (at an intuitive level) the important difference between such crimes. Thus, as far as I can gather from Austin's text, without such a justification, the distinction will rest primarily on our intutitions (remaining senseless). With this (albeit brief) plausible explanation, there is still the question of how this distinction is derived from the mixed hypothesis.

Ultimately, what I think Austin has in mind is this. The *jus gentium* of the positive law can be traceable back to the hypothesis of our moral senses, or what Austin calls our moral sentiments, which we have apart from any sort of education or reflection. Austin calls these sentiments "instinctive" or "moral instincts."[66] His illustrations of the feral individual indicate a class of (criminal) actions, which, as the Latin indicates, are wrong in themselves. Thus, the conditions are favorable to conclude that positive law gives testimony to *law natural*. The *jus civile* follows from the hypothesis of utility. This is so primarily because the principle of utility only makes sense within a context that contains *jus civile*. Although there are laws dedicated to preventing violent crimes, there are also laws that primarily focus on *law positive*. These laws, unlike the criminal laws, for a lack of a better term, are described as laws of public and civil coordination. These are laws which we need to facilitate the harmonization between the interests of the whole and the interests of the individual, and thus, justified by the principle of utility.

I will end with some final thoughts. First, by capturing the connection between the mixed hypothesis and the positive law, I have made Austin's views plausible that the distinction implied by positive law is not senseless. This is, of course, a narrow point and requires a qualification. On the one hand, to say that without the mixed hypothesis the notion of positive law is senseless means that the truth-value of the *content* of the positive law remains without warrant. Surely, it is obvious that I have not made this clear. On the other hand, maintaining the view that, without the mixed hypothesis, the notion of positive law is senseless, means that there is no *relationship*, deductive or otherwise, to think that the notion of positive law has no assignable truth-value, is false. Although many may disagree, there is a plausible way to describe the *relationship* between the mixed hypothesis and positive law that *makes sense*. Again, this is what I take to be the narrow interpretation of the *senselessness* Austin speaks about. Second, because of the amount of time it would take me to show how the *content* of the positive law follows from the mixed hypothesis, I will leave that discussion for another time.

JOHN STUART MILL (1806–1873)

In this section, I discuss John Stuart Mill's contribution to the discussion of the rules of positive law and classical legal positivism. To do this adequately, I will first briefly talk about Mill's utilitarianism. After that, attention will be paid to the connection between his view of utility and justice. Finally, I will underscore his principle of liberty.

Mill's utilitarianism is a version of consequentialism, which focuses primarily on pleasurable and painful psychological states. Thus, like Bentham before him, Mill's utilitarianism is correctly described as a mental-state hedonism.[67] Even though this may be the case, Mill is highly critical of Bentham's analysis of the principle of utility. The problem was not merely Bentham's quantitative hedonism. That is only part of the problem. As Rawls makes clear, Mill argues that Bentham's theory was too narrow to address the most basic social and political problems they faced. Rather, what is needed is something broader, which takes into account character formation and its relationship to the political context.[68] Without discussing such basic topics, the possibility of forming a specific national character, one in which relies on a specific form of government, will not address the urgency to cultivate the members of the culture.[69] To make this clear, I will briefly present the aspect of Mill's utilitarianism which address these concerns. There are three points to underscore: Mill's moral criterion, the quality/quantity distinction, and the application of the Principle of Utility.

Mill begins his discussion with a summary of his moral principle: "Actions are right in proportion as they tend to promote happiness; wrong as they tend to produce the reverse of happiness. By happiness is intended pleasure and the absence of pain; by unhappiness is intended pain and the privation of pleasure."[70] This passage is of paramount importance, and there are several points to underscore. First, Mill's moral principle is a teleological principle. This means that the normative status of an action, whether it is right/wrong or good/bad, is relative to a nonmoral good.[71] So, from Mill's perspective (and Bentham's view), if an act is right, then it is right because of its relationship to happiness. As the quote above indicates, the relationship is spelled out in terms of proportionality.

The notion of *proportionality* figures prominently in Mill's moral theory. For example, to speak of an action "in proportion" points to the ratio of happiness associated with an action, a ratio offset by unhappiness. So if we were to think of something like a sliding scale between two contrary ends, viz., between actions which produce an unqualified state of happiness and one which produces an unqualified state of unhappiness, we can then imagine the different proportions between both of the contrary ends. Although Mill doesn't make this clear, a right action is one in which the proportion of happiness is greater than the unhappiness associated with the same action. The implication is that when the amount of unhappiness overtakes the amount of happiness, then the action may be described as wrong.[72]

Another issue related to Mill's moral theory focuses on the *propensity* that actions may have to produce happiness. Naturally, the unspoken assumption behind the view that actions can *cause* happy or unhappy consequences often remains an open question. Unfortunately, what I add to this important discussion may not make his principle perfectly evident. Nevertheless, minimally what Mill may intend for us to understand is that the normative status of actions, which generate morally relevant consequences, are a part of the set of proximate causes—causes that are the focus of moral judgments. Of course, the proximate cause of the consequences is distinguished from the set of short-term and long-term consequences generated by the proximate cause.[73] Unfortunately, Mill does not make this difference explicit.

Perhaps this much may be expounded by the qualification he makes about the proximate cause. He writes that the proximate cause "tends to" bring about the resulting consequences. As far as causal considerations go, the language associated with the underlying conditions, i.e., the necessary and sufficient conditions, do not apply. First, if we apply the notion of sufficient condition, e.g., when a sufficient condition is present, the effect is guaranteed to occur, then the application of Mill's moral principle will not work because he argues that effect "tends to" occur. The same problem occurs with the necessary condition. So, without a necessary condition, the effect will not occur. What necessary condition is relevant? The answer is, of course, that an action is a necessary condition to produce the effect of happiness or unhappiness. But here is another problem: Is an action necessary to produce happiness? That is hard to answer. What about speech acts? For example, what about warnings, threats, or promises? Mill's point appears to be limited to only actions (in the narrow sense of the term). At least for now, this problem will have to be set aside.

One final facet of Mill's moral theory to mention involves what Mill means by happiness and unhappiness. Mill spells out happiness as pleasure and the lack of pain, and unhappiness in opposite terms. It is here that we get our first suggestion of Mill's mental-state hedonism. Minimally, what Mill means is that from a moral or normative point of view, only the mental states of pleasure and pain are morally relevant properties.[74] So, in terms of the right-making and wrong-making characteristics of an action, only the properties of pleasure and pain (conceived of as consequences) are the focus of our moral judgments. Such a view trumps other moral views which might put the focus solely on the motives or character associated with an action. In any case, Mill positions his own viewpoint within a specific tradition of teleology which has its roots in as far back as Epicurus (341–270 BC), including the atomism endorsed by Epicurus.

The second point concerns the distinction Mill makes between pleasures. While it may be tempting to identify pleasures as merely feelings or some sort of sensory experience, this is not the case at all.[75] Rather, Mill makes a quality/quantity distinction.[76] Here, we pick up Mill's discussion of how to tell the difference between these two types of pleasures:

> Of two pleasures, if there be one to which all or almost all who have experience of both give a decided preference, irrespective of any feeling of moral obligation to prefer it, that is the more desirable pleasure. If one of the two is, by those who are competently acquainted with both, placed so far above the other that they prefer it, even though knowing it to be attended with a greater amount of discontent, and would not resign it for any quantity of the other pleasure which their nature is capable of, we are justified in ascribing to the preferred enjoyment a superiority in quality so far outweighing quantity as to render it, in comparison, of small account.[77]

So, from this passage, apart from the role that the competently acquainted play in the determination of the quality/quantity distinction, we gather that there are pleasures which possess a quality that other pleasures do not. Such a passage is puzzling. Why make this distinction and what kinds of pleasures does he have in mind? I will begin with the former.

Mill makes this distinction in order to distance his viewpoint from any sort of ethical hedonism which makes the mental states of pleasure *simpliciter* the right-making characteristic of moral actions. Such a view is often attributed to Bentham, who argued that psychological hedonism is true. However, such a view often falls prey to the Swine Objection. Mill is conscious of this objection and brings it to the forefront in the early part of his text. I will briefly discuss this objection.

Mill describes the Swine Objection in this way: "To suppose that life has . . . no higher end than pleasure—no better and nobler object of desire and pursuit—they designate as utterly mean and groveling, as a doctrine worthy only of swine. . . ."[78] The intuition behind this objection is that if utilitarianism makes pleasure and pain the only right- or wrong-making characteristics of moral actions, then it would seem to endorse the view that the pleasure animals experience is the same kind of pleasure humans are capable of experiencing. Thus, as Mill makes clear: if this were true, then the rule of life for animals would be same for us.[79] According to Mill, such a view about utilitarianism is mistaken because, in general, utilitarians endorse pre-moral pleasures not typically associated with animals. For example, Mill includes the pleasure of the intellect, feelings, our moral sentiments. Such pleasures have a higher value than just sensations.[80]

So, to make a distinction between quality and quantity of pleasures is to focus on pleasures which are pre-moral pleasures or morally relevant pleasures.[81] Mill intends for us to understand that his moral theory will apply to only certain pleasures and pains. Still, the question remains concerning what pleasures our cultivated judges would endorse and which ones they would not. Mill hints at what he means when he speaks of the pleasures of the intellect and so forth. Nevertheless, he never fully describes what pleasures and pains might apply to his moral theory. There are two other problems with his view that I will briefly mention.

Apart from not knowing what pre-moral pleasures Mill has in mind as well as who are the cultivated judges, two other problems emerge. The first problem concerns whether we can become cultivated judges of pleasures which we intuitively know to be wrong. For example, do we have to experience the immoral pleasures associated with child pornography, necrophilia, rape, and so forth, to understand that such pleasures are not endorsed by Mill's utilitarian theory? No one would want to recommend such a view. Nevertheless, Mill's test seems to suggest that without first experiencing two pleasures, e.g., consensual sex versus non-consensual sex, we cannot pronounce our preferences for one or the other. Second, Mill does not discuss in any detail what he means by quality of pleasures. Of course, it may be tempting to say that quality of pleasures is just very heightened physical pleasures which may be difficult to quantify, but not impossible. Yet, while this interpretation makes sense, the spirit of Mill suggests otherwise.[82] Here is what I think he means: the qualities of pleasure, while present, are not quantifiable. Rather these are non-linguistic mental states which are grasped by our intuitions. Unfortunately, this passage remains a mystery, and so I will overlook it for the time being.[83]

The third point Mill brings to our attention is how and to whom the Principle of Utility is applied; it is not the agent's own happiness, but the happiness of everyone.[84] So, according to this quote, how and to whom is the Principle of Utility applied?[85] Mill raises two possibilities. The focus of the Principle of Utility is merely on the agent's own happiness or the greatest amount of happiness altogether. Clearly, Mill excludes the agent's own happiness as the proper application of the Principle of Utility. But why is this the case? Why make this point?

Mill is quite aware of the fact that there are competing teleological viewpoints where moral theories are concerned. Additionally, it is natural, when speaking of happiness as the nonmoral good, to assume that the most immediate application of the theory would be to benefit the agent who applies the theory. In fact, with this intuition in place, it is a small step to make the agent's own happiness the standard for the moral theory. Therefore, what makes an action right is the maximization of the agent's own happiness.[86] Although Mill does not make mention of this theory by name, he may have in mind what is known now as egoism.[87] Nevertheless, he sidesteps this view and refers to the greatest amount of happiness altogether. Unfortunately, such a phrase is ambiguous, because there is no clear referent to what he means. Ultimately, what Mill will say is that, depending upon the context, there is no expectation to apply the Principle of Utility beyond the particular persons concerned.[88]

This point brings up the following question: If the Principle of Utility does not focus on the happiness of the individual, but of all concerned, how does the utilitarian apply the Principle of Utility without, seemingly, taking his own happiness into account? Mill acknowledges this question and remarks that it is not the agent's own happiness but of all concerned: "As between his own happiness and that of others, utilitarianism requires him to be as strictly impartial as a disinterested and benevolent spectator."[89]

This passage brings to light the nicest little secret about Mill's viewpoint which is often overlooked by many interpreters and critics of Mill's classical Utilitarianism. The secret, which is unnoticed, is the role of cultivation.[90] Unlike Bentham, Mill implies that (character) cultivation is needed to apply the Principle of Utility in the right way. In fact, I should add that this cultivation is needed to train our intuitions to grasp the quality present in pleasures which would normally be overlooked. So, then, what does this passage add to our understanding of Mill which may help us to apply the Principle of Utility to the formation of a national character and cultivated legislative branch of government?

The key to this passage is obvious: to apply the Principle of Utility correctly, one must understand what he means by the notions of impartiality and disinterestedness. Indeed, there is nothing ambiguous about its meaning. What is unclear is how such an attitude is attainable. Unfortunately, although I have an idea about how to spell this out, I can only provide the barest bones of such a viewpoint. This much can be said: reminiscent of Aristotle's view of when the education of virtues begins, Mill subtly remarks that such an attitude must begin at a young age to teach children to associate their own happiness with the happiness of others.[91] Of course, it seems reasonable to assume that such an attitude may be attained later in life. But, more often than not, this attitude may be limited to familial ties. Mill's ideal is more reminiscent of a worldview. In other words, young children may be trained to associate their own good with the good of the whole of society, of course, whether that is attainable is certainly an undeveloped question. Apart from that question, there are smaller models which may illuminate what he means.

To maintain strict impartiality while also maintaining a benevolent attitude requires an individual to align their goals and projects with the goals and projects of the group. For example, in our own culture, the closest model we have to such an outlook are the individuals who become police officers or firefighters. On these models, a kind of collectivism emerges, e.g., a value that emphasizes a cohesiveness among the individuals of the group and prioritization of the group over the self. In the case of individual police officers or firefighters, there is an identification of the goal of the group to the extent that one may be willing to give their own life in the pursuit of the goal. Such an outlook may be found among members of the military and is even dramatically displayed in television series like the *Sons of Anarchy*. Two questions regarding these models seem necessary to bring up.

The first question concerns the status of the individuals within these collectivistic models. Are the individuals required to lose or suppress their own identity in order to be a part of the collective? The second question concerns whether being a member of the community requires an individual to set aside their ordinary rights, e.g., the right of liberty, welfare, and equality? Ideally, the answer to the first question is no. The reason is that individuals who enter such communities possess goals which, in some respects, are identical with the goals of the community. Thus, there is no need to suppress one's own identity if the goals of both are coextensive. In fact, I imagine organizations which are designed to protect the life and the liberty of other individuals will only accept those who are willing to make that sort of commitment.

The question of rights may be a little more difficult to answer. Certainly, unless one is a member of the military, we expect the individual members committed to protecting the public to live by and enjoy the same basic rights appreciated by ordinary people. And, yet, we tend to think that public servants who enjoy these basic rights must also meet the same standards and then go beyond. Perhaps this captures what is the case: on the one hand, no one would expect to be deprived of their basic rights to become a member of a public-service organization. For example, the right to freedom, whether conceived in negative or positive terms (i.e., the right not be physically constrained or coerced),[92] will remain intact as long as one remains a member of the community. On the other hand, we expect police officers to use their freedom to put themselves in harm's way to protect the public, a requirement not automatically expected of ordinary people. So, the point, in brief, is that while the basic rights of public servants are protected, we require more of them to satisfy their function to protect the public.

The last point to discuss brings to light a passage in which Mill gives us a synopsis of how to use the Principle of Utility and specifically the creation of national character and the legislators role. For example, the principle of ultility requires two things. First, it obliges "that laws and social arrangements should place the happiness or . . . the interest of every individual as nearly as possible in harmony with the interests of the whole."[93] It also requires that education and opinion be used "to establish in the mind of every individual an indissoluble association between his own happiness and the good of the whole.[94]

There are two parts to this passage which are, in fact, related. The first part illustrates, in the briefest terms, Mill's own interpretation of the Principle of Utility. The second part, mentioned earlier, describes (partly) the preconditions needed to understand how to use the Principle of Utility. Because I have spoken about the second part already, I will now concentrate primarily on the first part.

The text above follows directly upon the heels of Mill's disinterested and benevolent spectator. Additionally (in the sentence above it), Mill aligns the Principle of Utility with two Christian ideals of the New Testament.[95] With the Christian ideals in place, Mill then implies that using the Principle of Utility in a specific way will exemplify the commands of Jesus of Nazareth. The way to reach these goals, then, revolves around the harmonization of two items, viz., the happiness or interest of every individual with the happiness or interest of the whole. To accomplish this harmonization, we must design *laws* and *social arrangements* which will harmonize the interests of both groups.

No doubt, such a claim is quite interesting. Unfortunately, this passage appears to raise more questions than it answers. First, and foremost, Mill does not give us any examples to depict the harmonization he thinks is possible. Second, Mill initially explains the Principle of Utility by speaking of *actions* as being right or wrong. Here, Mill speaks of laws and social arrangement. What is the relationship, if any, between the actions spoken of earlier and the laws and social arrangement? Does this mean that Mill thinks the Principle of Utility will apply to both actions and rules? Personally, I am inclined to think he does. Third, while the term "law" is familiar, what is a social arrangement? Finally, how do we make sense out of the interests of individuals and the interests of the whole? As with the other questions, Mill leaves us with nothing to go on. Nevertheless, this much might be proposed.

Although Mill is highly critical of Bentham, he credits Bentham with a number of acknowledgments. Bentham exposed and challenged a number of erroneous and illogical legal maxims of the existing systems of jurisprudence, but he did more than that. Mill praises him for treating law like a science and bringing it back to a discussion of first principles. Bentham's influence is particularly important as he developed a complete body of law, including the Civil Law, the Penal Law, and the Law of Procedure. So, while Bentham made great strides in the areas of law, Mill complains that Bentham's account of human nature and moral psychology does not pass muster.[96] In fact, for all intents and purposes, Mill rejects Bentham's mental-state hedonism. He argues, among other things, that Bentham's view commits us to the view that "all our acts are determined by pains and pleasures *in prospect*, pains and pleasures to which he looks forward as the consequences of our acts."[97] Mill states that this is plainly false. Rather, which is often the case, "pain or pleasure which determines our conduct is as frequently one which *precedes* the moment of action as one which follows it."[98] Because Bentham's hedonism is off point, this leads to serious consequences for his theory of government and of law. There are two problems worth mentioning.

The first problem is minor. Mill sets up a destructive dilemma. On the one hand, as Mill interprets Bentham, if we assume that his account of psychological hedonism is true, then human nature is the same everywhere and at all times. At the same time, such an assumption creates two problems, given the kind of goals associated with creating a national character consistent with utilitarian collectivism. What reasons will motivate the citizens with dyed-in-the-wool hedonism to seek the good of the whole? Also, given Bentham's notion of human nature, how will we choose a leader to change the culture to an ideal that they think is not correct?[99] As minor problems go, Mill exposes Bentham's daring little liberties.

The prevailing error of Bentham, as Mill makes clear, is tinged with irony. Bentham imagines the average person "to be much cooler and more thoughtful calculators than they really are."[100] This means that Bentham assumes, contrary to his own assumptions again, that humanity, and humans in general, are receptive to change, especially change that takes place in a political and social setting. Mill, however, argues squarely against the viewpoint. In essence, Mill argues that the majority of individuals are afraid of change, even when that change brings a welcome respite from an inconvenient setting.[101] Thus, although Mill's utilitarianism may be discussed in a context dedicated to the explication of a moral theory, a historical placement of his document reveals something much deeper and broader than a narrow theoretical account. I will now discuss Mill's connection between justice and utility.

One may wonder how closely Mill followed in the footsteps of Bentham and Austin. Like both authors, Mill rejects the social contract theory.[102] Also, there's no room for the natural law in Mill's *Utilitarianism* or *On Liberty*.[103] Mill discusses attitudes toward law and whether justice is a product of nature or of law. After that, Mill spends his time talking about the nature of justice and its relationship to morality and expediency. I will start with Mill's discussion of the attitudes toward law and follow, very briefly, his discussion of the nature of justice.

Mill begins the last chapter of *Utilitarianism* with a discussion of the nature of justice. According to my interpretation of Mill, as with Bentham, justice is relative to a set of laws and an interpretation of those laws. This means that (as with Hume) there are no facts about justice prior to the formation of law (a view I also share). Thus, as the laws change and vary with the context, we expect the notion of justice to change as well. Even if this is not the case, the notion of justice, according to Mill, is notoriously difficult to pin down. To show this, there are five diverse applications to make about justice.

First, justice is often associated with what is legally required. For example, to deprive someone of their liberty or property is considered unjust. Unfortunately, depending what justice means, there may be strange notions of what is legal which aggravate what counts as a legitimate deprivation. Second, there are those who argue that regardless of whether the law is justified or not, it must not be disobeyed. The only way to alter the situation is to change the law through a competent authority.[104] Mill lands this objection against this view: To maintain this viewpoint would condemn many individuals who benefited mankind and to protect malicious governments. Others (following Aquinas and Augustine) maintain that any law judged to be bad may be disobeyed without blame.[105] Mill's objection to this latter view is less pronounced and shadowy. Although we are left uncertain to his meaning, what I gather is that this view fails to keep separate a law which is unjust from one that is merely inexpedient. The intuition, I imagine, is that justice applies to the former rule but not to the latter. Thus, despite the diversity of opinions about this matter, it seems to be universally admitted that there are just and unjust laws. Mill admits that this naturally leads to the conclusion that law cannot be the ultimate criterion of justice.[106] This is especially relevant when a law benefits a person or imposes an evil on someone which justice condemns. But is this really the case?

The third opinion about justice is fairness. Mill comments that this is perhaps the view that is the most manifest. This means that justice requires that each person receive what he deserves, whether he deserves good or evil. Unfortunately, such a view, while plausible, turns upon spelling out clearly what constitutes desert. Typically, what this means is that an individual deserves good if he does something right, and evil, if he does wrong. More specifically, good from those he has done good to and evil from those he has done evil to. Mill implies that such a view is fraught with problems because it is not clear, in either case, what recompenses are just. Likewise, the Christian injunction to return good for evil falls outside of the scope of justice.[107] The fourth and fifth notions of justice point to breaking faith with anyone and the requirement of impartiality. Of the former, to break faith is often required to employ different notions of justice when overriding conditions give us reasons to think breaking faith is permissible. The latter notion appeals to the universal intuition that it is unjust to be partial when partiality is clearly not required. Unfortunately, like the other cases above, it is not always clear that showing partiality is always automatically morally suspicious. The reason is that, under the majority of conditions, no one would blame an individual who consistently shows partiality to his family at the expense of a stranger (where duty is not owed).[108] There is one qualification to the latter view.

Mill comments that justice as impartiality is often synonymous with the idea of equality. Thus, the notion of equality is often treated as the essence of justice. The problem Mill exploits is the way this notion often becomes twisted to serve those whose notion of utility vary. To be sure, justice requires equality except when expediency overrides equality. Such a view has been used to justify slavery in different countries. Thus, in such countries, where riches and other privileges are at stake, for example, privileges afforded to skin color that do not support any reasonable treatment of inequality, nevertheless become the basis of inequalities.[109]

Thus, even if our intuitions connect justice to law, which is certainly the case, does Mill provide a bright line for us that demonstrates that this is what justice is and what it is not? He certainly seems to distance himself from all five views.[110] Much of what he eventually says about justice stems from his legal positivism. But is Mill wedded to such a view? I think he is. Here's what I take the argument to be:

1. Either Mill is a legal positivist about law and justice or Mill defends law with a deep account of justice and other moral considerations, which dictate what laws are good and which ones are bad.
2. It is not the case that Mill defends laws with a deep account of justice and other moral considerations which dictate what laws are good and which ones are bad.
3. Therefore, Mill is a legal positivist about law and justice.

The question now is whether this argument is sound. It certainly is valid, but are the premises true? Premise one is true, because both views are mutually exclusive and exhaustive. Why is this the case? As I made clear earlier, a nominalist account of law or morality is at odds with a metaphysical realist account of the same. Additionally, as far as any position which may be defended apart from these two positions, it is unclear what position that would be.

What about premise 2? That is, of course, the major question. So where do we begin? Let us begin with Mill's conception of law. Again, like those authors from the Enlightenment period, the essence of a law is the fact that its violation will involve punishment. Mill's view is no different.[111] So, when we talk about the violation of a law, we imply that some sort of punishment should be expected. Apart from law, no matter how much we may despise the action of another, we cannot invoke any penal sanctions unless there is a violation of a law. Justice in those cases is not relevant. No doubt, in any discussion of the essence or nature of law, we will expect our notions of justice to be tied very closely to law. In fact, like justice, law confers rights to those subject to the law. Justice, tied to those rights, insists that such laws be obeyed and that sanctions should be applied to those who violate the laws.

But now the question to consider is this: What are we to think when our notion of justice is at odds with a recognized law? It seems we are faced with a fountain of trouble.

First, it ought to be noted that even if legal positivism is true, and justice is relative to that set of laws, it should come as no surprise that our notion of justice will vary sometimes from what we take to be a law. In fact, there is plenty of evidence for such a view. For example, if we take the U.S. Constitution and the Amendments as a set of rules and instructions for the formation and the guidance of our government, rules which have historical significance but lack epistemic significance (a view consistent with H. A. L. Hart's rules of recognition), then, as the moral viewpoint of our culture changes, so will our notion of justice. So, even without a deep account of justice, as our own culture has shown, our ideas about slavery, women's rights, marriage rights, and so forth, may change. So, why do our moral views change if legal positivism is true and justice is relative to the current legal system? It's unclear why. Perhaps something like Richard Dawkin's notion of a meme may explain why our ideas change and become prevalent in a culture.[112]

Second, if there is nothing unusual about our notions of justice conflicting with our positive notion of law, then what kind of evidence do we need to maintain that justice is ultimately the criterion of law? The answer, as I have sought to discuss in this text, must ultimately turn to a deep account of justice, a justification consistent with the accounts developed by Aristotle, Plato, the Stoics, Aquinas, or Grotius. Does Mill have something like this in mind? The answer is no. Here's why.

Mill's discussion of justice is clear, but it is complex and fraught with many different qualifications. Essentially, Mill's view of justice is indispensably a sentiment.[113] It is a natural feeling of two other sentiments, viz., the natural instincts of self-defense and the feeling of sympathy.[114] Mill argues that such natural instincts are common to all animal nature. However, there is a crucial difference between non-human species and the human species. Although, several non-human species (especially those that follow a K-Strategy of sexual reproduction), like humans, are capable of sympathizing not only with our offspring, humans are also capable of sympathizing with all sentient nature. Additionally, Mill interleaves that humans have a more developed intelligence.[115] The advantage intelligence gives us is not just a greater capacity of sympathy. It also gives us the capacity to see ourselves as part of a community, a culture, and a society. This leads to a crucial aspect about the moral connection to justice perhaps not noticed, but important to understand.

Mill explains that the basic sentiment of justice is not necessarily a moral sentiment. The sentiment of justice itself arises naturally in us, but, as Mill makes clear, the resentment remains unfocused, because without moral cultivation, there is a tendency to begrudge indiscriminately anyone we find disagreeable. With that in mind, then, when does justice become, in Mill's own words, "moralized"? The answer draws us back to his moral theory, viz., the sentiment of justice becomes moralized when it is connected to the social feeling of the general good. Thus, justice is moralized when our sentiments are cultivated to desire the happiness of the community and ultimately our society.[116]

So, after this discussion, what are we to think about premise 2? It is clear that it is true. Again, this is so for two basic reasons. First, it is perfectly consistent to assume legal positivism is true and to argue that a legal system or a law is corrupt. Second, even though Mill argues that our notion of justice may dictate that our notions of law are mistaken, his notion of justice, until it is moralized, goes no deeper than the natural instincts we have about self-preservation and the narrow sympathy for our immediate family. Therefore, if premise 2 is true and premise 1 is true, the argument above is sound, and the conclusion is worthy of belief, viz., Mill, like Austin and Bentham, embraces legal positivistism.

CONCLUSION

The Counter-Enlightenment Period brings numerous changes. The focus of this chapter attempts to document some of the most important changes in political and legal philosophy. For example, natural law is rejected; the Social Contract Theory ridiculed and disparaged. The three notable scholars associated with the changes are Bentham, Austin, and Mill. Of course, the focus on these three figures is not meant to imply that that they were the only scholars dedicated to the status of the nature of law. The nineteenth-century school of historical jurisprudence (or the historical school of law) was not discussed.[117] This is not because the movement was not important. Rather, my own interest determined the focus of the scholarship dedicated to this text. Nevertheless, apart from the European movement of the study of law, the British and American movement deserves special attention. This is so because, from these roots, we can trace the preeminent legal scholarship from Hans Kelsen (1881–1973), Lon L. Fuller (1902–1978), H. L. A. Hart (1907–1992), and John Finnis (b. 1940) to Ronald Dworkin (1913–2013).

In the next chapter I focus on the views of three legal scholars before I develop my own view of legal naturalism. I focus on the legal philosophy of Austin, Hart, and Dworkin. After that, in chapter 6, I develop my own viewpoint by placing it in between the legal positivism of Austin and Hart and Dworkin's understated and thin account of natural law.

NOTES

1. Rommen, *The Natural Law: A Study in Legal and Social History and Philosophy*, 36.

2. Lon L. Fuller adds the is-ought gap introduced by Hume as an element in positivism which reflects the ethical subjection which emerged after Hume. The is-ought gap is reflected in the distinction between what law is and what law ought to be. See Lon L. Fuller, *The Law in Quest of Itself* (Clark, NJ: The Lawbook Exchange, LTD, 2012), 5. Charles Covell discusses the significance of the fact-value gap in Fuller's defense of natural law. See Charles Covell, *The Defence of Natural Law* (New York: St. Martin's Press, 1992), 31–38.

3. Rommen, *The Natural Law: A Study in Legal and Social History and Philosophy*, 97.

4. Rommen makes clear that there was another attack against natural law from a group called the German Historical School of Law. Although I would like to discuss this topic, I will concentrate on the efforts of British and American scholars. See Rommen, pages 101–105. This is also discussed briefly by Charles Covell, *The Defence of Natural Law* (New York: St. Martin's Press, 1992), 16–18.

5. Jeremy Bentham, *The Principles of Morals and Legislation* (Amherst, New York: Prometheus Books, 1988). Originally published in 1781. I will make reference to the Bentham text by indicating chapter and paragraph.

6. Ibid., I.ii.

7. Ibid., I.iii.

8. As well as his commitment to moral or normative hedonism, Bentham is also considered a psychological hedonist. This roughly means that all human behavior is motivated by pleasure or pain. Bentham writes: "Nature has placed mankind under the governance of two sovereign masters, pain and pleasure. It is for them alone to point out what we ought to do, as well as to determine what we shall do." Bentham, *The Principles of Morals and Legislation*, I.i.

9. William Frankena, *Ethics*, 2nd ed. (Upper Saddle River, NJ: Prentice Hall, 1973), 14–16.

10. Bentham, *The Principles of Morals and Legislation*, I.iii.

11. Bentham explains that the pleasures experienced by an individual are typically evaluated by it intensity, duration, its certainty or uncertainty and how close or remote it is. Ibid., IV.ii–iii.

12. Ibid., IV.iv.

13. Ibid., IViii–iv. Of these three, Bentham states that they are not really properties of pleasure or pain. Rather they are properties of the act chosen for its expected pain or pleasure. They estimate the tendency or the act or event. Ibid., IV.iii.

14. Ibid., IV.v.

15. Jeremy Bentham, "Anarchical Fallacies; being an examination of the Declaration of Rights issued during the French Revolution," in ed. Jeremy Waldron, *'Nonsense upon stilts': Bentham, Burke, and Marx on the Rights of Man* (London: Methuen, 1987), 46–69.

16. Ibid., 52.

17. Mill also complains of Bentham's lack of rigor and dismissive attitude toward his opponents. See John Stuart Mill, "Remarks on Bentham," in *Ultimate Collection: Works on Philosophy, Politics, and Economy* (Madison & Adams Press, 2017), loc. 47376–47410 of 53395, Kindle.

18. Bentham, "Anarchical Fallacies," 52.

19. Ibid., 53.

20. Ibid.

21. Jeremy Bentham, *A Fragment on Government* (Cambridge University Press, 1988), 86.

22. Frederick Schauer, "Positivism Before Hart," *Canadian Journal of Law & Jurisprudence* 24, no. 2 (July 2011): 455. It is worth noting that Schauer's article also includes a discussion about the significance of the term "positivism" (457–58). Charles Covell treats Bentham's legacy the same. See Covell, *The Defence of Natural Law*, 1. This is not to deny the significance of the early proto-positivism in Hobbes' *Leviathan* discussed in chapter 3.

23. Schauer, "Positivism Before Hart," 458–462; 464.

24. Ibid., 458.

25. Covell, *The Defence of Natural Law*, 1.

26. This claim, however, collapses two theses that should be kept separate. As Covell makes clear, Bentham distinguished *expository jurisprudence* and *censorial jurisprudence*. The for-

mer sets its sights on a description and analysis of law. The latter on the evaluation of law and legal concepts. Ibid., 2.

27. Schauer, "Positivism Before Hart," 460.

28. Ibid., 462.

29. Ibid., 464.

30. Bentham, "Anarchiacal Fallacies," 55. cf. Benthan, *A Fragment on Government*, 39, 116.

31. Bentham, *A Fragment on Government*, 39. cf. Philip Schofield, "Jeremy Bentham on Utility and Truth," *History of European Ideas* 41, no. 8 (2015): 1125–1142.

32. Bentham, *A Fragment on Government*, 51. cf. David Hume, *Treatise on Human Nature*, 2nd ed., ed. Lewis A. Selby-Bigge (Oxford University Press, 1978), III.ii.2. In particular, see pages 493–495 of the same edition. Covell also discusses Bentham's diatribe against Blackstone and discusses Bentham comments in the *A Fragment of Government*. Covell, *The Defense of Natural Law*, 3–4. Blackstone is interpreted as defending a deep account of natural law, one consistent with Aquinas, and which, ultimately, is the foundation of English common law.

33. Ibid., 52. Bentham describes this as a conversation with lawyers with no reference to whom he spoke with. It is an interesting piece of anecdotal evidence.

34. Paola Rudan, "Society as a Code: Bentham and the Fabric of Order," *History of European Ideas* 42, no. 1 (2016): 42.

35. Bentham, *Fragment on Government*, 42–43. See footnote P; 44.

36. Rudan, "Society as a Code: Bentham and the Fabric of Order," 43. After this point, Rudan explains that the conclusions Bentham draws about the fictions surrounding the original contract theory gives us insight into Bentham's critical remarks about the American Declaration of Independence. Ibid.

37. Bentham, *Fragment on Government*, 44. This is what Bentham seems to imply in paragraphs 16 and 17.

38. Ibid., 101.

39. Ibid., 116.

40. Ibid.

41. Ibid., 88.

42. Covell, *The Defence of Natural Law*, 12.

43. Wilfrid E. Rumble, ed. "Introduction," in John Austin, *The Province of Jurisprudence Determined*, ed. Wilfrid E. Rumber (Cambridge University Press, 2001): xi. My characterization of Austin and his life is overly simplistic and too brief.

44. Ibid., x–xi.

45. Ibid., xi–xii.

46. Ibid., xii. I should add that despite her efforts, Austin's lectures are poorly written, redundant, and tedious.

47. Ibid., viii.

48. Part of the reason why Austin spends little or no time in the justification of the principle of utility, unlike the efforts of Bentham and Mill, marks Austin's enterprise concerned primarily with the exposition of the science of jurisprudence—what positive law is—as opposed to what law ought to be. Austin's framework, then, becomes the foundation of the modern tradition of analytical jurisprudence.

49. John Austin, *The Province of Jurisprudence Determined*, ed. Wilfrid E. Rumber, (Cambridge University Press, 2001), 92.

50. Ibid., 116–117. Of the same topic, Austin describes three essential aspects of a strict law: "I. Laws properly so called are a species of *commands*. But, being a command, every law properly so called flows from a *determinate* source, or emanates from a *determinate* author. In other words, the author from whom it proceeds is a determinate rational being, or a determinate body or aggregate of rational beings." Ibid., 117–118. "2. Every sanction properly so called is an eventual evil *annexed to a command*." Ibid., 118. Finally, Austin makes clear: "3. Every duty properly so called supposes a command by which it is created. For every sanction properly so called is an eventual evil *annexed to a command*." Ibid. Italics occur in text.

51. Ibid., 91–92.

52. Austin, *The Province of Jurisprudence Determined*, 109–10.
53. Ibid. Austin discusses what he means by laws that are analogically similar to proper laws. The former he labels as improper laws. Ibid., 108. Thus, the third set of laws are improper laws, not proper. Later, Austin quotes and discusses John Locke's (1632–1704) view of the law of opinion or reputation found in Locke's *Essay Concerning Human Understanding*, II.xxviii. Austin, *The Province of Jurisprudence Determined*, 144–147. Although Austin does not think that Locke's law of opinion is a proper law, Locke argues otherwise because of the serious (painful) consequences associated with violating the law of opinion. Locke closely associates this third set with the law of nature, expressed in *aretaic* terms.
54. Austin, *The Province of Jurisprudence Determined*, 91.
55. Ibid., 45.
56. Ibid., 91.
57. Ibid., 83.
58. Ibid.
59. Ibid., 83–84.
60. Ibid., 86.
61. Ibid., 88.
62. Ibid., 91.
63. Ibid., 86.
64. Ibid., 92.
65. Ibid.
66. Ibid., 82.
67. Wendy Donner, "Mill's Utilitarianism," chap. 7 in *The Cambridge Companion to Mill*, ed. John Skorupski (Cambridge University Press, 1998): 257.
68. John Rawls, *Lectures on the History of Political Philosophy*, ed. Samuel Freeman (Cambridge and London: The Belknap Press of Harvard University Press, 2007), 255.
69. Ibid. cf. Mill, "Remarks on Bentham's Philosophy," loc. 47461 of 53395, Kindle.
70. John Stuart Mill, *Utilitarianism*, 2nd ed., ed. George Sher (Indianapolis and Cambridge: Hackett Publishing Co., 1979), 7. Originally published in 1861.
71. Frankena, *Ethics*, 14.
72. Several qualifications are relevant. First, as I mentioned above, characterizing the notion of "proportion" amounts to a bit of speculation on my part. Nevertheless, it is part of Mill's moral principle and, because we may not know what Mill intended, it remains permissible to interpret it as long as the interpretation does not paint his theory as something inconsistent with a traditional understanding of Mill's moral outlook. Second, although my interpretation of the notion of "proportion" could use numbers often associated with contemporary utilitarian discussions, Mill does not intend to spell out his moral principle in terms quantifiable with numbers. It is natural to describe proportions in terms of numbers, but Mill does not give us any indication that this is what he intends. Of course, if this is not what he intends, then what are the epistemic requirements for knowing when an action is a right action and one which is wrong? Soon, I will make a case that we when we discuss Mill's quality/quantity distinction, Mill's position is best captured by a naturalized (cultivated) intuitionism. The immediate implication for this issue is that, barring the suspicious option of merely guessing, we are left with taking into account the historical significance of the consequences associated with an action or using our intuitions to grasp, so to speak, the proportion of happiness relative to the unhappiness. Third, there is an unspoken assumption here that the consequences of an action, whether right or wrong, are mixed, so to speak, with happiness and unhappiness. Does such a view pan out with our experience? There may be some obvious cases. For example, suppose a car is traveling out of control and unbeknownst to an individual who is in the car's way, is rescued at the last minute by another individual. Unfortunately, the only way to save him is to push him with the result that he falls and breaks his arm. Initially, the injured individual may be tempted to classify this action as wrong especially in the light of the pain; however, once he recognizes that his life was spared, he may change his outlook about the consequences. If this case works, it is an obvious example of an action which is a mixture of happiness and unhappiness.
73. The short-term and long-term distinction is a contemporary distinction often associated with act-utilitarianism and rule-utilitarianism respectively. As far as I can tell, Mill never

makes the act/rule distinction explicit, but it seems to subtly appear in his discussion. I will make this clear momentarily.

74. Although it may be tempted to classify Mill, like Bentham, as a psychological hedonist, that would be a mistake. To make this point clear, Donner reproduces a rather large quote taken from Mill's text *Logic*. She writes that Mill makes clear that: "as we proceed in the formation of habits, and become accustomed to will a particular act or a particular course of conduct because it is pleasurable, we at last continue to will it without any reference to its being pleasurable." Again, from the same passage, Mill points out that: "It is only when our purposes have become independent of the feelings of pain or pleasure from which they originally took their rise, that we are said to have a confirmed character." Donner, "Mill's utilitarianism," 259–260.

75. Rawls, *Lectures on the History of Political Philosophy*, 259.

76. Mill also describes this distinction as higher and lower pleasures. Mill, *Utilitarianism*, 10.

77. Mill, *Utilitarianism*, 8–9. cf. Rawls, *Lectures on the History of Philosophy*, 259–263.

78. Ibid., 7.

79. Ibid., 8.

80. Ibid. Rawls makes clear that Mill's higher and lower distinction is a reaction to Bentham's view that the morally relevant pleasures point, not to the source of the pleasure, but its intensity and duration. Otherwise, "a pleasure is a pleasure is a pleasure." Rawls, *Lectures on the History of Political Philosophy*, 261.

81. Another important difference between Mill and Bentham is the following: although Bentham regards only the quantities of pleasures as normative, that is, productive of good, Mill does not solely regard the quantity as normative. He regards both quantity *and* quality of pleasures and satisfactions as normative or productive of good. Overall value or goodness is produced by quantity and quality, the two basic good-making characteristics.

82. For example, Mill writes: "When, therefore, those feelings and judgment declare the pleasures derived from the higher faculties to be preferable *in kind*, apart from the question of intensity, to those of which the animal nature, disjoined from the higher faculties, is susceptible, they are entitled on this subject to the same regard." Mill, *Utilitarianism*, 11. This passage points to the illusive nature of the quality of pleasures especially when he does not link it to the intensity one might feel with other physical pleasures. For an excellent discussion of Mill's qualitative hedonism and its critics, see Donner, "Mill's utilitarianism," 261–273.

83. As an attempt to explicate this unusual point by Mill, I submit the following illustration about the pleasures of love and friendship. My claim is that anyone who is competently acquainted with both will insist that love has a quality of pleasure which is not present in friendship. Thus, because of the presence of pleasure in love, there is decided preference for love (even as Mill makes clear that such pleasures are attended with a greater amount of discontent): Briefly, to recognize that one has a friend is to list the friendship-making characteristics, which typically add up to the conclusion that someone is a friend. So, for example, if John is friends with David, and Renee asks John why he is friends with David, John could point out the friendship-making characteristics which would, in a sense, add up to why John likes David. In other words, Renee may easily agree with John's reasons for why he is friends with David. But here is the interesting question: can we list the being-in-love-making characteristics as easily as the friendship-making characteristics? The answer is no. The main reason is that no matter how many being-in-love-making characteristics one can name, one can still ask, "But is that why you love her?" In general, the answer will always be no. Such a thought experiment points to, as I suggest, the quality of pleasure present in the pleasure of love which is not present in the pleasure of friendship. So, if we assume for the moment that my account of being in love is accurate, then what are we to make of it? My estimation is that the quality of pleasure is a non-linguistic property which is grasped at some sort of intuitive level.

84. Mill, *Utilitarianism*, 11.

85. The following discussion (reminiscent of Aristotle's discussion toward the end of Book X of the *Nicomachean Ethics*) moves slowly to Mill's vision of a national character and the legislator's role in this endeavor.

86. Feldman, *Introductory Ethics*, 83.

87. It is unclear who Mill specifically has in mind when he raises the specter of egoism. Unless he is referring to a prevailing meme, one contemporary writer Mill may be referring to is the German scholar, Max Stirner (1806–1856). He authored *Der Einzige und sein Eigenthum* (1844), which was later translated into English, *The Ego and Its Own*. It was widely read and critically reviewed by many scholars. Leopold, David, "Max Stirner," *The Stanford Encyclopedia of Philosophy* (Fall 2015 Edition), Edward N. Zalta (ed.), URL = https://plato.stanford.edu/archives/fall2015/entries/max-stirner/.

88. Mill, *Utilitarianism*, 19.

89. Ibid., 16.

90. Ibid., 9. Mill's focus on cultivation comes immediately after he discusses how to detect the qualities of pleasure in certain actions. Unfortunately, what is missing is a clear connection in the text between the two topics.

91. Ibid., 17. For an excellent discussion of Mill's classical training, and its influence in his writings, see T. H. Irwin, "Mill and the Classical World," chap. 12 in *The Cambridge Companion to Mill*, ed. John Skorupski (Cambridge University Press, 1998), 423–463.

92. John Rawls, *A Theory of Justice* (Cambridge: The Belknap Press of Harvard University Press, 1971), 210–05. cf. John Rowan, "The Moral Foundation of Employee Rights," in *Ethics for the Professions*, ed. John Rowan and Samuel Zinaich, Jr. (Belmont, CA: Wadsworth/Thomas Learning, 2003), 91. Previously published as John R. Rowan, "The Moral Foundation of Employee Rights," *The Journal of Business Ethics* 24 (2000): 355–361.

93. Mill, *Utilitarianism*, 17.

94. Ibid.

95. Ibid. Mill aligns the principle of utility with the Golden Rule: Treat others as you would want to be treated, and, what has come to be called the second part of the Greatest Commandment: love your neighbor as yourself. Mill writes that both rules capture the spirit of the utilitarian ideal.

96. John Stuart Mill, "Remarks on Betham's Philosophy," in *Ultimate Collection: Works on Philosophy, Politics & Economy (Including Memoirs & Essays)* (Madison & Adams Press, 2017), loc. 47511 of 53395, Kindle.

97. Ibid.

98. Ibid.

99. Ibid., loc. 47597 of 53395, Kindle.

100. Ibid., loc. 47614 of 53395, Kindle.

101. Ibid., loc. 47609–47626 of 53395, Kindle. This issue, oddly enough, is brought up in Locke's *Second Treatise*. On a tangential issue, when a government is mismanaged, the individuals tend to put up with many wrongs and inconveniences. And yet, Locke optimistically stipulates that when the long term designs of a government becomes tyrannical, humans "rouze themselves" to secure a government which they first consented to. Locke, *Treatises*, II.xix.§225.

102. Mill, *Utilitarianism*, 56; cf. John Stuart Mill, *On Liberty*, Elizabeth Rapaport, ed. (Indianapolis and Cambridge: Hackett Publishing Company, Inc., 1978), 73. Original work publish in 1859.

103. Mill does address the law of nature in *Three Essays on Religion* and cannot resist taking it down a peg or two: "Under their influence the Roman jurists, when attempting to systematize jurisprudence, placed in the front of their exposition a certain Jus Naturale, "quod natura," as Justinian declares in the Institutes . . . and as the modern systematic writers not only on law but on moral philosophy, have generally taken the Roman jurists for their models, treatises on the so-called Law of Nature have abounded; and references to this Law as a supreme rule and ultimate standard have pervaded literature. The writers on International Law have done more than any others to give currency to this style of ethical speculation; inasmuch as having no positive law to write about, and yet being anxious to invest the most approved opinions respecting international morality with as much as they could of the authority of law, they endeavoured to find such an authority in Nature's imaginary code." John Stuart Mill, *Three Essays on Religion*, in *Ultimate Collection: Works on Philosophy, Politics & Economy (Including Memoirs & Essays)* (Madison & Adams Press, 2017), loc. 36434 of 53395, Kindle. Likewise, with little charm to the eye, Mill writes: "The people of this generation do not commonly

apply principles with any such studious exactness, nor own such binding allegiance to any standard, but live in a kind of confusion of many standards; a condition not propitious to the formation of steady moral convictions, but convenient enough to those whose moral opinions sit lightly on them, since it gives them a much wider range of arguments for defending the doctrine of the moment. But though perhaps no one could now be found who like the institutional writers of former times, adopts the so-called Law of Nature as the foundation of ethics, and endeavours consistently to reason from it, the word and its cognates must still be counted among those which carry great weight in moral argumentation. That any mode of thinking, feeling, or acting, is "according to nature" is usually accepted as a strong argument for its goodness. Ibid., loc. 36437 of 53395, Kindle.

104. Mill, Utilitarianism, 44.

105. Ibid.

106. Ibid.

107. Ibid., 45.

108. Ibid., 45–46.

109. Ibid., 46.

110. Rawls argues that Mill's notion of justice comes very close to his own view of the two principle of justice as fairness. In light of the discussion above, this view may be difficult to justify. Rawls, *Lectures on the History of Political Philosophy*, 267.

111. Mill, *Utilitarianism*, 48.

112. This is not meant to be a complete or partial explanation for the change of our intuitions concerning justice. It is just a bit of speculation.

113. Mill, *Utilitarianism*, 51.

114. Ibid.

115. Ibid.

116. Ibid., 52.

117. See Covell, *The Defence of Natural Law*, 16–19. Also, see Rommen, *The Natural Law*, 101–108. Rommen clarifies that the historical school, also a movement in the Romantic era, was hostile toward natural law as well.

Chapter Five

Austin, Hart, and Dworkin

INTRODUCTION

In this chapter, I intend to examine the views of Austin (again), H. L. A. Hart, and Ronald Dworkin. I argue that each scholar has significant problems justifying their views with regard to the foundations of a legal system. Austin's views are harried by uncertainties because of his command theory of law. Hart's rule of recognition is exceedingly doubtful because, from a foundational point of view, his secondary principle will possess only historical significance. Finally, Dworkin's view is full of misgivings primarily because of his alignment with natural law.

A THOUGHT EXPERIMENT

I would like to begin this section with a thought experiment. Let us assume that there is some society, which, essentially, is a well-organized society. This is, no doubt, a controversial claim to make, because the concept of a "well-organized society" points to aspects about which no agreement is forthcoming among scholars. For example, pros and cons aside, there is no agreement whether a Monarchy, Aristocracy, Oligarchy, or even the various forms of a democracy may serve as the proper foundation of such a society. Nevertheless, what does not seem as controversial is that such a society have a legal system, which consists of a set of fair and stable procedures or processes for interpreting and a method for the coercive enforcement of the law.[1] Minimally, such a legal system will concern itself with adjudicating cases where the rights and obligations of its citizens may conflict or be at risk. Another qualification is needed before I spell out my thought experiment more thoroughly.

To speak of a well-organized society with a just legal system does not imply that the legal system has a legal rule to cover every problem that may arise between the members of this society. This means that while there is a perfectly consistent, possible world in which a legal system is flawlessly complete, the concept of a legal system within a well-organized society does not commit us to any necessary truths about the legal system. Rather, any thought experiment about a just, but incomplete, legal system in these terms makes perfect sense for the purposes of this text. So, with this qualification in mind, I will proceed to raise an issue brought forward by Dworkin.[2]

Let us suppose that within society a legal case arises between two groups of people. Additionally, the court, which agrees to adjudicate the situation, is keenly aware that there is no legal standard or rule which applies to the case at hand. So, as the situation stands, there are no secondary principles or first-order rules that spell out for the court the rights or obligations which may shed light on who may be at fault or otherwise legally responsible.[3] The way to answer this question, then, would be to appeal to some sort of justification for the foundation of the legal system for the hypothetical society.

So, with no case law or legal rule to appeal to or follow, what options does our factious court have available to settle the case? A list of options might include the following items: the Judeo-Christian scriptures, moral theory, moral intuitionism/innate ideas, or positivism. Although this list may not be exhaustive, in the light of the history of ideas rehearsed in this text, of the four options just mentioned, there is only one option our court should use, viz., legal positivism. Why is this?

In the simplest terms, the first three positions fail to act as legitimate foundations for a legal system to handle cases which fall outside case law. This is because, historically speaking, they are no longer scientifically or philosophically respectable. For example, there is no evidence to justify moral intuitionism or innate ideas. As I indicated earlier, Locke raises the issue of innate ideas to a level of doubt that dominated the academic landscape for years. Even the intuitionism (following on the heels of the Romantic period) that later emerges, and is defended by Henry Sidgwick (1838–1900), G. E. Moore (1873–1958), and W. D. Ross (1877–1971), did not survive.[4] Alternatively, consider the Judeo/Christian scriptures. Will appealing to the Christian scriptures work in a pluralistic society? No. What reasons can be given to accept the scriptures as authoritative? There are no reasons other than a leap of faith to accept such a claim. In any case, from the political doctrine of liberalism, we would not expect our legal system to favor any religion in terms of case law. Finally, are we in a better position when it comes to using a moral theory? The answer is no.[5] Of course, we could enlist the utilitarians. For example, we may be inclined to think that consequentialism is the best choice to use as a foundation for our legal system; however, what version of consequentialism should be used? Should we use the mental state hedonism of Bentham and Mill? What about the viability of preference, welfarist, or even perfectionistic consequentialism? These problems and others not mentioned here lead to the conclusion that, of the four mentioned, legal positivism looks like the only best option left. If this is so, what makes positivism the best choice? That is, what can we say, if anything, in favor of positivism?

Perhaps one way to do this is to spell out what legal positivism means. Rommen has an interesting take on positive law.[6] The main point is the renunciation "to know the essence of things (nominalism)" and the "repudiation of the metaphysics of hierarchized being and value." Elsewhere, of positive law, Rommen writes: "Consequently there is no eternal justice, nor is there unalterable moral law. The state is the creator of morality and law, but the state in turn is merely a product of the struggle of social classes and servant of the class that rules at any given time."[7] Such quotes make clear that positivism proceeds under the assumption that philosophical nominalism is true, i.e., there are no mind-independent truth-conditions that make the rules found in a legal system true. For example, the rules that forbid murder, robbery, and so forth, are rules largely arbitrary stipulated by the state. Of course, if we embrace the political subjectivism discussed earlier, i.e., what the state (or legislator) stipulates as true *is* true, our legal rules may be considered true or false relative to what the government stipulates. Nevertheless, in light of what legal positivism means, although I was optimistic earlier, I dare say that legal positivism would not fit too well with our hypothetical society (not to mention our current form of government). Let us delve into this matter a little deeper to make sure we are not mistaken about this point. So, now the issue may be focused in the following manner. First, I will briefly discuss Austin's brand of legal positivism and then Hart's version of legal positivism.

Again, returning to the earlier thought experiment, let us suppose that within society, a legal case arises between two groups of people. Additionally, the court, which agrees to adjudicate the situation, is keenly aware that there is no legal standard or rule that applies to the legal case at hand. So, as the situation stands, there are no rules that spell out for the court the rights or obligations which may shed light on who may be at fault or otherwise injured. How will Austin handle this problem?

JOHN AUSTIN

Again, Austin enunciates legal positivism in a straightforward manner—the sovereign authority makes the laws. The question of the origin of the sovereign authority becomes focused on the sanctions settled by a single authority or aggregate of individuals. The sanctions represent the commands from the sovereign authority, which go no deeper than its desires or preferences.

Thus, in a similar fashion to Hobbes and Locke,[8] , the authority of the law follows from the fact that sanctions are attached to pronouncements of legal laws. Nevertheless, how does such a viewpoint fit our thought experiment? If there is a question about how to answer a legal dispute which does not fit into the current case law of the legal system, then one has only to look at the current sovereign to make a decision. At the same time, as Dworkin makes clear: "Therefore (according to Austin) the sovereign grants those who enforce the law (judges) discretion to make fresh orders when novel or troublesome cases are presented. The judges then make new rules or adapt old rules, and the sovereign either overturns their creations or tacitly confirms them by failing to do so."[9]

Of course, as many scholars argue, for example Dworkin, there are problems with Austin's account. How do we account for laws within a pluralistic society, and how do we distinguish between the (seemingly arbitrary) commands of the sovereign and the commands of a gangster?[10] There is one problem he does not discuss, which is the problem of strange laws.[11] Briefly, this means that without criteria to judge the warrant of a legal law, other than appealing to the desires, preferences, and beliefs of the sovereign and his judges, there is no reason why a law may be created to solve an issue which stands at odds with our legal intuitions, and seriously so. Here is an example of what I mean:

Strange Law Objection (SLO)
1. If there are no objective standards (partial or otherwise) to guarantee that our ideas of "law" are true, then even if our laws may vary significantly from culture to culture, there is no way to determine whose laws are true even if they are strange.
2. There are no objective standards (partial or otherwise) to guarantee that our ideas of laws are true.
3. Therefore, even if our laws may vary significantly from culture to culture, there is no way to determine whose laws are true even if they are strange.

Is this objection sound? Let us begin with premise 1. Is it true? Premise 1 is true because without some sort of objective standard to determine which law is true or false, then we are, in a sense, cut off from formulating a true and deep account of some of the most basic concepts, which guide our understanding of the world. For example, suppose an individual argues in favor of a law-like claim like this: All people should be treated equally and fairly. However, one day he is confronted with a contrary claim: Some people should not be treated equally or fair because of their gender or race. If there is not an objective standard, then there is no way to determine which claim is correct even if our intuitions favor the former over the latter, strange account of law. Thus, premise 1 is true.

What about premise 2? It is true as well. In fact, Austin agrees with this view. Again, as I have rehearsed throughout this text, with the advent and rise of nominalism, the best account we can give for the foundation of law may rest upon some version of legal idealism. So, whether we appeal to subjectivism or intersubjectivism, we are no closer to an *objective* standard (partial or otherwise). There is one qualification. Austin's political subjectivism is a realist account of legal justification. This is so because, on his view, the following claim must be true:

Political Belief Subjectivism
Only the legal ideas dictated by the political authority are true.

So, on this view, a legal statement is true or false relative to the sovereign's pronouncement. On the most charitable interpretation of this view (a view often attributed to Hobbes), Hobbes argues that the political authority will not only determine what is legally right and wrong, but also morally right and wrong. Additionally, though this may not be apparent, the sovereign will also have absolute authority, i.e., there will be no rule of law. Such a view, from our own point of view, is atrociously mistaken and incapable of defense. Even if the political authority is a benevolent dictator, there is no guarantee that he will know what laws are best for our culture. Thus, premise 2 is true, and the objection is sound.

Perhaps H. L. A. Hart's rule of recognition will fare better. In the current hypothetical situation, the lack of a primary rule may be remedied by appealing to Hart's secondary rule or the rule of recognition. I will now turn to Hart's viewpoint.

H. L. A. HART (1907–1992)

The crucial question to focus upon concerns whether Hart's viewpoint is multilayered enough to handle hard cases which, like mercury, are visible but unable to pin down. Perhaps Hart's notion of law possesses such a breadth of outlook. To test Hart's theory I will begin with a viewpoint not typically associated with Hart. That is, his theory of law is a form of foundationalism. Of course, the term "foundationalism," as far as I know, is not used in his text *The Concept of Law*. The language associated with foundationalism is certainly at work. For example, the language of foundationalism, as I mentioned earlier, makes a distinction between basic and non-basic judgments. While he does not say, some sort of relationship also exists between Hart's secondary rules and the primary rules.[12] It seems reasonable to assume that the relationship is one of deduction. Nevertheless, the latter guide specific human behavior at an ordinary level. The former are different from the primary rules: "They specify the ways in which the primary rules may be conclusively ascertained, introduced, eliminated, varied, and the fact of their violation conclusively determined."[13] The secondary rules are the principles which make up the rule of recognition.

The question now to consider is what sort of foundational validity does the rule of recognition possess? I will discuss Hart's views and then raise objections.

Hart's foundationalism exhibits what Michael R. DePaul calls a historical foundational structure.[14] Again, among the two set of beliefs, Hart's secondary rules, or what he calls the rule of recognition, represent such a historical foundation. I will first discuss his historical foundationalism. After that I will address two qualifications.

From a historical point of view, whether we are talking about our imaginary legal system or an actual one, Hart indicates that a more complex society will incorporate a rule of recognition to guide the formation of many of the primary rules. So, at some point in the history of the society, the rule of recognition will be made explicit and acknowledged by the legislature and the judicial branch of the government. Even though that may be true, Hart explains that the rule of recognition is very seldom expressed or even stated in the day-to-day life of a legal system.[15] Nevertheless, legal officials, like the umpires of a hockey, soccer, or a football game, will still make decisions about legal cases against the backdrop of the rules of recognition.[16] Hart explains this tendency by legal professionals (and even the public) as "the internal point of view."[17] What does this mean?

Hart distinguishes two points of view which indicate two different attitudes one may take toward a legal system, i.e., the internal point of view and the external point of view. The former is an attitude by individuals who have some sort of stake in the use and integrity of the law. For example, individuals who share this attitude have internalized the rules of the system. Such an attitude represents the acme of judges. Additionally, we expect such an attitude by ordinary individuals who also identify with the legal system.[18] The other view reflects a different kind of attitude.

The external point of view maintains a spectator outlook of the legal system. Hart describes these individuals who, for whatever reason, do not accept the rule of recognition, and yet understand that others do.[19] Of course, Hart makes clear that individuals with this attitude may live in a culture where the law has no efficacy on the behavior of any individual. In such a situation, Hart explains that the legal system either never established itself or once established, ceased to be the legal system.[20] Historically speaking, both scenarios seem plausible. In this regard, in a well-established society, such an attitude is still possible. Take, for example, Dr. Martin Luther King's refusal to obey rules that he thought were unjust:

> How can you advocate breaking some laws and obeying others? The answer lies in the fact that there are two types of laws: just and unjust. I would be the first to advocate obeying just laws. One has not only a legal but a moral responsibility to obey just laws. Conversely, one has a moral responsibility to disobey unjust laws. I would agree with St. Augustine that "an unjust law is no law at all." Now, what is the difference between the two? How does one determine whether a law is just or unjust? A just law is a man-made code that squares with the moral law or the law of God. An unjust law is a code that is out of harmony with the moral law. To put it in the terms of St. Thomas Aquinas: An unjust law is a human law that is not rooted in eternal law and natural law.[21]

What Dr. King's letter indicates is the possibility of taking Hart's "external viewpoint" about some aspect of the legal system that may have become corrupt. Dr. King's letter reflects such an attitude and one in which he condemns the predominately white churches which refused to give up an internal standpoint of the current legal situation.

The last point to discuss is Hart's view of the justification of the rule of recognition. This may seem like a bit of a stretch, certainly by the scholarship, which critically assesses the rule of recognition. Of course, I am part of the throng of critics. Nevertheless, what I intend to do is capture why the rule of recognition has a historical foundational character, especially when applied to the United States Constitution, but ultimately lacks the epistemic justifications that scholars so desire.

Hart's attempt to justify the rule of recognition is of no little moment. It begins with a distinction between two different terms: "assuming the validity" and "presupposition."[22] What does this mean and how does it apply to his notion of justification? First, the notion of validity, at least from a legal point of view, points to, as Hart may imply, the (possible) epistemic status of the primary rules that follow from the rule of recognition. Thus, the primary rules are said to be *valid* when they follow from the rule of recognition.[23] I certainly agree with this point. Nevertheless, Hart appreciates that the rule of recognition is understood in different terms. That is, it is typically thought to be assumed, postulated or it is considered a hypothesis. In other words, to express the same thing, the rule of recognition is a legal presupposition. To make such a claim does not automatically mean that what is postulated or treated as a presupposition is not justifiable. On the contrary, as most arguments go, the language game requires presuppositions or assumptions to get the argument off the ground.

So, what does Hart want us to understand about the justification of the rule of recognition? It is clear that a historical foundationalism has very limited, if any, epistemic warrant. Nevertheless, here is the problem. If a hard case presents itself, a case outside of the historical aspect of the rule of recognition, there is little hope for the judge to solve the case. Thus, the judge must face the unenviable position of using extra non-legal sources to adjudicate.

Perhaps what I argue does not capture what Hart provides as a limited epistemic status to the rule of recognition. In fact, what he says is subtle and overlooked. If my interpretation is correct, Hart not only develops a historical foundational structure for the rule of recognition, but he also attempts to develop an epistemic foundational structure. This may give us reasons to rethink Hart's rule of recognition. Of course, the historical aspect of the rule of recognition is clear. What about its epistemic relevance? Additionally, what does this mean?

In order to illustrate the epistemic nature of the basic beliefs that form the foundation of the rule of recognition, Hart makes two points. First, the nature of the rule of recognition is represented in a favorable light on the occasion that an individual seriously asserts the validity of a primary rule. Hart implies that the individual assumes that the rule of recognition possesses legitimate authority.[24] Second, Hart makes clear that if there is an individual who seriously asserts the validity of a primary rule against the backdrop of the rule of recognition, then it is only reasonable to assume that the rule of recognition possesses a tribute of reverence by others as the foundation of the legal system.[25] To demonstrate this point, Hart expounds that (using a counterfactual argument), if the rule of recognition were doubted (and in my own terms, if they did not possess some epistemic authority), there would be no recognition that the primary rules would count as law. In other words, on the assumption that there are rules which count as law, and taken to be so by those who are internally related to the rule of recognition, there is a consensus that the rule of recognition possesses (epistemic) authority.

Thus, to deny that (in the spirit of Hart's own view) the rule of recognition has no epistemic authority would miss the best possible testimony to the soundness of the method Hart can muster. The question now is whether his method will give him what he needs and supply us with an air of quiet, unaffected assurance. Unfortunately, there are many doubts. I will first discuss my own objections. After that, I will bring forward objections from Dworkin.

To analyze Hart's position as a form of foundationalism represents (only) my understanding of his view of the rule of recognition. To make such an analysis brings with it the virtues and the drawbacks associated with foundationalism. Thus, my critical comments will be consistent with such an assumption. So, I will bring forward two related objections.

The first objection concerns Hart's historical foundationalism. Here is the issue: Foundationalism is typically an ambiguous endeavor. On the one hand, it seeks to capture the way beliefs are organized (or may be organized). Thus, historical foundationalism brings forward the intuitions that a belief (or a set of consistent beliefs) may play an important role in someone's life because of its chronological significance. It may become cherished or otherwise structurally dominant. On the other hand, the fact that a belief is chronologically significant does not guarantee that it is true. This is so because such beliefs do not bring with them anything that might make them true (even if they are much-loved beliefs) except that they are true for those who take them to be historically accurate. What about whether Hart's rule of recognition (and ultimately, the U.S. Constitution), is epistemically basic? This is the second objection.

No doubt, from an anthropological point of view, the historical beliefs of a culture, e.g., the history of the legal rules of its Supreme Court or the evolution of, say, a society's culture faith viewpoints, may interest historians (legal or otherwise), sociologists, religious apologists, political pundits, and so forth. Regrettably, such histories generate little or no philosophical interest. On the contrary, the question of whether the rules of recognition are *simply* basic to a set of individuals or not, is to cast such a view into the winds. The interest, rather, focuses on whether they are *properly* basic. This is the work of paramount significance.

So, of course, the question of whether the rules are properly basic raises the question of what such beliefs are like. Again, a basic belief is a belief "that . . . is not accepted on the evidential basis of other propositions."[26] Such beliefs may normally arise spontaneously from the perceptions of objects presented, or appeared to, by one or more of my senses. It is not a belief deduced or inferred. It is the causal result of the mental states associated with sense perceptions. Whether such beliefs are properly basic follows from an addition condition. For example, as Alvin Plantinga explicates, the belief is basic for an individual and "he is justified in holding it in the basic way: he is within his epistemic rights, is not irresponsible, is violating no epistemic or other duties in holding that belief in that way."[27] Thus, with this distinction in mind, we can turn to Hart's rule of recognition.

Earlier, two points were made which, from my point of view, may indulge the hope that the rule of recognition has epistemic significance. This means that the rule of recognition is exemplified whenever an individual seriously asserts the validity of a primary rule and such exemplification assumes that it is accepted and used by others as the foundation of the legal system. Otherwise, if the rule of recognition did not possess (epistemic) authority, there would be no primary rules that would count as law. Certainly, there is the hint that individuals who are internally oriented toward the legal system take the rules of recognition to be basic. Nevertheless, are they properly basic? The answer is yes only if the beliefs possess warrant. So, what are the conditions for warrant?

Plantinga makes clear that the warrant is relative to the proper functioning of our cognitive faculties, and so, a small percentage of our beliefs may only be properly basic. He includes perceptual beliefs, memory beliefs, and some *a priori* beliefs.[28] So, the implication of this viewpoint is that epistemic justification in foundationalism may have a limited set of justifying conditions. Now, the question for Hart's rule of recognition is whether it has such warrant. Unfortunately, this is a rather complicated issue.[29] It is complicated because of the different forms the rule of recognition can take. For example, it can be as simple as "Whatever the Queen in Parliament enacts is law" and as complicated as the U.S. Constitution. Thus, to make a judgment about the proper basic justification of the rule of recognition may be impossible to do. So, if we take the rule of recognition to be a set of guidelines designed to (minimally) enact laws for an established legal system, then it seems reasonable to raise serious doubts about whether the gold standard of epistemic warrant can apply to such rules. My suspicion is that, a set of rules (unconnected by a basic norm) like this resist *a priori* warrant. But before we give up, there is one more approach that may work and perhaps we can apply the notion of reflective equilibrium to Hart's rule of recognition.

There is one qualification I need to make before I proceed. The notion of reflective equilibrium (whether wide or narrow) may be applicable here even though it is an approach designed specifically for an ethical context and discussion. In particular, following Norman Daniel's notion of wide reflective equilibrium, such an approach "is an attempt to produce coherence in an ordered triple of sets of beliefs held by a particular person, namely, (a) a set of considered moral judgments, (b) a set of moral principles, and (c) a set of relevant background theories."[30] Unfortunately, there is always the problem of applying a theory meant for one context to another that it may not be intended to fit. So, barring the problem just mentioned, there may be an unexplored analogy for Hart's rule of recognition. I will briefly explore this issue. Ultimately, even if this does not give us the kind of justification we hope for, reflective equilibrium may still be useful for a discussion of the unexplored coherence requirement for rules of recognition.

The analogy begins by assuming that Hart's notion of law can be interpreted as an ordered triple, (a) a set of primary rules, (b) a set of secondary rules (i.e., the rule of recognition), and (c) a set of background theories. From Daniels' point of view, the set of background theories sets the view of narrow reflective equilibrium apart from wide reflective equilibrium. Narrow equilibrium is concerned with the coherence between the principles and judgments of a moral theory.[31] Wide reflective equilibrium adds a set of background theories in order to make sure the moral principles are not accidental generalizations.[32]

So, the background theories are analogous to the auxiliary assumptions used to confirm or disconfirm a scientific hypothesis.[33] In the same way, the backgrounds theories in ethics, whether they address what role a moral theory might play in a society or the nature of persons, perform the same role.[34] Daniels argues that the proper choice of our set of relevant background theories should show that the set of moral principles is more acceptable than alternative principles, or perhaps, better explanations for the truth of the set of relevant moral principles. Thus, on this view, if it is possible to defend such an explanation, we will achieve independent support for the set of moral principles.[35] Such an approach is applicable to Hart's discussion of the rule of recognition.

But what background theories could a legal system employ to guarantee that the rules of recognition are not accidental generalizations?[36] It is unclear if there are any background theories that may produce the kind of coherency in the triple ordered pair of beliefs in Hart's view of law that could give the rule of recognition epistemic warrant. Nevertheless, before we give in to the rising tide of victory, perhaps an example may help illustrate Hart's project. Let us take the U.S. Constitution as an example of a rule of recognition. So, what background theories could we enlist to show that the legal (secondary) principles in the U.S. Constitution are more acceptable than alternative principles? Could a view of human nature work? Maybe, if there is such a thing as human nature, which has more than just flinty support. Nevertheless, could we make minimally some claim to our social nature? Are we strict psychological egoists or predominately psychological egoists (See chapter 3, note 21)? Does not the latter capture our intuitions? What about a theory of personhood?[37] Unlikely, because the scholarship dedicated to personhood is as vast as it is varied and opaque. What about an appeal to a social theory or a theory of the role of morality society or religion?[38] For reasons earlier stated, I am inclined to reject both morality and religion.[39] What about the former? Will a social contract theory work? In light of Hume's and Bentham's critique of the social contract theory, it is unclear whether Hobbes', Pufendorf's or Locke's view will work. What about Rawls' viewpoint? What about Marxism or a Postmodern Social Theory? Of the latter three, only Rawls' Theory will work. What about a political theory that spells out the goal and structure of a political economy? Of the former, two passages appear to be applicable. Of such an economy, Plato writes: "You are forgetting again that it isn't the law's concern to make any one class in the city outstandingly happy but to contrive to spread happiness throughout the city by bringing the citizens into harmony with each other through persuasion or compulsion and by making them share with each other the benefits that each class can confer on the community."[40] Aristotle's political viewpoint deserves attention too: "The conclusion is evident: that governments which have a regard to the common interest are constituted in accordance with strict principles of justice, and are therefore true forms; but those which regard only the interest of the rulers are all defective and perverted forms, for they are despotic, whereas a state is a community of freemen."[41] These quotes are relevant support because both quotes are consistent with the U.S. Constitution.

What of the structure of our government? As Locke maintains, monarchism is beyond redemption. Rather, our Constitution bears the fruits of separation of powers found in Locke's *Two Treatises* and Montesquieu's *The Spirit of Laws.*[42] Until these background issues, and other issues not mentioned, are worked out, there does not appear to be a way to escape the problem of justifying the U.S. Constitution. Thus, this seems to be another dead end to save Hart's rule of recognition from the inevitable conclusion: like Austin's viewpoint, I cannot see a way to save Hart from the appellation of legal positivist, and thus, there is no way to deal with hard cases using background theories.

There is one more problem that must be discussed. Part of the set background theories discussed by Hart and brought to nearly an axiomatic truth is Hart's own view of the limitations of his view with regard to hard cases.[43] Hart saddles his own view with a commitment to what Leiter calls Empirical Rule-Skepticism.[44] This view consists of two theses: 1. The indeterminacy of legal rules, and 2. The decisions of judges are not constrained by legal rules.[45] As Leiter makes clear, according to Hart, the first thesis is true because "In all fields of experience, not only that of rules, there is a limit, inherent in the nature of language, to the guidance which general language can provide."[46] This is due primarily to the "open texture" of language in general. This means that words, when applied consistently to a specific context, may find a clear expression of connotation and denotation. However, in contexts where a conventional understanding of the meaning of words is not expected, especially in the canons of the legal profession, such terms resist a clear signification. In such cases, we can only hope for a partial understanding of the term.[47]

Such an understanding of the indeterminacy of language seems plausible. In fact, it is often common to hear deprecations of the vague or ambiguous character of a specific philosophical text. Philosophers are well aware of this problem and often take advantage of this problem. So, the question is why this protestation is looked upon in the legal profession with a jaundiced eye. According to Leiter, the results of the problem are apparent when judges must interpret the contents of the rules spelled out in statues and precedents.[48] Here is a summary of the problem.

When deciding a case using a statute or precedent, a judge may interpret either one in a strict or loose reading. While this does not automatically seem like a problem, especially if both interpretations are consistent, the problem is that a dash of recklessness arises when contradictory rules may be exegeted from, say, the same statute. No doubt, the situation becomes manifestly suspicious when both rulings are treated as legitimate rulings (on two separate occasions). So, given the ambiguity associated with the meaning of words, and little direction or structure to interpret legal statutes, and so forth, some hard legal cases are indeterminate, and thus, hard cases will be decided using irrelevant, non-legal reasons.

While the problem of ambiguity is a common phenomenon in all forms of communication, especially a prevalent problem among the academic disciplines, the ambiguity of which Hart speaks goes a little deeper. Brink specifically identifies the premise in question: "All general terms are "open textured": they contain a "core" of settled meaning and a "penumbra" or "periphery" where their meaning is not determinate."[49] In other words, the problem of the "open texture" of the general terms guarantee that the meanings are not determinate. Thus, as Brink makes clear, to assess correctly Hart's legal indeterminacy, we must uncover his semantic assumptions.[50]

Given the length and complexity of this issue, I will highlight the essential aspects of Hart's semantic hypotheses brought to light by Brink and his critical assessments. Brink locates Hart's semantic conjectures within the traditional empiricist semantic theory. Such a theory has historical significance and (according to Brink) can be traced as far back to Locke's *An Essay Concerning Human Understanding.*[51] There are two characteristics: "(i) the meaning of a word or phrase is the set of (identifying) properties or descriptions which speakers associate with it, and (ii) the meaning of a word determines its reference."[52] With such a plausible account, what could be the decided opposition to Hart's semantic theory?

When the need arises, under normal conditions of legal interpretation, both characteristics are satisfied according to the conventional meaning of legal terms concomitant within the legal profession. Unfortunately, when faced with hard cases, the theory is faced with a serious, nearly intractable, problem. As Brink makes clear, when the facts associated with a case sit outside of a shared or conventional understanding of the (available) legal terminology, the judge has no other option but to step outside of the conventional meaning of legal terms and, instead, defend a decision based upon her own personal discretion.[53] But, still, why is this a problem?

Here is the issue. To illustrate this problem, Brink promotes a perfectly relevant distinction between a conventional and an individualistic interpretation relative to the traditional empiricist semantic theory. Of these distinctions, Brink writes: "An individualistic theory makes the meaning of a word depend upon the criteria which the speaker associates with the word, while a conventionalistic theory makes the meaning of a word depend upon the criteria with which the word is conventionally associated or with which it is associated by a majority of speakers."[54] Thus, as Brink makes clear, on the assumption that Hart endorses the conventional theory when a set of individuals are faced with a set of legally relevant facts, even though there may be a disagreement about the interpretation of those facts, there still remains a shared understanding of the relevance of the legal terms relative to the facts. However, when faced with a hard case, Hart cannot take advantage of the shared understanding of the conventional meaning of the legal terms relative to the set of facts. This is so precisely because "in hard cases people disagree about whether the legal terms apply; the features of these cases are not conventionally associated with any legal terms. Legal language has no determinate meaning in such cases, and so, according to (ii), the cases are legally indeterminate."[55] Thus, in such cases, the judge is forced to use her own individualistic (non-conventional) interpretation of the case.

Although Brink's article contains many other essential details about Hart's viewpoint, it is necessary to give way to a discussion about Dworkin.

RONALD DWORKIN (1931–2013)

Dworkin's critical remarks of Hart's viewpoint are well rehearsed. The first major point is that, as Dworkin makes clear, "a rule of recognition cannot itself be valid."[56] Roughly, this means that there is no ultimate, mind-independent, truth-making conditions for a rule of recognition.[57] Rather, the truth-conditions for any rule of recognition, if any, go no deeper than what a particular community historically has adopted or follows. No doubt, as Hart himself indicates, there may be evidence provided by the members of the community to bring some sort of epistemic significance to the rule of recognition. For example, in the question of the legality of automatic weapons in our own culture, the primary rules used to allow the purchase of such weapons, including handguns, appeals to the Second Amendment of the Constitution including, concomitant case law and a historical defense of the original interpretation as a justification for the rule.[58] But, if such a defense is to work better than just an interesting, cultural historical description of the origins of our own gun laws, the discussion must turn to why such an account has epistemic significance.[59] In the end, Hart cannot gives us the kind of warrant we may seek to justify the Second Amendment or even the U.S. Constitution (taken as a rule of recognition).

But now the question is this: If Dworkin is correct and Hart's rule of recognition is also a nominalist account of legal positivism, then, like Austin, we may also wonder whether his viewpoint will lead to counterintuitive conclusions. For example, will the problem of strange concepts of justice reemerge? How is it possible to avoid such problematic conclusions?

There may be another position, not mentioned yet, defended by Dworkin, called constructive interpretation. Dworkin's constructive interpretation, no doubt, is highly intuitive and celebrated by scholars as a natural response to the positivism of Hart. For Dworkin, it is the aim of all legal interpretation to constructively interpret the social practice of law, by imposing purpose upon it such as, "to make of it the best possible example of the form or genre to which it is taken to belong."[60] Dworkin immediately qualifies this point in three different ways. Initially, he reasons that because constructive interpretation is part of creative interpretation, which is analogous to art interpretation, not every interpretation will work. On the contrary, like works of art, he appears to insist that we must limit our interpretations to the author's intention[61] if appropriate or at least to an obvious interpretation of the object itself.[62] Dworkin also qualifies this view that, like a work of art, a social practice may possess data that underdetermines the value of the art work or social practice. So, competing interpretations may be equally valid. Later, Dworkin adds another qualification. Constructive interpretation, while similar to creative interpretation, of the artistic kind, is slightly different. It is a counterfactual point which may go unnoticed. Here is what he says:

Apart from the endeavor to understand the artist's conscious mental states, which in most cases is unavailable, we may gather, in a creative sense, what the artist nevertheless may have intended. We may, as Dworkin suggests, engage in an imaginary conversation with the artist, asking from a contrary to fact perspective, what the author thinks about a new (proposed) interpretation. It is an interpretation the artist is unfamiliar with; nevertheless, we can imagine asking the artist his opinion about the new interpretation. If this new interpretation, somehow, satisfies, what the artist may have had in mind, i.e., if it captures the feeling he could have had, and (from our creative endeavor we estimate that) he now accepts this interpretation, then our understanding of the work of art will be a part of our constructive interpretation of the work of art.[63] But how does this viewpoint apply to social practices?

Unlike with works of art, it may be difficult to interpret social practices in the same way. This is so because social practices typically do not have an author or any identifiable event that may be responsible for the origin of a social practice. Nevertheless, it may still be possible to construct an interpretation, which may represent the practice in the best possible light. However, unlike a work of art, where physical features may guide our aesthetic intuitions, a social practice, like any (Lockean) mixed mode, does not have physical features. Rather, it is an abstract concept that resists any sort of physical representation.[64] So, in this case, what is Dworkin's recommendation? He gives us two: conversational interpretation and constructive interpretation. I will begin with the former.

Dworkin expounds that if we assume conversation interpretation as the recommendation, there are only two real possibilities. The interpreter must distinguish two options: he must decide what the other members of the community think the social practice, say, courtesy, means or he must decide for himself what it means.[65] Dworkin rejects the latter approach first. This is because, if we suppose a social scientist undertakes such an endeavor, he has two options. First, he can ask different individuals what the practice demands. Unfortunately, no interpretation (or definition) of the practice would be forthcoming based only the examples of what courtesy requires.[66] The other option requires joining the practice itself. Dworkin concludes that the social scientist must proceed in the same manner as he did in the first option. This means he must move from his own examples of courtesy (examples which others may or may not agree with) to a conceptual understanding of what courtesy means.[67] Like the first option, the second approach will be wrapped in doubt. He also rejects the former approach for roughly the same reason. If we suppose that we could ask the community conceived as some sort of super entity or collective consciousness, we still end up facing the same problem. Conceiving the community as a distinct entity with the same perspectives as an individual will only give what the social practice requires, not what it means.[68] Thus, conversational interpretations will not work. What other options, then, do we have left? Constructive interpretation. Dworkin draws our attention back to constructive interpretation of a different sort.

Constructive interpretation is part of Dworkin's third conception of law called "law as integrity." Prior to that, Dworkin discusses two other conceptions of law, that is to say, conventionalism, and pragmatism and personification, and rejects both views. Thus, according to Dworkin's third conception of law, "propositions of law are true if they figure in or follow from the principles of justice, fairness, and procedural due process that provide the best constructive interpretation of the community's legal practice."[69] Of course, Dworkin makes clear that the first two conceptions of law involve interpretation, but not the kind involved with constructive interpretation. This is so because conventionalism merely requires judges to base their rulings on past legal decisions that are available and conventionally recognized to have legislative power.[70] Once case law has been established, interpretation stops. Pragmatism stipulates that judges must decide what rules will best work for the legal future of the society. Once such a view is stipulated, interpretation stops.[71] Constructive interpretation is different. It combines both backward and forward interpretations of legal claims.[72] Additionally, as Dworkin makes clear, interpretation continues throughout the entire process even if the case law has been thought to be successfully interpreted.[73]

Three Interpretative Stages

To make clear Dworkin's view of law as integrity, it is important to start with his stages of interpretation. There is the "preinterpretive" stage, the "interpretative stage," and the "postinterpretative stage."[74] The first stage identifies the material to be used to interpret some sort of issue. In this context, we might imagine the famous cases of *Riggs v. Palmer* (1889) and *Henningsen v. Bloomfield Motors, Inc.* (1960).[75] The second stage considers some sort of justification which fits, so to speak, the facts or the elements of the case or cases at the preinterpretive stage. The last stage attempts to adjust the justification given at the second stage and may include making clear the apparent disanalogies that may count against the second stage.

Of course, the sum and substance of the whole matter is Dworkin's second stage—the interpretive stage. It is at this stage that the judge works to fit a case into the judicial history of the culture in which the case occurs. Although such an attempt may involve originalism, whether the appeal is to the original intent or original meaning of the authors of their own rule of recognition, Dworkin subtly qualifies this point. On the one hand, he states that law as integrity does not aim to recapture the ideals of the original framers of an amendment. On the other hand, he elucidates that integrity as law aims to justify what they did (including the ideals when necessary) in order to create a story that connects the past and future together.[76] Thus, the decisions about a new case, especially hard cases like *Riggs*, *Henningsen*, and *McLoughlin*, will see the interpretive proposal fit and justify the decision that law as integrity requires. To illustrate this viewpoint, Dworkin introduces his interesting discussion of the chain novel.

The Chain Novel

Dworkin familiarizes his viewpoint with an approach that is analogous to the interpretation often taken to interpret a literary novel. The approach does not aim to discover what the author's purpose is for the novel. Rather, as Dworkin makes clear, the interpreter aims to impose a creative interpretation on the text, which interprets the text in the best possible light. Therefore, likewise, creative interpretation within law aims to treat legal documents in the same way. Creative legal interpretation, then, seeks to impose an interpretation on the text that represents the best possible interpretation of the text.[77]

In particular, then, the analogy Dworkin advocates is something akin to the interesting phenomena of the "Chain Novel." On this view, a group of authors intends to write a novel. On a standard collaborative interpretation, the novel would represent the collective results of the authors in the same way as a scientific or philosophical article might represent the collaborate efforts of an article. A chain novel, however, is slightly different. Surely, the novel is written as a collaborate effort, but each chapter of the novel is written by a different author. In such an endeavor, each author (except the first author) intends to add consistently to the plotline of the preceding authors. Thus, the presupposition (warranted or otherwise) of such a novel is that each author intends to make it the best novel possible.[78] Before Dworkin turns this discussion to the application of a legal context, he considers two qualifications.

Dworkin partially wraps up the nuts and bolts of his view of the chain novel discussion by considering two dimensions which act as qualifications for his view of interpretation. The first qualification he calls the dimension of fit.[79] This issue, as I understand it, concerns the requirement that no interpretation of the novel that can be recruited will be worthy of confidence. It must be the best fit. Nevertheless, although there may be the assumption that there must be a perfect fit, Dworkin clarifies that the contribution of the chapter must not reflect or capture perfectly the main plot, subplots, themes, and readings of character, and so forth, of the previous chapters.

The second dimension concerns the possibility of having at least two interpretations that fit the text. Like the first dimension, such a situation presents a similar problem. How does one judge or make an assessment that one interpretation fits better than another interpretation? Although a precise answer is not forthcoming, the writer (apart from flipping a coin) eventually should be able to develop a *sense* of when an interpretation fits poorly and one that fits, all things being equal, as a hand might fit a glove.[80] Nevertheless, all guarantees aside, Dworkin comments that it may turn out that the interpretation he chose and uses as his model to write his own chapter may fail. Thus, if this is possible, then our author must return to the text to reconsider and decide upon a new interpretation.[81]

The next point to consider before I turn to my critical remarks of Dworkin's viewpoint concerns his application of the chain novel thought experiment to his law as integrity outlook. So, instead of focusing on the further illustration of the chain novels application to Scrooge and *A Christmas Carol* by Charles Dickens, I will move instead to discuss his view of Hercules.

Hercules (and Herbert)

Hercules is discussed at length in Dworkin's *Taking Rights Seriously* and later in *Laws Empire*.[82] There is continuity between the two texts concerning the character of Hercules with one exception—the former text introduces a character unlike Hercules—Herbert. Here is what I mean. As both texts indicate, Hercules is a philosophical judge who has "superhuman skill, learning, patience and acumen."[83] Hercules, with his special powers, is enlisted to handle hard cases, and for the present purposes, Hercules must decide a case where there is no answer from prior case law or the Constitution. Ultimately, he must set aside both sources to decide whether, for example, it is unfair for a state to outlaw abortion in the first trimester.[84] But why Hercules? To make this point clear, Dworkin's Hercules character is part of his ideal judgment theory. This is the view that moral principles are made true or false by whether they would result from the assessment of an ideal judge who is in the ideal conditions to make judgments.[85] So, appealing to an ideal judgment theory requires us to follow the metaethical principle that states that whatever the ideal judge claims is true or false, *is* true or false. In this case, whatever Hercules decides is legally true or false is, in fact, legally true or false.

Herbert is a different kind of judge. It is unclear what characteristic Herbert shares with Hercules. Nevertheless, in *Taking Rights Seriously*, both are enlisted to address the problem of abortion. I will briefly discuss the judgments of Hercules and Herbert in Dworkin's *Taking Rights Seriously*. After that, I will discuss the rulings Hercules must face in *Laws Empire*.

To understand what Hercules may face in his possible world actually took place in our world when the USSC ruled in *Roe v. Wade*.[86] As Dworkin makes clear, because the due process clause and prior case law did not point to an answer to settle the abortion issue, both were set aside. Nevertheless, the court decided that it is unfair for the state to outlaw abortions during the first trimester.[87] With this in mind, how does Herbert address the issue?

Dworkin makes clear that in classical jurisprudence, there are two steps to decide a case where case law is underdetermined or the Constitution is silent: "they find the limit of what the explicit law requires, and they then exercise an independent discretion to legislate on issues which the law does not reach."[88] Dworkin explains that this approach brings with it the objection that a judge, then, must rely upon his own notions of political morality.[89] Herbert accepts this way of adjudication. So, if this is the case, he may argue in one of two ways. On the one hand, he may begin with and accept the conjunctive options: women have a right to end a pregnancy when they desire to do so *and* the majority of people in our culture think otherwise. How shall he proceed? He may decide that a democratic approach will solve the issue. So, regardless of his own viewpoint, he will claim to deny his own view in favor of the majority's moral opinion. Dworkin comments that Herbert's decision is disingenuous because he has to use his moral viewpoint to decide in favor of the majority.[90] Thus, Herbert is still relying upon his own view of political morality. The second approach is also problematic.

Suppose Herbert argues in favor of a woman's right to have an abortion. If he judges against the majority opinion, then he is still mistaken because he did not give enough weight to the principle of democracy. Thus, in either case, Herbert cannot avoid the objection that he is deciding upon his own convictions at the expense of the rule of law and democratic principles.

If Herbert fails to bring about an appropriate interpretation, then how will Hercules fare? According to Dworkin, Hercules will reject the approach of the classical jurisprudence supposes to be true. Instead, by sidestepping in a sense the classical jurisprudence approach, Hercules immediately will use his own judgment, based upon his own political morality, to weigh whose rights have the preponderance of evidence in their favor and make a judgment based upon that evidence, viz., in favor of his own view or the public's morality. In this way, as Dworkin makes clear, Hercules can reach an intuitive decision by not simply duplicating the decisions of other judges, but deal directly with the institutional rights the case deserves.[91] That said, has not

Hercules fallen prey to exactly the same problem he accused Herbert of? Dworkin does not think so. Unfortunately, his response is rather opaque.

In order to clarify what he means, Dworkin makes clear that there are two ways a judge might rely upon his own viewpoint when making a decision. One is offensive and the other is inevitable.[92] The former, Dworkin describes as the fallacy of the appeal to authority. Here is what he means. Suppose an official or (an elected) judge may be required to vote on an anti-abortion statute, which has never been ruled on. Suppose the official rules in favor of it because this is what his constituents believe is true. If he makes such a rule, he is not making a decision based upon whether there is any warrant for the statute, but simply appealing to the authority of his constituents. I may add to that criticism that such an appeal is more accurately an appeal to an *unreliable* authority! Hercules does not make this mistake.

The second view, described as the "inevitable view," is the way in which Hercules must rely upon some of his own moral views. If that is the case, what does Dworkin mean? The example is not very illuminating. Nevertheless, I will try to make it clear. Hercules makes a decision about the abortion case which looks like, for all intents and purposes, a decision that Herbert just made. So what is the difference? Dworkin focuses our attention to the due process clause of the Constitution, which states that Congress shall not deprive any person of "life, liberty, or property, without due process of law." Hercules believes that this clause is inconsistent with any anti-abortion law, because it deprives a woman the liberty to choose her own reproductive future. In fact, he holds this viewpoint even though the majority of his colleagues, the editors of significant law journals, and the majority of individuals of an electorate district have voted in favor of anti-abortion laws.[93] Like Herbert above, Hercules decides that it is his duty to defer to the judgments of the individuals above, even though he thinks they are all mistaken. Again, what is the difference? Here is what Dworkin says: "But in that case he relies upon the soundness of his own convictions that his institutional duty is to defer to the judgment of others in this matter."[94] To do this, Dworkin correctly points out that, unlike Herbert's reliance upon the authority of his constituents, Hercules must rely upon his own judgment to make such a decision.

Perhaps the difference is unclear why Hercules, like any judge with integrity, will *inevitably* have to use his political moral viewpoint. Having said that, there is still a question, at least to me, of how his political moral viewpoint influences him to defer to his colleagues, and so forth. Nevertheless, Dworkin is confident that there is a clear difference between Herbert and Hercules. In fact, Dworkin remarks that Hercules, and his superior intellect, was able to understand that the community morality that he deferred to "is the political morality presupposed by the laws and institutions of the community."[95] I will now turn to Dworkin's account of Hercules in *Law's Empire*. After that, I will begin my critique of Dworkin's viewpoint.

Dworkin spends a significant amount of time discussing Hercules in *Law's Empire*. I will try to limit my comments to Hercules' relationship to political morality. We pick up the discussion, so to speak, with Hercules attempting to adjudicate another hard case—the very famous *McLoughlin* case.[96] The emphasis Dworkin places upon this discussion is not so much on what he decides about the *McLoughlin* case, but *how* he decides the *McLoughlin* case. To decide this case, Hercules must choose between six available interpretations.[97] Ultimately, Dworkin explains that Hercules "must decide which interpretation shows the legal record to be the best it can be from the standpoint of substantive political morality."[98] Hercule's decision is fully consistent with the House of Lords, that the best way to solve the *McLoughlin* case is by granting compensation to the wife but not compensation which would impose draconian financial burdens on those who were careless. Why is such an interpretation the best one? Here is what I take to be Dworkin's answer.

Dworkin agrees with the interpretation above because Hercules' view of political morality keeps distinct the notions of justice and fairness. Dworkin, earlier in his text, argues that fairness and justice are independent of one another. This means that fair institutions may endorse unjust decisions and unfair institutions may produce just decisions.[99] Of course, this is an interesting and controversial position to defend, but how does it help us to understand the problem Hercules faces now? Here is what I take the text to say. Unfortunately, it is a complicated story.

First, Hercules may think that a decision to limit compensation is warranted by justice (even though he does not say why). At the same time, Hercules may recognize that such a view may be promptly and vigorously disposed of by the majority of the public and be "unknown in the political and moral rhetoric of the times."[100] Hercules may instead side with the state on the view that draconian measures are unfair (which makes sense), but that the people's need for justice appears to override such a decision. Thus, as Dworkin makes clear, Hercules, nevertheless, prefers fairness to justice in this case. As a result, Hercules' preferences reflect a deeper account of his own moral convictions, convictions about the role that justice and fairness should play in a decent government.[101]

The reason why Hercules prefers fairness to justice, and how this reflects his moral convictions, including how this relates to the role of political morality, is unclear. I imagine that the answer simply turns on how we should decide whether fairness or justice applies. In this case, to decide between two such important moral outlooks, we need a meta-moral principle of some sort to make such a decision. In this case, Hercules' political morality, viz., in Hart's terminology, a secondary principle may be needed. Again, if such a basic principle is needed to decide between two primary principles, we may need to apply the natural law. The reason is that it was designed to discriminate between what rule or law deserves focus or which law or rule is just or unjust. Unless I am mistaken, it is my view that Dworkin's political morality is a natural law account.

Unfortunately, if Dworkin's viewpoint is a natural law point of view, then it is flawed. At first glance, there does not appear to be a clear identification of the role of natural law in Dworkin's three major works. In fact, Dworkin articulates that a moral reading of the U.S. Constitution, for example, is possible. If that is the case, then what sort of moral reading is he talking about? The answer to this question is difficult to answer. On the one hand, to proclaim that there is a moral reading of the constitution as he does in *Freedom's Law*[102] implies that some sort of moral standard is employed. Why speak of a *moral* reading without some sort of standard in mind? Such a position would not make much sense. If that is the case, Dworkin may have (at least) three standards in mind when he speaks about a moral reading of the U.S. Constitution. For example, in light of the justification of the human positive law, he may have in mind the moral view of natural law discussed in the earlier chapters of this text. On the other hand, maybe Dworkin has in mind a consequentialist interpretation or deontological interpretation. If so, then in both cases, he may have in mind rule, rational accounts[103] or rule, intuitionist accounts.[104] But these different accounts resist accurate textual interpretations and scholarly interpretations of Dworkin's texts. Barring any other moral theories, for example, an *arête* viewpoint, does Dworkin's view appear to be consistent with a natural law account? Thom Brooks argues that Dworkin is best interpreted as committed to the contrary viewpoints of natural law and logical positivism.

Brooks argues that, like Hegel, Dworkin's theory of law has a foot in natural law and logical positivism, but neither scholars sit comfortable in either outlook.[105] If this is true, then Dworkin's viewpoint has serious issues. The reason is that both positions, for the lack of a better term, are contraries. This means that both positions can be false, but both viewpoints cannot be true at the same time. Again, one might push Dworkin into the following dilemma:

1. Either Dworkin's viewpoint is a natural law position or his view is a legal positivist account.
2. If it is a natural law account, then he is committed to a deep account of morality (and to the truth-making conditions that make those moral statements true).
3. If he is a legal positivist, then he is a nominalist.
4. Therefore, Dworkin is committed to a deep account of morality (and to the truth-making conditions that make those moral statements true or he is a nominalist.

Such a dilemma, if sound, would prove to be a devastating objection to his view. Both views, no doubt are mutually exclusive. Still, the question remains whether and how much he is committed to a natural law account. I will try to make a case that he is, in fact, committed to a natural law account. So, to save Dworkin from the dilemma, I argue that premise 1 is false. This is so because (on the assumption that the disjunction in premise 1 is inclusive), while it is true that Dworkin is committed to a natural law account, it is contingent whether Dworkin is a logical positivist.

It is interesting to note that the evidence that Brooks brings forward for Dworkin's view of natural law, looks like, essentially, an offhand and obscure remark by Dworkin in which he grudgingly identifies his view as a natural law account.[106] But this is not the case at all. Although Dworkin seems to distance himself from a natural law point of view, in much the same way that one may distance oneself from a bad marriage, he endorses natural law. Dworkin's article "Natural Law Revisited" is a defense of a natural law account.[107] Even though this may be the case, as Brooks indicated, it is not a typical defense of a natural law that one might expect.[108] Nevertheless, it is a natural law account, and it is pretty obvious, it is the foundation of morality implied in *Taking Rights Seriously* and *Law's Empire*. If I am right, then what makes it a natural law account?

Dworkin recognizes that his view has been criticized because of its alignment with a natural law account. His response to this claim appears to be ignored: "Suppose this *is* a natural law. What in the world is wrong with it?"[109] What proceeds in this article is not a defense of the metaphysical underpinnings of the theory so much as a discussion of its necessity to maintain the close connection between law and morality. Moreover, what is also misleading is that throughout Dworkin's article he uses the term "naturalism" instead of the locution "natural law." At first glance, the former reference does not automatically resemble what we might expect from Dworkin's article. The reasons is that the term "naturalism" has its roots in different legal and philosophical contexts which do not resemble a natural law discussion at all.[110] That said, what appears to be overlooked is Dworkin's defense of natural law in two paragraphs on pages 165 and 166.

Dworkin begins his argument by making clear that the crude character of his viewpoint is more appropriately called "naturalism." That said, Dworkin does not give any reason why the ambiguous term "naturalism" is better than "natural law." With this brief qualification, I will try to spell out Dworkin's role of natural law in his viewpoint. Unfortunately, this is not easy to do because his argument does not fall clearly into any (truth-functional) recognizable pattern of valid reasoning. Nevertheless, I will try to spell out his argument as clearly as possible.

Dworkin writes: "According to naturalism, judges should decide hard cases by interpreting the political structure of their community in the following, perhaps special way: by trying to find the best *justification* they can find, in principles of political morality, for the structure as a whole, from the most profound constitutional rules and arrangements to the details of, for example, the private law of tort or contract."[111] So, with a focus on hard cases, perhaps cases with little or no prior case law available or nothing within the Constitution to help illuminate the case, our judge may be forced to interpret the political structure of the community by finding a principle in political morality that will act as the best justification for the case at hand.

But such an abstract approach does not quell our reservations for what this might entail. Fortunately, Dworkin does not leave us hanging. On the contrary, he directs our attention to the parts of the *McLoughlin* case and pushes us to consider how a judge should decide, if at all, for emotional and psychological damages on behalf of the plaintiff.[112] That is, the process begins with the judge looking for an interpretation to apply to the *McLoughlin* case with the hope that the interpretation, i.e., the moral principle, which reflects the content of the natural law, will justify the adjudication of the judge. Of course, what may not be noticed, is the following qualification. The interpretation must be consistent with the *entire* body of law.

The qualification raises Dworkin's need to seize with avidity the opportunity to introduce Hercules. As I discussed earlier, Dworkin's Hercules character is part of his ideal judgment theory. But how does such an ideal judge in this situation work?

Initially, Dworkin stipulates that the principle needed to deal with the hard case will have to be the best translation that will fit with the different principles and rules within the entire body of law. That said, as Dworkin makes clear, only the superior intellect of Hercules can determine how a principle of political morality will fit so closely within the political structure *as a whole*. He illustrates this ideal position by contrasting it with real judges.[113] Real judges, Dworkin explains, are not capable of making such an intellectual effort. Rather, because the whole truth is not known to a real judge, he will not be able to provide a complete justification for the principle. Nevertheless, following Hercules' ideal approach, tapping into, so to speak, the doctrine of natural law, real judges will also have to adjudicate at times by making use of the natural law to solve hard cases. As a result, Dworkin comments: "It is obvious why this theory of adjudication invites the charge of *natural law*. It makes each judge's decision about the burden of past law depend on his judgment about the best political justification of that law, and this is of course a matter of political morality."[114]

From my point of view, then, it makes sense that Dworkin's viewpoint in this article, and its commitment to natural law, would find its home in *Taking Rights Seriously*, *Law's Empire*, and his more popular text *Law's Freedom*. Without a commitment to natural law, how else will he be able to stand against the logical positivism of Hart? This question is certainly rhetorical.

Nevertheless, what should we make of contemporary view that relies upon a natural law account to adjudicate hard cases? I will now turn to that issue.

From a historical point of view, there are, at least, six different versions of natural law identifiable in the history of philosophy, viz., versions by the Stoics, Aquinas, Grotius, Hobbes, Pufendorf, and Locke. Not only that, but each one varies in terms of the truth-making characteristics for the law of nature. So, to reclaim a natural law view as part of the justification of legal claims, ignores the problems associated with the metaphysics to establish a natural law viewpoint.[115] In fact, I argue that such a return will ultimately fail, and in the end, the only way to establish the justification for some (basic) legal principles is to develop Analytical Legal Naturalism, which I discuss in the next chapter.

So, briefly, why will an appeal to natural law ultimately fail? The reason is that, from a historical point of view, no account of the law of nature has been successfully defended. Of course, this text discusses six different accounts of natural law, none of which survived the acid test of philosophical scrutiny. Barring the fact that there may be other versions of natural law which may escape notice, the six in question point to the Stoics, Aquinas, Grotius, Hobbes, Pufendorf, and Locke. The first three qualify as deep accounts, and the last three do not. I will now turn to discuss the significance of these six accounts.

The first three versions of natural law (attributed to the Stoics, Aquinas and Grotius), represent deep accounts of natural law because the truth-conditions of natural law claims are objectivistic. That is, their truth-values do not refer or *need not* refer to anyone's subjective states or to the capacities, conventions, or practices of any group of people. As I pointed out in chapter 2, the two possible exceptions point to the viewpoint of the Stoics and Aquinas. The Stoics rely in some sense on the handiwork of Zeus. On one interpretation, Zeus creates and structures the world in specific way, including the natural law, which is implanted in the minds of humanity. For Aquinas, the natural law is part of the eternal law, which is coextensive with the mind of God. Like the Stoics, the law of nature is also implanted by God into the minds of humanity. Nevertheless, does such a view have any current significance? There are reasons to doubt that it does so, and I articulate the same in chapter 2. Of the first three, only Grotius articulates a pure objectivistic account of the natural law. Again, the natural law would exist even if God did not exist.

Apart from some of the puzzles associated with the Stoics and Aquinas, the first three accounts of the natural law remain rejected because, as the new changing ideal of science took root within the scientific community, the metaphysical machinery needed to support the views of the Stoics, Aquinas and Grotius are no longer available or even feasible.[116]

The last three accounts, viz., Hobbes, Pufendorf, and Locke, do not represent deep accounts of the law of nature. To make such a claim seems counterintuitive. Do not all three scholars talk about the law of nature? The answer is yes. Still, the last three positions do not represent a deep account of the law of nature. This is so because all three positions, unlike the metaphysical realism of the Stoics, Aquinas, and Grotius, assume the truth of nominalism. Again, as I explained earlier, such a view denies the metaphysical machinery needed to offer a deep account of the law of nature. Nevertheless, Hobbes, Pufendorf, and Locke offer accounts of the law of nature which, in certain respects, resemble the first three. That notwithstanding, when their positions are examined more closely, the resemblance may only be superficial. Here's why.

Hobbes, Pufendorf, and Locke clearly understood the tenuous foundation of the law of nature without the appeal to metaphysical realism. Logically speaking, then, we might expect all three authors to reject the doctrine of the law of nature. However, instead of rejecting the law of nature, each writer turned to what we might call a naturalized version of the law of nature. This means that each respective author turned to facts that they took to be morally relevant. And, in all three cases, the morally relevant facts are facts about human nature.[117] For example, Hobbes defended and emphasized the antisocial nature of humans, Pufendorf defended the social aspect of human nature, and Locke defended the view that all humans are born free and equal. No doubt, all three accounts, at first glance, seem reasonable. Unfortunately, while their accounts of human nature may act as a partial justification for positive law, they fail to work as natural law accounts because the teleology necessary for a natural law account is circumvented by nominalism. Thus, any appeal to an account of human nature will ultimately fail to serve as the foundation for the law of nature.

CONCLUSION

This chapter was dedicated to the views of three major legal scholars: Austin, Hart, and Dworkin. There are other legal scholars I did not discuss, scholars who also deserve the highest tribute for their contributions to legal philosophy. Of course, Lon L. Fuller and John Finnis are both famous examples (I will make clear why I chose not to discuss these authors momentarily). The reason I chose to only discuss Austin, Hart, and Dworkin points to what I am attempting to accomplish. Surely, all three deserve attention because of their impact within the legal and philosophical communities. That is plainly certain. I chose these three because they represent positions that serve as the foundation of my own viewpoint in two ways. Here is what I mean.

On the one hand, it is clear that all three suffer from different problems. Austin's view (political and ethical subjectivism) resembles and falls prey to the objections generated against Thomas Hobbes. Hart's rule of recognition suffers from epistemic concerns, which cast a shadow over its justification. Like Austin, Hart's view gets thrown into the poison well of legal positivism. Dworkin's view, although extremely complicated, ends up characterized as a natural law viewpoint. Such a view, as I make clear, cannot survive the kind of metaphysical scrutiny to satisfy the truth-making conditions for natural law claims. I contend that any view like it will also lack the same epistemic foundations to make natural law work. This applies to Fuller's account as well as Finnis' account.[118] So, part of my strategy to discuss Dworkin's thin account of natural law was partly motivated to show that not only is it a natural law viewpoint, but also try to explain what it would take to develop the truth-making conditions for such a position. Thus, if Dworkin's view cannot satisfy those conditions (in fact, as far as I know, Dworkin never discusses the epistemic foundation for such a view), then Fuller's view and Finnis' view (which seem to articulate such epistemic concerns) will also fall as well.

While the focus of this text, so far, supports a negative thesis, there are two positive reasons why I chose just to focus on Austin, Hart, and Dworkin. First, all three positions can be used to develop a superior alternative to legal positivists (Austin and Hart) and the natural law accounts (Dworkin and others). For example, from Austin we understand the nature of law and the connection of coercion. This shows that we can clearly demarcate the boundaries between law and morality. From Hart, we understand the nature and complexity of constitutional-based law. His rule of recognition serves to show how we may clarify the complexity of the legal profession by talking about secondary principles and primary rules. I speculated that a combination between Hart's rule of recognition with wide reflective equilibrium may reveal a fruitful endeavor to give constitutions epistemic warrant. Dworkin's view of constructive interpretation is worthwhile and a mine of wealth in itself. Thus, a case can be made that all three views have a unique and abiding value.

The other positive aspect, at least for my project, demonstrates what kind of position that needs to be developed to address hard cases. So, the position I develop in the final chapter is constructed to benefit from and to avoid the pitfall from the three authors examined in this chapter.

NOTES

1. One question here is raised by Robert C. Hughes. Whereas my thought experiment begins with a conception of a well-ordered society which hinges on an appropriate legal system in place with justifiable enforcement procedures, Hughes argues that it is possible to conceive

of an entirely non-coercive legal system. His claim in particular is that the entitlement to make law does not require an associated entitlement to coerce. The two are not unrelated. Hughes argues that "Showing that there can be law without coercion is a necessary first step to showing that there can be an entitlement to make law without an associated entitlement to coerce." Robert C. Hughes, "Law and the Entitlement to Coerce," *Philosophical Foundations of The Nature of Law*, ed. Wil Waluchow and Stefan Sciaraffa (Oxford University Press, 2013): 185. Ultimately, Hughes intends to show that "in a society of morally very good people, there could be a system of legislative and judicial bodies that satisfies these conditions and that does not use or threaten coercion." Ibid., 186. With this in mind, here is what I take to be Hughes' argument. First, minimally, Hughes is treating the following claim as a necessary truth: Necessarily, if x is a law of a government G and x is part of a legislative body that makes rules of G, then x is enforced by the judicial body of G. The intuition behind this claim is that only laws enforced by the judicial body of G, are considered to be legitimate laws. Hughes proposes to show that the claim is not a necessary truth by giving the following counterexample: Possibly, x is a law of a government G and x is part of a legislative body that make rules of G, but it is false that x is enforced by the judicial body of G. The counterexample allegedly attempts to show that it is possible to conceive of a law of some government G without enforcement and it is still a legitimate law.

To demonstrate the plausibility of the counterexample, Hughes lists three jointly sufficient conditions for the existence of a legal system of an effective government (with a legislative and judicial branches) which does not, and need not, make mention of any powers of the judicial branch dedicated to the enforcement of the laws the legislative branch generates. Ibid., 187. Briefly, there is a system of legislative and judicial bodies which makes laws, the laws are morally binding, and the bindingness of morality is in virtue of the pronouncements of the legislative body. Thus, Hughes concludes that "An entirely non-coercive legal system is thus a conceptual possibility." Ibid., 188.

There are two objections about Hughes' counterexample. First, two reasons emerge whether this counterexample will work. The first reason is that counterexamples work best when the possible world they generate to challenge a necessary truth are convincing. This is especially important when the claim in question has deep intuitions attached to it. For example, the intuition behind the claim that the legitimacy of law is determine partly by whether it is enforced or not is a deep and guiding intuition with historical significance. Hughes proposes to convince us that it is merely conceivable to list three sufficient conditions for the existence of legal system without the judicial body of that system committed to the enforcement of at least one law. Although an interesting attempt, it remains unconvincing. The second reason to doubt Hughes' counterexample is the problem associated with precising definitions. Hughes presumably has his focus on certain borderline cases (which I will mention momentarily). Precising offers us the method to make the meaning of important terms more precise to deal with hard cases. Thus, the looming problem is whether Hughes' unique view of law remains consistent with the word's common and ordinary usage. I am sympathetic with his attempt, but I have doubts. Both problems cast a shadow of doubt over his counterexample.

The second problem follows on the heels of the first objection. Hughes' intuitions dictate that as long as coercion is connected to the notion of law, we are blind in some respects to an important issue. What is that issue, then? Hughes makes clear that if he can establish that the legitimacy of law is conceptually disconnected from its enforcement, he can then demonstrate that the entitlement to make law does not imply the entitlement to coerce. I gather from his article that his arguments raise to the forefront the (borderline) real-world cases that there may be laws where coercive enforcement is not *practically* necessary. Ibid., 191. Thus, this pushes the legal and philosophical communities to generate arguments which defend the view that if anything qualifies as a law, it must also be enforced.

Unfortunately, Hughes' argument is unsound because his conclusion, namely, the entitlement to make laws does not imply the entitlement to coercion, does not follow from his premises (his second premise is false: the legitimacy of law is conceptually disconnected from its enforcement). Just the same, there may be other reasons to think the conclusion is worthy of belief. Let's take a real-world example. The members of the USSC are entitled to make laws, but they are not entitled to enforce the laws they make. The enforcement of the laws falls within the purview of the federal government. If this is the case, then this shows that within our own legal system the intuition to keep both aspects separate is already in place. Additionally, with this in mind, such a view is entirely consistent with the view that only legitimate laws are enforceable laws. In fact, keeping the entitlement to make laws separate from the entitlement to enforce them maybe to the advantage of a legal system because of the fact that the USSC and Congress may, from time to time, create laws which should not be enforced. See, for example, *Korematsu v. United States*, 323 U.S. 214 (1944).

2. Ronald Dworkin, *Taking Rights Seriously*, 22–28. For the lack of a better term, Dworkin raises the issue of what other scholars' call "hard cases." Although this term is ambiguous, it typically points to cases where no case law or legal rules, relative to the set of an established legal system and its constitution, can be adjudicated.

3. Three such cases are discussed in Dworkin's *Taking Rights Seriously*, 22–28; 123–130.

4. One contemporary exception is the development of intuitionism by Robert Audi. See Robert Audi, *Moral Knowledge and Ethical Character* (Oxford University Press, 1997).

5. The USSC concurs with this point as well by making clear that moral judgments are not for the Government to make pronouncements about. For example, see *Brown v. Entertainment Merchants Association* 564 U.S. 786 (2011) and *United States v. Playboy entertainment Group, Inc.* 529 U.S. 803 (2000). See also the Dissent opinions of Justices Black and Stewart, in *Griswold v. Connecticut* 381 U.S. 479 (1965).

6. Rommen, *The Natural Law: A Study in Legal and Social History and Philosophy*, 36. A more contemporary account of positivism is developed by Brian Leiter. He describes positivism as the combination of two theses, the Social Thesis and Separability Thesis. The former indicates that a law with in society reflects a social fact about that society. The latter reflects the is-ought distinction made so famous by Hume. This means that there is a clear distinction between what law is and what it ought to be. See Brian Leiter, *Naturalizing Jurisprudence: Essays on American Legal Realism and Naturalism in Legal Philosophy* (Oxford University Press, 2007), 66–68. See also Jules Coleman and Brian Leiter, "Legal Positivism," in *A Compainion to Philosophy of Law and Legal Theory*, 2nd ed., ed. Dennis Patterson (Chichester, West Sussex: Wiley-Blackwell, 2010): 228. At least for the purposes of this text, Rommen's view is appealing because he clearly understands the metaphysical outlook for legal positivism to emerge.

7. Rommen, *The Natural Law: A Study in Legal and Social History and Philosophy*, 112.

8. Zinaich, *John Locke's Moral Revolution* 118–21.

9. Dworkin, *Taking Rights Seriously*, 18. Fuller also maps out this issue with rigid precision. He simply points out that the legal positivists are quite apprehensive about hard cases and legal gaps. Such gaps represent opportunities for morality and natural law to enter into the discussion. So, Fuller makes clear that positivists simply deny the possibility of such gaps. The assumption is that what the sovereign has not explicitly forbidden, he implicitly permits. Fuller, *The Law in Quest of Itself*, 38–39.

10. Ibid., 18–19.

11. Ultimately, this is problem for any positivist's account of legal justification.

12. Hart, *The Concept of Law*, 94.

13. Ibid., 94.

14. Michael R. DePaul, "Reflective Equilibrium and Foundationalism," *American Philosophical Quarterly* 23, no. 1 (January, 1986): 61. Leiter argues that Hart's Rule of Recognition satisfies the first thesis of positivism, i.e., the Social Thesis of legal positivism. It also satisfies the Separability Thesis because it states that whatever satisfies the Rule of Recognition will be a law. Leiter, *Naturalizing Jurisprudence*, 67–68.

15. Hart, *The Concept of Law*, 101.

16. Ibid., 101–02.

17. Ibid., 102.

18. Ibid., 102–03.

19. Hart, 103.

20. Ibid.

21. Martin Luther King, Jr. (1963). "Letter from Birmingham Jail" (PDF). Stanford, California: The Martin Luther King, Jr., Research and Education Institute .

22. Hart, *The Concept of Law*, 109.
23. Ibid., 108.
24. Ibid.
25. Ibid.
26. Alvin Plantinga, *Warranted Christian Belief* (Oxford University Press, 2000), 175. Other than the late Gordon H. Clark (1902–1985) or the late Cornelius van Til (1895–1987), Plantinga is perhaps this century's greatest Christian apologist rivaled only by Richard Swinburne.
27. Ibid., 177–78.
28. Ibid., 178.
29. Hart, *The Concept of Law*, 94.
30. Norman Daniels, "Wide Reflective Equilibrium and Theory Acceptance in Ethics," *The Journal of Philosophy* 76, no. 5 (May 1979): 256–282; 258.
31. Ibid., 258.
32. Ibid., 259.
33. Herrick, *The Many Worlds of Logic*, 552.
34. DePaul, "Reflective Equilibrium and Foundationalism," 59.
35. Daniels, "Wide Reflective Equilibrium and Theory Acceptance in Ethics," 259.
36. There is an important note to make here about the background theories. On my understanding of what this means, background theories are not equivalent to a basic belief. Rather, they are theories incorporated to prop up, so to speak, some aspect of the moral principles or the rules within the rule of recognition. Of course, we expect such theories to be grounded in reality. Nevertheless, they act as horizontal support but not vertical support.
37. Daniels, "Wide Reflective Equilibrium and Theory Acceptance in Ethics," 260.
38. Ibid.
39. Dworkin expresses doubts about religion too. See Dworkin, *Justice for Hedgehogs*, 339–344.
40. Plato, *Plato Complete Works*, 520.
41. Aristotle, *The Complete Works of Aristotle*, 1279a15–20.
42. Montesquieu, *The Spirit of the Laws*, eds. Anne M. Cohler, Basia C. Miller, and Harold S. Stone (Cambridge University Press, 2014).
43. Hart, *The Concept of Law*, 126–136. cf. Brian Leiter, *Naturalized Jurisprudence*, 73–80 and David O. Brink, "Legal Theory, Legal Interpretation, and Judicial Review," *Philosophy & Public Affairs* 17, no. 2 (Spring, 1988): 105–148.
44. Leiter, *Naturalized Jurisprudence*, 73.
45. Ibid.
46. Hart, *The Concept of Law*, 126.
47. Ibid., 126–27.
48. Leiter, *Naturalized Jurisprudence*, 75.
49. Brink, "Legal Theory, Legal Interpretation, and Judicial Review," 106.
50. Ibid., 111.
51. Ibid., 113. Locke's theory of language is in Book III of *An Essay Concerning Human Understanding*.
52. Ibid.
53. Ibid., 113–14.
54. Ibid., 113.
55. Ibid., 114.
56. Dworkin, *Taking Rights Seriously*, 18–19.
57. There appears to be a controversy surrounding the meaning of the term "validity" as it is applied to Hart's Rule of Recognition. Part of this debate concerns Matthew H. Kramer's critical assessment of Scott Shapiro's interpretation of Hart's view of legal validity. Shapiro interprets Hart's notion of validity in reference to the role that it plays in Hart's Rule of Recognition as conferring a duty-imposing norm on the primary rules that follow from the secondary rules. Kramer disagrees and makes the case that such an understanding of Hart's notion of validity is off point. Rather, what Hart means is that "Hart took the Rule of Recognition to be the array of ultimate standards by reference to which the officials of a legal system

identify the norms that belong to the system as laws. Matthew H. Kramer, "In Defense of Hart," *Philosophical Foundations of The Nature of Law*, ed. Wil Waluchow and Stefan Sciaraffa (Oxford University Press, 2013): 24. My interpretation appears to be consistent with Kramer's view because the identification, Kramer speaks about, includes the identification of the partial epistemic warrant of the primary rules.

58. This method of constitutional interpretation is called the method of originalism. When such a method is used, an appeal may be sought from the original intent or original meaning from the original writers of the Constitution. The former looks for evidence about what the framers wanted to do. The latter considers what the framers meant to those who enacted it. See, Lee Epstein and Thomas G. Walker, eds., *Rights, Liberties, and Justice*, 9th ed. (Thousand Oaks, CA: CQ Press), 23.

59. From Hart's point of view, given the concurrence of the legality of guns by individuals who own weapons (including the tacit acceptance of the 2nd Amendment by these same individuals), and even the United States Supreme Court's ruling in favor of the right to keep and bear arms, e.g., see *District of Columbia v. Heller* 554 U.S. 570 (2008), there remains a historical aspect, but not so much an epistemic aspect to the U.S. Constitution. The method of originalism is very apparent in this ruling and it becomes the basis for reinterpreting the 2nd Amendment, viz., the prefatory clause of the 2nd Amendment, i.e., "A well-regulated Militia, being necessary to the security of a free State," is no longer applicable. Nevertheless, Justice Scalia argued that the operative clause is perfectly consistent to protect the right of gun owners today, even though the right is not unqualified. See Epstein and Walker, *Rights, Liberties, and Justice*, 385–86. Unless stated otherwise, references to Epstein and Walker's text will be to pages of the partially reproduced decisions of the USSC.

60. Ronald Dworkin, *Law's Empire* (The Belknap Press of Harvard University Press, 1986), 52.

61. See Dworkin's discussion of the role the artist's intentions may play, 55–65.

62. Ibid., 52

63. From an aesthetics point of view, this view is commonly called "Hypothetical Intentionalism." There are two versions. First, as Robert Stecker makes clear, a hypothetical intention is an ideal audience's best hypothesis regarding the actual artist's intentions. On this view then, like the ideal judgment theory in moral theory, statements about artist's intentions are made true or false by whether they would issue from an ideal audience under ideal conditions of judgment. On this assumption, the ideal audience is one that is historically situated so that it knows the corpus of the artist's work as well as other publicly available features of the context of creation. The second version is different in two ways: First, although it appeals to a hypothetical intention, the hypothetical intention proceeds from and is fixed by a hypothetical artist, who is fully aware of context and conventions and uses them flawlessly to say or do what she intends. See Stecker's discussion in Robert Stecker, *Aesthetics and the Philosophy of Art: An Introduction*, 2nd ed. (Lanham, MD: Rowman & Littlefield, 2010), 158–161. At first glance, Dworkin's analogy to art casts a creative and intuitive approach to the kind of interpretation that must take place when hard cases need interpretation. Unfortunately, Arie Rosen tactfully points out such a view is not shared by herself or other scholars. Although Rosen states that the analogy is open to easy attacks, and perhaps she is correct, there are no examples in her excellent article. Arie Rosen, "The Normative Fallacy Regarding Law's Authority," *Philosophical Foundations of The Nature of Law*, ed. Wil Waluchow and Stefan Sciaraffa (Oxford University Press, 2013): 96. With this in mind and in the spirit of Rosen's intuitions, Dworkin's hypothetical intentionalism raises doubts. For example, what sort of epistemic respectability can warrant the conclusions of a hypothetical artist? It seems unlikely that there would be a way to meaningfully distinguish the conclusions of the hypothetical artist from our own culturally determined artistic biases.

64. Dworkin's understanding of his own creative interpretation and the scientific method may be worth mentioning. He makes two points. First, Dworkin makes clear that both viewpoints share similarities. Among the obvious similarities are the commitments to simplicity, verifiability, and so forth, which lead to the best explanation of the data. Second, while there may be a speaking likeness between the two, Dworkin recognizes the important difference. In the simplest of terms, the difference resides in the fact that we use different standards to judge

works of art from those we use to judge physical data. Dworkin, *Law's Empire*, 53. Dworkin's clear conviction of the difference between both projects raises a question about Arie Rosen's comment that Dworkin is "moving away from the foundation his conceptual methodology has in . . . science." Rosen, "The Normative Fallacy Regarding Law's Authority," 96.

65. Dworkin, *Law's Empire*, 64.

66. See, for example, Dworkin's discussion of courtesy in *Law's Empire*, 68–70.

67. Ibid.

68. Ibid., 64–65. There is additional opposition the social scientist will face. For example, the social scientist must also face the fact that (acts of) courtesy will evolve. For example, what may historically constitute an act of courtesy, say, opening the door for a woman, may not be a socially accepted requirement later on.

69. Ibid., 225–27. Imer B. Flores raises an important issue directed at Dworkin's notion of "law as integrity." Flores, "The Nature of Law vis-à-vis Legal Rationality Revisited," 111–15. Flores directs our attention back to O. W. Holmes. On the one hand, Flores makes clear that Dworkin shares the same sort of rigor Holmes advocates concerning the study of jurisprudence. Holmes writes: "We have too little theory in the law rather than too much, especially on this final branch of study." Oliver Wendell Holmes, "The Path of the Law," *Harvard Law Review* 110, no. 5 (March 1997/1897): 1007. On the other hand, Flores attributes to Holmes that jurisprudence and legal reasoning must take advantage of the disciplines of "language and logic, history and tradition, sociology and philosophy, economics and statistics, ethics and morals. . . ." Flores, ""The Nature of Law vis-à-vis Legal Rationality Revisited," 112. We should also add history to this list as well as Dworkin cautiously recommends. Dworkin, *Law's Empire*, 227. Nevertheless, while it sounds like legal reasoning is under the domination of great ideals, a more realistic approach, tempered by careful considerations, may reduce this goal to a romantic ideal, which ignores the limits of one's own knowledge.

70. Ibid., 226.

71. Ibid. Steven D. Smith brings forward serious complaints against Dworkin's characterization of legal pragmatism. Against legal pragmatism, Dworkin argues (in the briefest terms) while such judges adjudicate cases for the community's future, they (largely) treat past decision as merely possessing instrumental value but not intrinsic value. Dworkin, *Law's Empire*, 95. See Steven D. Smith, "The Pursuit of Pragmatism," *Yale Law Journal* 100 (1990): 412–420. Smith argues persuasively that Dworkin's emphasis on the intrinsic value of past decisions resembles a straw man attack, a kind of misrepresentation of legal pragmatism that deflects our attention to the real issue. So, as Smith makes clear, the legal pragmatist cannot help but maintain a continuity with the past and to use those past decisions when it is necessary. Under conditions, which do not favor maintaining continuity with the past, like nonpragmatists, such appeals are demurred. Smith, "The Pursuit of Pragmatism," 413. I am indebted to Professor Frank Colucci for bringing my attention to Smith's excellent article.

72. Dworkin's point appears to be reminiscent of Munroe Smith's claim that case law decision should never be treated as final truths; rather, the rules of case law should be treated analogously to working hypotheses in an experiment. Thus, depending upon the explanatory power of the rules, reformulation, retesting, and re-examination should be the ultimate recourse for the interpretation of case law. Munroe Smith, *Jurisprudence* (New York: Columbia University Press, 1909), 21. Smith's text was brought to my attention by Imer B. Flores' article "The Nature of Law vis-à-vis Legal Ratinality Revisited," *Philosophical Foundations of The Nature of Law*, ed. Wil Waluchow and Stefan Sciaraffa (Oxford University Press, 2013): 113.

73. Dworkin, *Law's Empire*, 226.

74. Ibid., 66–67.

75. Dworkin, *Taking Rights Seriously*, 23–24.

76. Dworkin, *Law's Empire*, 227–28.

77. Ibid., 228–32.

78. Ibid., 229.

79. Ibid., 230.

80. Ibid., 231.

81. Ibid., 232. As part of his critique of Dworkin's analysis of pragmatism, Steven D. Smith offers an insightful appraisal of Dworkin's "chain novel" analogy. Attacking Dworkin's view

that pragmatism does not "count continuity with the past as 'valuable for its own sake'," Smith argues that the analogy fails for two reasons. First, Dworkin merely assumes that the unity of the chapters of the "chain novel" is analogous to the kind of unity desirable in law. Second, Dworkin fails to understand that his analogy does not establish that the (later) authors of the "chain novel" will treat earlier information in the (earlier) chapters for its own sake. See Steven D. Smith, "The Pursuit of Pragmatism," 417–420.

82. Dworkin, *Taking Rights Seriously*, 105–30. Dworkin, *Laws Empire,* 239–275. Dworkin discusses Hercules in his article, "Natural Law Revisited," *University of Florida Law Review* 34, no. 2 (Winter, 1982). I will discuss this article very shortly.

83. Ibid., Dworkin, *Taking Rights Seriously*, 105.

84. Ibid., 125.

85. Stephen Darwall, *Philosophical Ethics* (Boulder, CO: Westview Press, 1998), 236.

86. *Roe v . Wade* , 410 U.S. 113 (1973); *Doe v. Bolton* , 410 U.S. 179 (1973).

87. Dworkin, *Taking Rights Seriously*, 125.

88. Ibid.

89. Ibid., 123.

90. Ibid.

91. Ibid.

92. Ibid.

93. Ibid., 124.

94. Ibid.

95. Ibid. 126.

96. Here is a brief description of the *McLoughlin* case: "The husband and children of the claimant were involved in a road traffic accident at around 4 p.m. with a lorry driven by the first defendant and owned by the second defendant. McLoughlin, who was home at the time, was informed of the accident at around 6 p.m. by a neighbour, who drove her to hospital to see her family. Upon arrival, she learned that her youngest daughter had been killed and witnessed the nature and extent of the injuries suffered by her husband and other children. McLoughlin alleged that the impact of what she heard and saw caused her severe shock resulting in psychiatric illness and brought an action in negligence against the defendants." https://www.lawteacher.net/cases/mcloughlin-v-obrian.php.

97. Dworkin, *Law's Empire*, 240. The six interpretations are spelled out on this page.

98. Ibid., 248.

99. Ibid., 177.

100. Ibid., 249. Although it is not clear what this phrase means, Hercules may recognize, because of his superior knowledge of the democratic context in which he lives, that no such view exists to support such a decision.

101. Ibid., 249–50.

102. Ronald Dworkin, *Freedom's Law: The Moral Reading of the American Constitution* (Cambridge, Mass: Harvard University Press, 1996), 7–12.

103. Here Dworkin might have in mind Kant's rule, rational, deontological account or Mill's mental-state hedonism consequential account.

104. Likewise, Dworkin might have in mind Henry Sigwick's rule intuition, consequentialism or Ross' rule intuitionism deontology.

105. Thom Brooks, "Between Natural Law and Legal Positivism: Dworkin and Hegel on Legal Theory," *Georgia State University L.aw Review* 23, no. 3 (Spring 2007): 517.

106. Brooks documents Dworkin's comment about his apparent connection to natural law in a footnote. In fact, it is part of his thesis in the essay Brooks lifts it out of.

107. Ronald Dworkin, "Natural Law Revisited," 34 *University of Florida Law Review* 165 (1982).

108. Thom Brooks, "Between Natural Law and Legal Positivism: Dworkin and Hegel on Legal Theory," 517. Brian Bix makes the same kind of claim about Dworkin too. See Brian Bix, "Natural Law Theory," in ed. Dennis Patterson, *A Companion to Philosophy of Law and Legal Theory*, 2nd ed. (Blackwell Publishing, Ltd., 2010), 221. This is important to note because, as I have indicated in the first four chapters of this text, to align oneself with a natural

law account is no longer a viable theory to use as a foundation for morality, and as a result, no longer a viable method to use as a measure for worthiness of a just legal principle.

109. Dworkin, "Natural Law Revisted," 165. Italics are in the text.

110. For example, see the "naturalized jurisprudence" defended by Brian Leiter or the naturalized movement inspired by W. V. Quine's discussion of "Epistemology Naturalized." For an excellent discussion of these distinctions see: Roger A. Shiner, "Law and Its Normativity," in *A Companion to Philosophy of Law and Legal Theory*, 2nd ed., ed. Dennis Patterson (Blackwell Publishing, Ltd., 2010), 439.

111. Dworkin, "Natural Law Revisted," 165. Italics are in the text.

112. Ibid., 165–66.

113. Ibid., 166.

114. Ibid. Italics are mine.

115. Although Lon L. Fuller's account of natural law as well as John Finnis' account will fall prey to similar objections, both accounts deserve serious attention to show why my claim is true.

116. Hans Kelsen writes: "Consequently a metaphysical theory of law pretends to discover a natural law immanent in nature. From the point of view of a scientific view of the world, however, within which only a positivistic theory of law can be established, the difference between the (causal) law of nature and the rule of law must be maintained with all emphasis." Hans Kelsen, *Pure Theory of Law* (Clark, NJ: The Lawbook Exchange, 2009), 77.

117. Finnis raises a serious issue with this viewpoint. Although his critical remarks aim at Blackstone, Finnis' remarks could equally apply to Hobbes, Pufendorf, and Locke. And, in fact, they do. According to Finnis, Blackstone is guilty of endorsing the view that natural law may be derived from "the naked individual in his state of nature as a standard." However, if this is the case, then, as Finnis makes clear, there is little derivation between natural and positive law. In fact, there is no derivation at all. Thus, it stands to reason that there is little or no human laws justified against the natural law. In fact, natural law has all but disappeared because the concept of the common good, or in Locke's terminology, the *summon bonum*, has been replaced by the concept of the pre-social individual. Thus, Finnis concludes that Blackstone's view fails as a natural law account, and (I might add that) by implication, so do Hobbes, Pufendorf, and Locke. J. M. Finnis, "Blackstone's Theoretical Intentions; Note," *Natural Law Forum* 12 (1967): 181. cf. Covell, *The Defence of Natural Law*, 197. I am indebted to Covell's text which brought to my attention Finnis' 1967 article.

118. Both views are complicated, and spelling out their views in the detail they deserve is beyond the goals of this text. Nevertheless, some indications of the problems both positions face may be pertinent. Fuller's defense of natural law proceeds in the following manner: Natural law and legal positivism are mutually exclusive viewpoints. Fuller, *The Law in Quest of Itself*, 5–6. This is so because while natural law presupposes the notion of purpose within nature, legal positivism effectively removes the concept of purpose. The demise of (Aristotelian) purpose within nature is a result of the new scientific ideal. That said, Hume (and later Kant) are interpreted as underscoring this issue by making the is-ought distinction. The result of this distinction effectively creates the contemporary tension between the cognitive camps of value statements and the non-cognitivist camps. The result is that statements which express moral value (or disvalue) or legal value (or disvalue) become, at least on a non-cognitivist account, merely reflections of our sentiments. Fuller stands opposed to the is-ought gap or fact-value distinction. In fact, to effectively block legal positivism, as Fuller makes clear, we need only to reject the is-ought gap and put normative claims back on their proper footing. Therefore, if it is possible to defend a cognitivist account of value-laden, moral and legal statements, natural law will regain it hegemonic position in constitutional adjudication. cf. Covell, *The Defence of the Law of Nature*, 31–43. Covell's account elucidates Fuller's complicated critique of Hume and Kant.

Two problems immediately emerge. First, there is a crucial misunderstanding of Hume's fact-value distinction. I make this clear in my discussion of Hume in chapter 3. Although my alternative analysis of the fact-value divide will not ameliorate Fuller's problem, there is still another serious problem. It is the problem of nominalism. Thus, the (perceived) metaphysical machinery utilized by Plato, Aristotle, Aquinas, and Grotius to make moral and legal judgments true, have disappeared and skirted the edge of justification. Thus, Fuller's defense of natural law will be met with a flat refusal.

Finnis aligns himself with Aquinas. I spelled out the metaphysical assumptions of Aquinas in chapter 2. What is it about Finnis' theory which makes him subject to my complaints about the lack of epistemic warrant? Finnis begins his account of natural law spelling out seven basic values for human flourishing which are universal and self-evident: life, knowledge, play, friendship, practical reasonableness, and religion. John Finnis, *Natural Law and Natural Rights* (Oxford: Clarendon Press, 1980), 85–90. Each basic value corresponds to an inclination. The basic values are not deduced from the inclinations nor is the list of inclinations exhaustive. We have contrary inclinations of selfishness, cruelty, and so forth. Unlike the untoward inclinations, the worthiness of the seven requires no explanation. Ibid., 91. The seven basic values are analogous to Aquinas' three basic values I discussed in chapter 2. That said, Finnis resists placing any of the basic seven an hierarchy. Ibid., 96. Covell explains that in order to generate moral judgments which reflect the warrant from natural law, we must follow nine methodological requirements which amount to normative contraints upon rational deliberation. Covell, *The Defense of Natural Law*, 201. The requirements are as follows: our decisions must be practically reasonable, (on occasions) they must be consistent with a coherent plan of life, no arbitrary preference of any of the basic seven values, no arbitrary preferences amongst persons, a certain amount of detachment from the projects we undertake, the relevance of consequences when necessary, respect for the basic value in every act, a requirement to foster the common good, and finally, we must follow our own conscience. Finnis, *Natural Law and Natural Rights*, 100–126.

There is no doubt that Finnis' theory is a masterly exhibition of adroitness and philosophical skill. Just the same, there remains a burning issue for me. What is the epistemic warrant for the seven basic values? If Finnis aligns himself with Aquinas (more or less), then he should be aware of the metaphysical machinery needed to justify the seven basic values. If so, then what sort of defense can he enlist to justify the epistemic warrant of the values? Suppose Finnis insists the basic value are universals (which he does). How can he consistently maintain such a view in a world dominated by nominalism? It seems unlikely that such a project will be successful.

Chapter Six

Toward a Theory of Analytical Legal Naturalism

INTRODUCTION

What is Analytical Legal Naturalism (ALN)? ALN is the view that what has legal value or disvalue is related to what is common to and rooted in our experience.[1] The goal of ALN is to develop truth-making conditions in order to show that *some* legal principles are true. To accept that they are true requires not returning to the mysterious properties of metaphysical realism, Aristotelian substances, morality, or suspicious accounts of human nature. Although such a project remains the primary aim of this text, for the purposes of this endeavor, even though filled with lofty aspirations, my goal is much narrower. My purpose is merely to make recommendations about how judges may decide some hard cases.[2] Thus, if the objections to the Austin, Hart, and Dworkin viewpoints work, without a fundamental principle like ALN to fall back on, when faced with hard cases, serious problems will emerge. In other words, if we are put in such a position, the influence of legal indeterminacy will open the gate to extra and suspicious non-legal considerations.[3]

FACTS AND VALUE

To avoid these and other outcomes (including the problem of the strange notions of justice), legal naturalism, which is the backbone of ALN, may be formulated against the backdrop of three theses, which spell out the relationship between facts and value. The first thesis is this:

The Ontological Principle of Supervenience (OPS)

Necessarily, whenever anything has value (disvalue) of any kind, then there is some feature(s) of it *in virtue of which* it has it.[4]

This principle states that if anything has value or disvalue, then, whatever it is, it must possess a characteristic(s) that gives it the value or disvalue. In this discussion, the focus is on a sentence expressible as a legal principle connecting (legally relevant) factual properties with a legal property.

The second thesis formulated by Cohen is this:

Epistemic Principle of Supervenience (EPS)

Necessarily, a person knows *firsthandedly* that a thing has value (disvalue) only if the person knows what feature(s) the thing has in virtue of which it has the value (disvalue) in question.[5]

The second principle states that the feature mentioned in the first principle must be perceptible in some way. So, according to this principle, in the analysis of any legal principle which connects factual predicates with a legal property, the facts in question must be observable or distinguishable in some way.

The last principle, which I develop, is called the Logical Principle of Supervenience (LPS):

Necessarily, this feature(s), whatever it may be, must be such that its presence makes anything which has this feature(s) have value (disvalue) or tends to make anything which possesses this feature have value (disvalue) for a person.

This third principle spells out some relationship between the facts and the value in question. The relationship is primarily deductive. In this discussion, then, the relationship which connects facts with legal properties, will produce this value or tend to do so. Two deductive formulations may work for a theory of legal naturalism: 1. Factual predicates *entail* legal predicates or 2. Factual properties *imply* legal properties.

Following the model of ethical naturalism developed by Robert B. Scott Jr., two types of legal naturalism may be formulated. ALN is the first type. It specifically states that some factual properties *entail* some legal properties. As the notion of entailment implies, the relationship between the factual properties and the legal properties are captured by an analytical connection. The other way of talking about the second formulation of legal statements may be called contingent legal naturalism

Contingent legal naturalism, unlike ALN, spells out the logical relationship between a factual property and the legal property by means of material implication instead of the analytical connection: Some factual properties materially imply some legal properties. The difference, of course, between the two statements is that the analytical statement supplies a conceptual connect between the subject and predicate, whereas material implication does not furnish such a link. In due course, the goal is to capture a principle of universalizability, one with both cross-cultural significance and trans-historical significance. Thus, my attempt will be to defend the strongest viewpoint, which will also be the most controversial, viz., ALN. Here is my argument for why analytical legal naturalism is true. After that, I will discuss the implications that such view will point toward. Thus, the question, then, is what is ALN and why is true?

ANALYTICAL LEGAL NATURALISM

ALN, a foundational theory (reminiscent of Kelsen's "basic norm"), states the following: Necessarily, for any being you chose, if this being is a person, then this person is born free and equal,[6] and for any other being you might (arbitrarily) select, if this being is also a person, then this person is also born free and equal, then (no matter who we chose from the set of persons born free and equal) it follows that no one should harm one another.[7] What does this mean and what are the reasons to believe it is true? I will conjoin both questions and answer them at the same time.

To answer what this means and why it is true, I must first prove that my version of legal naturalism is analytically true.[8] Here is my semantic proof. Let us suppose for the moment that we can select an individual (a nonspecific individual) who is a person and, by implication, born free and equal. Additionally, let us suppose that we can randomly select another (nonspecific) individual from the same set of individuals who is also a person and, by implication, born free and equal. With that in mind, let us assume for the moment that it is false that these two individuals should refrain from harming each other. What would this mean? This means that it is permissible to harm (unjustifiably) each other. If this is true, then it is permissible to neglect the fact that whoever harms another is born free and equal and yet, such a claim is false. This conclusion, then, leads to the contradiction that it is permissible *and* forbidden to harm another individual who is a person that is born free and equal. Therefore, the assumption that it is permissible to harm one another is false, and therefore, it is true that no one should harm one another. So, because this assumption is true, and the other two assumptions (for conditional proof) are both true, then ALN is true.

Unfortunately, this semantic proof may raise more questions than it will answer. First, I have listed natural characteristics, which I take to be legally relevant, viz., that all persons are born free and equal.[9] These characteristics follow from the fact of the new scientific ideal, an ideal alive today, which reveals (minimally) that no one is born morally superior to another.[10] Therefore, if we take these facts seriously, as we should, then it leads us to the legal property that no one should harm another. However, such a conclusion may lead to the objection that my legal naturalism is just a disguised moral theory. This is not the case, because while there may be moral theories consistent with my view, none have any hegemonic authority, including any sort of legal enforcement. What I mean more specifically is that, as Feinberg has demonstrated, a useful distinction may be maintained between a legal right and a moral right.[11] Of the former, for example, are legally valid claims we can make against the state not to interfere unjustly in our private affairs or a valid claim against the state to enforce legally valid claims we might have against other private citizens. Moral rights point to valid claims we have against other private citizens, which aim at the conscience of the offender. Such claims may or may not be enforceable. This is (part of) the difference between legal theory and moral theory. Thus, my view remains primarily a naturalistic *legal* standard, that is, a standard enforceable by a legal system.[12]

The Question of Harm

Next, although harm plays the role of the legal predicates in the statement above, it is not clear what harm means or what harms are legally relevant. Defining "harm" for the purposes of this text would be impossible. Even though this may be true, some of the framework of the notion of harm may be laid in place to eliminate some of the fuzzy edges.[13] Therefore, whether the harm is intentional or not, minimally it involves some sort of loss, or a setback, that an individual takes to be in his interest.[14] The list of interests one may have is their desire to maintain (at least once) the homeostasis of their physical, psychological, financial, spiritual, and emotional well-being.[15] On this view, an individual may be harmed even if he is not aware that his stability has been interrupted.[16] In most cases, unless death occurs, once the instability (perhaps measured as a setback, made worse off, diminished opportunities)[17] is recognized, we may (typically) expect a negative psychological response to the harm which diminishes or deprives the autonomy of the injured party.[18] It is here that my view rests (partly) on Results Continuity doctrine. This means that, occasionally, it will be necessary to consult the successful scientific theories to discern the degree of harm.[19]

This leads, then, to the next issue. What sort of harms may be enforced by a legal system? Following Locke, since this (partially) takes Locke's approach in the *Second Treatise* of the *Two Treatises of Government*, the list of harms includes harms to one's life, health, liberty, or possessions.[20] Notably, Locke does not indicate that this is a complete list. Nevertheless, it is what free and equal individuals should refrain from doing to one another. Given the design of this account, the attempt is to limit the consultation of non-legal, irrelevant facts. There is one qualification to the list of harms mentioned above. Locke makes clear that, under abnormal conditions, if we become aware that an innocent individual is being attacked, we may be obligated, when we can help without harm to ourselves, to preserve the life of an individual whenever their life, liberty, health, limb, or goods are at risk.[21]

Before I move on, there is one more issue to discuss. My claim is that ALN is true. Thus, it is true in virtue of the meaning of its terms as the semantic proof above demonstrates. Additionally, I maintain that it is also a necessary truth. This indicates that ALN is a necessary truth, which implies that the statement of ALN is also true in all possible worlds.

Conventional Necessity

Now, any one versed in metaphysics may understand that my statement of ALN may object that my viewpoint relies on a deep account of reality in many ways like the metaphysical realists I rejected earlier.[22] In this case, necessity requires an independently existing modal structure of reality to make my analytical legal naturalism a necessary truth.[23] However, this is not the case. In fact, I can still maintain the necessity of this claim, including its universality, by explaining the modal force in terms of us. That is, its force will be laid out in terms of the way we carve up the world without resorting to the mysterious properties of a modal reality.[24] How is this possible, then?

To begin, let us discuss my statement of ALN in a little more detail. It is a necessary truth and known *a posteriori*. Here is what I mean. Take, for example, the statement: Hesperus is Phosphorus. This example (also known as the "Evening Star is the Morning Star" illustration), is based on the story that, for many years, stargazers thought that Hesperus and Phosphorus were different stars. Eventually, it was discovered that they were both the same. As a result, the following statement is true: Hesperus is (identical to) Phosphorus. Thus, the latter claim is knowable *a posteriori*. This means that we would never know apart from experience, that is to say, never from an *a priori* point of view, that they were the same. Additionally, because of the identity relationship between both referents, the claim is also a necessary truth. In other words, the identity claim expresses a claim that is true (just in case it is true) in all possible worlds.[25]

In the same way, my statement of analytical legal naturalism is known *a posteriori*. First, it is not known *a priori*. This means that apart from experience, we cannot know that the non-legal facts of freedom and equality (facts about persons) are logically connected to the legal property of not harming. In other words, the connection is not simply a matter of reflection. We need to study the world. It is also a necessary truth, because the logical connection between the non-legal facts *strictly imply* the legal predicates. With this in mind, what are the truth-conditions that make this statement true? As I mentioned earlier, it may be tempting to assume that the conditions adopt a realist interpretation, i.e., it is true in virtue of metaphysically deep facts about the world (in this case, the existence of modal facts). That having been said, it may be possible to interpret my claim from a conventional point of view without being committed to the strange occult properties of modality, forms or essences. I will turn to this point now.

Turning away from a realist account requires us to reframe the issue of justification. It requires us to find a middle ground between a deep metaphysical foundation consistent with the metaphysical realists (consistent with Plato, Aristotle, and so forth) and one that is a nominalist's account (consistent with Austin's and Hart's legal positivism). To begin, then, we may start with the fact that ALN is a necessary truth and known *a posteriori*. This means that it is true in all possible worlds and it requires experience to come to understand that it is true. Indeed, as Allen Sidelle makes clear, if it turns out to be false (which is apparently imaginable), we would merely retract our modal claim of necessity and attempt to reformulate it.[26] In other words, even if, as I claim, there is a strict entailment between the legally relevant (factual) properties and the legal properties, then we would not expect to retract our concepts. Still, it may be required under certain circumstances in order to maintain the modal claim of necessity.

Next, with this point in place, I will follow the line spelled out by Sidelle. That is, I will try to show how I can maintain the necessity of my first principle without being labeled a metaphysical realist. Here is what I mean. Sidelle discusses two different claims typically thought to be necessary and known *a posteriori*. For example, Water is H_2O and Margaret Truman is the biological daughter of Bess Truman. Both claims are known *a posteriori*. This is so because we need experience to know whether they are true, and both claims have been defended as necessary truths. This means, minimally, that (if the truth-value of these statements are settled, so to speak) we will be at a loss to imagine a possible world where water is not H_2O and to imagine Margaret's mother other than she actually is.[27] Sidelle makes clear that the assumption of the truth-making conditions of these claims typically presuppose a realist account of a modal reality.

The next step elaborates how a conventional approach can explain the necessity of these claims without positing the existence of the strange properties of modal reality. Sidelle begins with the assumption that we can take a claim like the two just mentioned, abstract away the particular predicates of the statements (and even their subjects), and find a class of "relevant alternatives" that will make the statement a necessary truth.[28] Let us say, as Sidelle demonstrates, that we remove the predicates of the statements of Water is H_2O and Margaret Truman's biological origin was *Bess Truman*, e.g., Water is ____________, and Margaret Truman's biological origin was ______________. What we can prove is this: if we can fill in the blanks with a predicate from the set or class of actual "relevant alternatives," each alternative will result in the truth of that statement. The problem is, what constraints or relevant alternatives will work to make the sentence true? Presumably, the set of relevant alternatives would be determined by what Sidelle calls General Principles of Individuation (GPI).[29]

So the question is, what are GPI? Sidelle describes these principles as truths behind truths. The former truths determine the relevant alternatives to make other latter truths necessary statements. So, for example, here is a simplified version of the GPI applied to the statement "H_20 is water": "Whatever is water's deepest explanatory feature is specifically, then water has it necessarily."[30] Thus, the feature(s) in question will make the statement "H_20 is __________" a true statement as long as the blank will be filled in with (truth-making) empirically verifiable feature(s), and the same statement will also be a necessary truth as long as it instantiates the GPI. The same will apply to Margaret Truman's biological origins. The question now is this: How will this apply to my first premise?

Following the Logical Principle of Supervenience (LPS), let us start with my statement of ALN:

Necessarily, for any being you chose, if this being is a person, then this person is born free and equal, and for any other being you might (arbitrarily) select, if this being is also a person, then this person is also born free and equal, then (no matter who we chose from the set of persons born free and equal) it follows that no one should harm one another.

Again, there are two issues here. First, is ALN true? And, second, is it a necessary truth? The first question is yes. I provided a semantic proof above to show that it is analytically true (i.e., it is true in virtue of the meaning of its terms). The second is yes too, but it is a little harder to show why. Even though ALN states that it is a necessary truth, I must still show why it is necessary and how that necessity can be explained from a conventional point of view. If Sidelle is right, then I will need a general principle of individuation as well.[31] This will not be easy to do, but this might work:

ALN General Principle of Individuation (ALNGPI)

For any property you can choose, if it correctly characterizes a certain kind of being and any being like it, and if this property limits what these beings may do to one another, then if any statement which expresses the limits of this behavior is analytically true, then it is a necessary truth.

So, as the argument goes, if ALNGPI is true, then it shows that ALN is a necessary truth which is established by our own conventions. In other words, because ALN satisfies the first two antecedents, e.g., that there are persons who are born free and equal, and because of these facts, it limits the harm each person may inflict on another and if this statement is analytically true, then it follows that ALN is a (conventionally determined) necessary truth. Before I move on, there are two qualifications.

The first qualification is this. What reasons, if any, should we think make the ALNGPI true? Following Sidelle, one way to approach this issue is to argue that if there are good reasons to believe that the characterization of ALN is analytically true, then the ALNGPI should be true as well.[32] For example, suppose I make the following claim: $Pa \supset Ra$, where P stands for "person," R stands for "rights," and "a" is a non-specific, individual variable. This says, then, if *a* is a person, then *a* has rights. From this claim I may move to a universal generalized statement using the rule of Universal Generalization:[33] $(x)(Px \supset Rx)$, which says, for any x you choose, if x is a person, then x has rights. But here is the interesting step. I can now provide a rule not unlike Sidelle's GPI rule: Where the domain of x is restricted to persons, if a universally quantified statement (where one statement implies a second statement) results in a true statement, then any instantiation of that claim (following the rule of universal instantiation[34]) will result in a true statement. Is the GPI rule for this example true? The answer is yes. This is so because it accurately spells out the condition under which an instantiated rule is true when it is correctly followed. The same thing applies to my ALNGPI and illuminates, I hope, what Sidelle means. Therefore, if there are reasons to believe that ALN is true, so (some version of) the ALNGPI should be true as well. No doubt, there may be problems with my characterization of the ALNGPI. Nevertheless, there should be a way to get as close to the proper portrayal of ALNGPI as possible.

The Relativity of Justice

It is now essential to discuss the relationship between ALN and justice. Here is my argument:

Argument for the Relativity of Justice (ARJ)

1. Analytical Legal Naturalism is true.
2. If Analytical Legal Naturalism is true, then justice is relative to a legal standard.
3. Therefore, Justice is relative to a legal standard.

Before we begin by asking whether this argument is sound, why is this argument relevant? The concept of justice is a nebulous concept, especially within the current debate. The notion of justice can vary depending upon the context and other practical matters. Nevertheless, the notion of justice must be placed in some sort of relationship with a standard like ALN. Here are two comments.

At the end of the day, I will give a nominalist account of justice. Still, even if we require a nominalist account of justice, it will be treated the same way whether the account is nominalist or not. Nevertheless, raising the question of the relationship between a legal standard and justice would seem to require a robust account of what justice means. Unfortunately, for the purposes of this text, this would be obviously too much to accomplish. Nevertheless, someone might reasonably object that if I am going to apply ALN in a meaningful way to hard cases, I will need to develop some sort of theory of justice; otherwise, without the constraints that a theory of justice will provide, it is likely that decisions about hard cases may reflect my own cultural biases instead of a principled approach. This is no doubt a worry. That notwithstanding, even with a robust theory of justice such a worry does not disappear. Without identifying my notion of justice with a specific viewpoint, say, Rawls' two principles of justice as fairness, I follow Mill's minimal conception of justice. This means that, apart from any moral considerations, justice implies a rule of conduct and a sentiment to sanction that rule.[35] Again, in line with my view that justice is relative to a basic legal norm, the norm will spell out what rules of conduct are relevant from a point of view of justice. With these (albeit brief) comments in place, I will discuss the premises of the argument above.

So, the question, now again, is whether AJR is a sound argument. If it is, then both premises must be true. What about premise 1? I have already argued that it is true. Although, premise 1 is controversial, the second premise is equally, if not more, controversial. Is premise 2 true? The answer is yes. Why is this so and what does it mean? I will begin with the latter question. First, what the antecedent of premise 2 means should be obvious even if is thought to be false. Where the domain is restricted to persons, given the fact that all persons are born free and equal, it follows that no one should harm one another. To harm another person without a clear justification to do so denies the other individual's freedom and equality. What does the consequent mean?

The consequent states simply that what we take to be principles of justice are determined and justified by a legal standard. First, historically speaking, under the traditional relationship between what is legal and what is just, the legality of an action is straightforwardly measured against the prevailing concept of justice. Such an approach goes as far back as Plato. Of course, up until the late sixteen hundreds and into the early seventeen hundreds, such a view made sense because of the metaphysical machinery philosophers thought supported such a view. Eventually, as the Aristotle and Plato viewpoints lost their authority and were replaced with the new scientific ideal, the relationship between justice and what is legal became strained. In fact, by 1777, in his *An Enquiry Concerning the Principles of Morals*,[36] Hume discusses justice in terms of its instrument value supported, at times, by an instinctual sentiment. Like Mill, the foundation of justice goes no deeper than that. Justice is relevant only when the context gives us reasons to think it is needed. Additionally, it is notable again that this tradition becomes an Archimedean point for Bentham as well. There is "no necessary or conceptually guaranteed connection between law and morality."[37] Thus, following the nominalist tradition, justice cannot be tied to a moral theory, and as a result, the validity of what is just must be relative to a legal standard. Thus, premise 2 is true and the ARJ argument is sound.

To follow this line of inquiry still further, defending premise 2 avoids the pitfalls of aligning our legal standard with some sort of moral theory. To make this claim does not deny that there are moral theories, especially action-based theories (deontological or consequential) which have been defended to the satisfaction of many scholars. Rather, we face a different problem. First, given the constituents of the universe (minimally described in terms of trope nominalism), it remains an open question whether there is a moral theory which, of those currently defended, comes close to making a moral criterion true.[38] Second, even under the assumption that a moral theory may be, more or less usable, there still remains the question of which moral theory should be used to determine when a legal standard or positive law is justified. Will we require a deontological account or a consequential account? A consequential account seems reasonable when applied to potential hard cases and problematic social arrangements. Nevertheless, which account of consequentialism will we use? It is unclear even where to begin.

The next step in the discussion to developing (partially) the truth-making conditions that make some principles of law true, I continue to spell out the relationship between ALN and the ARJ. So, the idea here is that if justice is relative to ALN, this raises the question of the relationship justice will have to moral theories. Here is my argument:

The Separatist Thesis of Justice (STJ)

3. Justice is relative to a legal standard.
4. If justice is relative to a legal standard, then justice may or may not be consistent with the ordinary requirements of morality, viz., the standards of virtue theory, natural law, deontology (contractarianism) or consequentialism (or any moral theory whatsoever). In other words, the consequent of premise 4 is a statement of The Separatist Thesis (ST).

5. Therefore, justice may or may not be consistent with the ordinary requirements of morality, viz., the standards of virtue theory, deontology (contractarianism), or consequentialism (or any moral theory whatsoever).

Again, is this argument sound? We may assume that premise 3 is true for the sake of argument. After all, it is the conclusion of the ARJ. Therefore, premise 3 is true. What about premise 4? To understand why premise 4 is true, it is important to make clear why legal judgments may or may not be consistent with the ordinary requirements of morality.

ALN is placed in between two commonly held positions. On the one hand, there is a handful of positions that understand that (sometimes) legal principles fashioned and designed to deal with hard cases (because of the lack of case law) must be judged against what morality may constrain us to do. Dworkin's view is, of course, a celebrated version.[39] On the other, there are the legal positivists that make clear that the formation of legal principles is something analogous to the political subjectivism of Hobbes. On this account, what is legal and just is whatever the sovereign dictates. ALN brings with it the logical necessity to avoid being labeled a logical positivist account and because it is a conventional account, it avoids the metaphysical machinery of the moral accounts associated with Dworkin, Finnis, and Fuller. Additionally, ALN also avoids the positivist's account that makes the notion of justice relative to the will of sovereign. Rather, ALN makes justice relative to the principle spelled out in ALN. Thus, although the notion of justice in ALN is a nominalist account, it is not an arbitrary account of justice either. Justice, minimally, follows and is determined by the harm principle in ALN.

Thus, with these distinctions spelled out, I am now in a better position to spell out the truth of premise 4. If justice is relative to ALN then, when deciding hard cases, the conclusions one might make may or may not be consistent with the requirements of ordinary morality.[40] The standard of justice will be relative to only what is legally relevant and enforceable. Thus, premise 4 is true, and the STJ argument is sound.

There is one qualification to make concerning the notion of the Separatist Thesis (ST), which is part of the STJ. Of course, the intuition behind the ST is that the notion of justice is separate from what we would normally think is obligatory by ordinary morality. Ordinary morality is not a term with any special significance. It refers simply to what we would expect a deontological or consequentialist account of morality to conclude about truth-telling, promise-keeping, reparations, non-maleficence, and so forth. That said, it is normally thought that the judicial system bears the burden of finding the truth. So, even though lawyers are officers of the judicial system, such a project is not a part of the lawyer's goal while representing a client.[41] An attorney's primary focus is the representation of his client, and no other. Following the analogy at a local level, so to speak, the issue here for STJ is that, in the adjudication of hard cases, judges are under no obligation to appeal to the ordinary requirements of morality. The standard that judges will use requires a special standard, one separate and specific to the legal profession, perhaps something like ALN, which I have outlined. Nevertheless, while the separatism remains a part of the ALN, it does not curtail the use of statistical or science-based data (or even anecdotal evidence). Relevant and scientifically solid data may be used to decide hard cases to determine harm (even cases that may be ambiguous). Here is what I mean.

PRELIMINARY OBSERVATIONS

Let us consider some hard cases that the courts deliberated which involved a lack of case law (partial or otherwise) to guide the courts decisions and involve the potential harm of the members of our society.[42] The first case is *Brown v. Entertainment Merchants Association* 564 U.S. 786 (2011). Although there is some case law that is relevant to the adjudication of this issue, Scalia, writing for the majority opinion, made clear that the State of California could make a better case for the restriction of children's access to violent material if there was a long-standing tradition to do so. Unfortunately, there is no case law or restrictions to speak of. In fact, as Scalia correctly points out, our culture actually has a long tradition of exposing children to different forms of violence particularly through children's stories and literature.[43] In this regard, the interactive videos which are the target for California's restrictions, videos like *Postal*, *Grand Theft Auto*, and so forth, represent a special class of potential harms for children not addressed before. How can this issue be fixed? The State of California, quoting the findings of research psychologists, attempted to make the case that there is causal link between playing these interactive games and the harmful effects on minors.[44] Of course, if the evidence could establish such a link, then there would be prima facie reasons for the state to restrict minors from purchasing violent, interactive videos. At this point, what may not be noticed is the implied principle of harm employed by the State of California of which ALN represents one version. Thus, if the harm to children is significant, then the necessity of ALN can be invoked to protect the rights of children not to have their interests violated or made worse off, and to do so without invoking a moral theory.

Justice Scalia made clear that the research used by California does not prove that violent, interactive video games *cause* minors to act aggressively. The empirical evidence, Scalia outlines, is based on correlation and the studies suffer from methodological flaws.[45] Thus, because the state's case was not compelling, the USSC ruled that the state's act imposes a restriction on protected free speech outlined in the First Amendment and, as a result, is invalid unless it passes strict scrutiny.

ALN may be applicable here as a useful legal standard to make a principled decision about the lack of compelling evidence of harm. Again, minors who satisfy the antecedent of the ALN, necessarily should be granted protection from harm. Failing to do this would violate the principle of harm of the ALN and fail what we take to be the just treatment of minors. In this case, without empirical evidence to show that there is causal link between minors playing violent video games and the aggressive behavior that it will cause, the government is not compelled to restrict protected speech even the protected speech of minors. Finally, what may be an interesting turn on this view is that the majority opinion flies in the face of what we might take to be a morally appropriate course of action. This points to the relevance of STJ, which may or may not capture what our moral intuitions dictate. In fact, Justice Breyer's dissent comes close to making this point. Part of what he argues is that the state has an independent interest in the "well-being" of the youth of our country. Although he has in mind the illegal violent behavior the video games might cause, his comments point to the potential harm of the well-being of the minor whose diet consists of violent video games.[46] In the end, two points are notable.

First, even as Justice Breyer appears to appreciate, there is a clash here between which theory (or hypothesis) best explains the facts. Thus, Justice Breyer shifts the focus to individuals and organizations who have a professional familiarity with the literature. With this in mind, Justice Breyer accuses Justice Scalia too quick in reproof of organizations which support the violent behavior thesis, including the prestigious American Academy of Pediatrics and the American Psychological Association.

Second, this case illustrates the need for a bright line to make explicit what remains implicit, in some ways, in the text of *Brown v. Entertainment Merchants Associations* (2011). This is part of the value of ALN; it makes clear that harm must be determined, at times, by a theory which is the best explanation for the preponderance of evidence.[47] Thus, barring the problem of relying on (the mysterious) direct cause or the imprecise characterization of what a cause may mean, the use of ALN relies on the best accounts available to determine the degree of harm even if such accounts may fall short of our Cartesian addiction.

Another case in point that raises doubts about pertinent and relevant case law is *Bowers v. Hardwick* 478 U.S. 186 (1986) and *Lawrence v. Texas* 539 U.S. 558 (2003). At first glance, it is not clear whether consensual (sexual) homosexual activity violated the right to privacy articulated in *Griswold v. Connecticut* 381 U.S. 479 (1965). Again, like the case above, there is some relevant case law but it does not speak directly to this matter of the sodomy laws which were still laws in many Southern states. *Bowers*, which was eventually overturned in *Lawrence*, upheld the sodomy laws of Georgia stating that there was no fundamental right to engage in homosexual sodomy.

Justice Burger also added that such laws, which prohibit such actions, are consistent with the "ancient roots" of proscriptions against sodomy and the Judeo-Christian moral and ethical standards.[48] Of course, although Burger is correct, it is not clear why the Christian Scriptures (both the Old Testament and the New Testament) present a consistent picture against homosexual activity. So, while it may be true that such activity is inconsistent with a theological viewpoint prominent in some Christian communities, should it be illegal? No doubt, a traditional natural law account could make a case against homosexual activity.[49] Apart from these "ancient roots," is there any reasons to prohibit such activity as long as it is between to consensual adults? In other words, where is the harm? Like the State of California in the *Merchant* case above, the majority opinion, written by Justice White, failed to make any sort of case that homosexual activity constituted a harm that was not protected by the privacy rights found in the penumbras of the Amendments of the U.S. Constitution.[50] Thus, from an ALN perspective, if both of the individuals are born free and equal, and their sexual activity does not harm each other (or anyone else), i.e., their sexual activity does not make them worse off or constitute any sort of physical, emotional, psychological setback to themselves (or anyone else), the state should not restrict their liberty of action.

Seventeen years later, the same issue was brought to the attention of the USSC, via *Lawrence v. Texas*, for a second time. Again the focus of the issue was very similar to *Bowers*. Two individuals, Tyron Garner and John Geddes, were arrested for engaging in a sexual act. Unlike Georgia, where sodomy was proscribed on the whole, Texas made it a crime for two individuals of the same sex to engage in sodomy. This time, unlike the *Bowers* case, the USSC ruled against the state. What is interesting to note is that the majority opinion invoked the equal protection law to protect the privacy rights of homosexual men because there was no legislative purpose to restrict such behavior. In fact, toward the end of the majority opinion, Justice Kennedy writes that *Lawrence* does not involve minors or anyone who might be injured or coerced. Moreover, it does not involve any sort of (embarrassing) public conduct or prostitution, and so forth. Rather, this case simply about two, consenting adults engage in sexual practices which is consistent with a homosexual lifestyle.[51]

Another way that may be useful to speak about this ruling is that there are two individuals born free and equal, who are not harming each other or anyone else. Thus, unlike *Bowers*, *Lawrence* reflects the sort of equality that necessarily all people must share regardless of their sexual preferences. That said, the *Bowers* case correctly points out that the Christian community in the United States, for the most part, rejects a homosexual lifestyle. So, in such a case, a decision like *Lawrence* will remain an unpopular decision relative to the mores of that demographics. Nevertheless, as I mentioned earlier, a legal decision may or may not reflect the moral or religious intuitions of the population. Such a claim is supported by the STJ.

There are three other cases that are worth reasoning about: *Griswold v. Connecticut* 381 U.S. 479 (1965), *Riggs v. Palmer* 115 N.Y. 506, 22 N.E. 188 (1889), and *McLoughlin v. O'Brian* [1983] 1 AC 410. I will begin with *Griswold.*

Griswold v. Connecticut represents another hard case in which the USSC had to make a decision about the right of privacy with little or no case law and, what makes the case even more interesting, no explicit mention of privacy in the U.S. Constitution. In the simplest terms (and, at first glance, seemingly irrelevant), the majority opinion, delivered by Justice Douglas, struck down a Connecticut law which prohibited dispensing contraceptives to married couples.[52] Although such decision makes sense, the reasons to do so remained elusive. Eventually, Griswold's attorney developed the argument that the Connecticut law violated the right to privacy implied by five of the Constitution's amendments. Justice Douglas, with the concurring opinions of Justices Goldberg, Harlan, and White, found favor with this line of argument and strengthened Thomas Emerson's (Griswold's attorney) argument in the following manner.

Justice Douglas reasoned that several amendments have penumbras (in metaphorical terms, viz., a space of partial illumination) which refers to an implied restriction against the federal government. In fact, these penumbras create zones of privacy. Thus, because the Constitution reflects, at some level, the fundamental right to privacy, there is fundamental right of privacy protected by the U.S. Constitution.[53] Concurring with the decision, Justices Goldberg and Brennan reason that the idea that privacy is a fundamental right older than the Bill of Rights. Thus, it becomes apparent that, as the majority of the Justices recognized, like the fundamental notion of liberty, privacy is also a fundamental part of our traditions and collective conscious. Thus, privacy emanates from the Constitution and is therefore a fundamentally protected right.[54]

Right after the majority opinion, Justice Black (joined by Justice Stewart) brought serious objections to the majority opinion. I will briefly discuss their dissent. After that I will bring two objections against the majority opinion. First, the majority opinion rests on a logical fallacy. Second, I will try to show how the ALN may be applied to the issues brought up in *Griswold* and in an earlier case: *Poe v. Ullmann* 367 U.S. 497 (1961). Perhaps addressing the anti-contraception law will save us from twisting the U.S. Constitution to say whatever we want it to say.

Justice Black's dissent follows a two-prong attack. Black's first attack aims at the fact that there is no explicit mention whatsoever of privacy in the Constitution. Black does recognize that certain Amendments are written to protect the privacy of individuals at certain times and places. Nevertheless, to interpret narrowly the Amendments as just speaking to privacy is an absurdly distorted view. The second attack is substantive and complex. Ultimately, Justice Black's criticism focuses on what role the USSC should play when faced with such a decision with no case law to fall back on. In such cases, Black argues that the Court should *remain silent* rather than strike down laws with no justification to do so, legal or otherwise. Such State laws, he argues, are the primary function of the legislative branch of the government, not the USSC. Additionally, the courts appeal to the "collective consciousness of the people" is nothing but a disguised attempt to appeal to a "mysterious and uncertain natural law" to strike down the law.[55] Subjective considerations used here, Black makes clear, were laid to rest years before.

To Black's rare combination of audacity and calculation, I add the following critical remarks. The majority opinion rests on the (informal) fallacy of composition.[56] This fallacy involves the mistaken transfer of a property from the part to the whole. In particular, it involves the mistaken assumption that what is true of the part of the whole must be true of the whole.[57] Examples of such mistakes are numerous. For example, one silly and homely example is that since sodium is a poison and chlorine is a poison, salt must also be a poison. Another example, less humorous, is committed by Aristotle. He argues that since each part of the human body has a function, then all humans must have a function as well. If such reasoning is problematic, how does this apply to *Griswold*?

The argument presented by Thomas Emerson goes roughly like this:

1. The First, Third, Fourth, Ninth, and Fourteenth Amendments are a part of the U.S. Constitution.
2. The First, Third, Fourth, Ninth, and Fourteenth Amendments contain penumbras which create zones of privacy.
3. Therefore, privacy is a fundamental right, which emanates from the totality of the U.S. Constitution.

Perhaps the argument is a little more complicated. Nevertheless, it is represented here in its bare bones to show the problematic nature of the majority opinion. Just because (at least) one Amendment implies some aspect of privacy does not mean that there is fundamental right protected by the U.S. Constitution. Having said that, perhaps the ALN may speak to this issue. My view is that we can address the original issue brought forward in *Griswold* and maintain the exceptional value of the dissent of Justice Black.

The case advanced by Griswold was similar to a case discussed in *Poe v. Ullmann* 367 U.S. 497 (1961). The facts of the case involve two married women who suffered extensive psychological and physical harm from their attempts to conceive and deliver healthy babies. Both women sought from their physician Dr. Charles Lee Buxton for the provision of contraceptives.

Neither of the women, nor their spouses for that matter, wanted to take the risk of getting pregnant again. However, the state's attorney Ullman threatened and deterred Buxton from providing contraceptives and advice because of an 1879 law that made it illegal for Buxton to do so.[58] The two women (referred to as Poe and Doe) including Buxton appealed their case all the way to the USSC claiming that the Connecticut law violated their 14th Amendment right to due process.

Unfortunately, the Court ruled against the plaintiffs. Like the lower court of appeals, the USSC ruled that because the law had never been litigated, the statute was a threat of the application of the Connecticut law and not an actual application of the law.[59] Against this background, the dissent by Justice Harlan raised a profoundly significant point, which he describes as his core disagreement. The Connecticut statute has the potential of leaching into the privacy of the marital bedroom.[60] The question is this: Who should decide when a couple should choose to decide to procreate or not? Of course, it needs no great play of imagination to see that the state should not. With this point in mind, it seems as if privacy is the relevant issue here (as Justice Douglas and Justice Harlan unreservedly concur). This is clearly the case. But does that mean that there is fundamental constitutional right to privacy?

Four years later, *Griswold* raised a similar case and, by design, pushed it all the way to the USSC. In order to get arrested to show that the law in Connecticut was in fact more than just a threat, Estelle Griswold and Buxton opened up a birth control clinic in 1961. Shortly after it opened, both were arrested for violating the 1879 Connecticut law which prohibited the sale and dispensing of contraceptives. But what may not be known are the reasons for the 1879 law. Here is a brief account of the background of the law.

On February 7, 1879, the Connecticut state legislature passed a bill entitled, *An Act to Amend an Act Concerning Offenses against Decency, Morality and Humanity*. It was a version of the Comstock Law passed by Congress in 1873. The Comstock Law, among other things, made it illegal to sell or distribute materials that encouraged contraception or abortion. It attempted to discourage women from entering the workforce as they were beginning to occupy jobs, which were traditionally held by males. The presence of women in the workforce, it was also argued, undermined the institution of marriage. Apparently, though, while each state began to pass their own versions of the Comstock Law, regulating the use of contraceptives, Connecticut banned the use of contraception altogether.

Whether we approach this case using ALN as a patch or to jump-start the case, what is clearly problematic about the Comstock Law and Connecticut Law is that both deny the freedom and equality of both men and women. As a result, the laws, especially when applied to women, prevents each individual or couples the right to the health benefits of contraception, the liberty to choose when and when not to procreate, and the liberty to pursue employment when qualified to do so. It is noteworthy that some of what ALN captures is partly consistent with the arguments of Griswold's attorney. In other words, because the ALN clearly identifies the harms associated with the Connecticut law and the necessity of rights against the State to avoid interfering in such matter, it makes sense, then, to evoke due process law of the 14th Amendment. Using the ALN here, then, illustrates need to abrogate the Connecticut law. What is not clear to me, though, is why the spurious argument for privacy was added to the case. Striking down the law was enough to protect the necessity of the sanctity of the home and the intimacy of marriage.[61]

The next case is *Riggs v. Palmer* 115 N.Y. 506, 22 N.E. 188 (1889). This case is discussed by Dworkin because it is an example of a hard case that had no probate or criminal laws available to help the justices adjudicate the case. That said, the case is fairly simple and straightforward. The families of Riggs and Preston, daughters of Francis B. Palmer, and the grandson of Francis B. Palmer, Elmer E. Palmer, were listed to inherit his estate upon his death. Apparently, Elmer E. Palmer reasoned that when his grandfather married Mrs. Bresee in March 1882, he might change his mind and change his will, effectively eliminating him from his inheritance. To prevent this, Elmer poisoned his grandfather and murdered him. *Riggs v. Palmer* reflects the attempts of the daughters of Francis B. Palmer to prevent Elmer from receiving his inheritance.

Justice Earl, who wrote the court opinion for the New York Court of Appeals, penned the following:

> Shall he acquire title by murdering him? If he had gone to the testator's house and by force compelled him, or by fraud or undue influence had induced him to will him his property, the law would not allow him to hold it. But can he give effect and operation to a will by murder, and yet take the property? To answer these questions in the affirmative, it seems to me, would be a reproach to the jurisprudence of our state, and an offense against public policy.[62]

As a result, Earl maintains that "My view of this case does not inflict upon Elmer any . . . greater or other punishment for his crime than the law specifies. It takes from him no property, but simply holds that he shall not acquire property by his crime, and thus be rewarded for its commission."[63] Such a ruling makes sense. At the same time, ALN may focus our attention in this way.

Elmer's murder of his grandfather indicated that he did not take seriously the obvious fact that all people are born free and equal, and as a result, no one should unjustly kill another individual no matter how profitable it might be to do so. The forbiddenness of such an action bears the fruits of necessity, and while such a ruling is consistent with any viable moral theory, the ruling by Justice Earl, nor the facts isolated by ALN, does not require a moral theory to confirm the criminality of the grandson's action. Additionally, although this is not formally a part of the ALN, a decision in favor of Elmer would also condone enabling others to kill an innocent third party in similar situations. Thus, ALN illuminates an important aspect not mentioned or developed by New York State of Appeals.

The last case I will discuss is, perhaps, the most interesting case (and one discussed at length by Dworkin). It is a British tort case, *McLoughlin v O'Brian* [1982] UKHL 3 (06 May 1982).[64] The facts of the case are fairly straightforward. Nevertheless, it is unusual because of what the claimant desires. Around 6 p.m., the claimant was notified by an individual, who was a witness to the accident, that her husband and children were involved in a serious accident two hours earlier. She was taken to the hospital and discovered that one of her daughters was dead and she witnessed the stark injuries her husband and other children suffered. The claimant sued the driver of the truck (who admitted negligence) that caused the accident because she claimed that what she witnessed caused her severe shock, which resulted in a psychiatric illness.

Like *Riggs v. Palmer*, this is an unusual case because of the lack of case law to adjudicate the facts. The closest case was *Chadwick v British Railways Board* ([1967] 1 WLR 912). The claimant, Chadwick, who witnessed a terrible train wreck close to his home, endeavored to rescue and offer comfort to the survivors of the train wreck. Later, Chadwick successfully sued British Railways for a severe psychiatric illness he claims that resulted from what he witnessed. The Chadwick decision, based partly on his proximity to the accident and his personal involvement in the case, brought to the forefront of the *McLoughlin* case the issue of whether she was sufficiently proximate to the event to recover damages. Initially, the lower court denied her appeal because her case (compared to the Chadwick case, where the claimant was at the accident site immediately after the accident) were distinguishable, namely, the psychological harm of the mother was not foreseeable.[65] McLoughlin appealed this decision to the next highest court, the Court of Appeal. Although the Court of Appeal also denied her request, they did so for different reasons. On the one hand, they did agree that the psychological response of McLoughlin was foreseeable. On the other hand, awarding her compensation would set a policy that would lead to untoward and absurd consequences.[66] Finally, McLoughlin appealed to the House of Lords, which upheld her appeal. The House of Lords did not think that the potential for untoward (absurd) consequences identified by the Court of Appeals should be used to deny her the compensation for her suffering.[67] Thus, in order to adjudicate future cases and to avoid the potential abuse for similar but spurious cases, the House of Lords set the following parameters: 1. The class of persons whose claims should be recognized. 2. The proximity of such persons to the accident. And 3. The means by which the shock is caused.

The class of persons is limited to the closest of family ties, specifically, of parent and child. The husband-and-wife relationship is excluded because adults should be able to endure such tragedies. Excluded are the ordinary bystander who may witness an accident. This is so because the defendants "cannot be expected to compensate the world." The proximity of the claimant to the accident must be close both in time and in space. This requirement does not insist upon a direct perception of the accident to account for the "nervous shock." Rather, it relies on the "Aftermath Doctrine," which includes anyone who (presumably satisfies the first condition), comes from close proximity very soon upon the scene. Finally, the "nervous shock" must come through sight or hearing of the event or of its immediate aftermath. Excluding third parties accounts, the House of Lords stipulates something comparable of sight or hearing which does not necessarily exclude what may be revealed by television.[68]

As noted above, Dworkin devotes a lot of intellectual energy discussing this case and uses it to develop his idea constructive interpretivism. Again, using Hercules as the representative in his ideal judgment theory, Hercules must choose between six interpretations to decide the *McLoughlin* case.[69] So, given Dworkin's chain novel analogy, Hercules must find an interpretation which will be the best fit in the light of *Chadwick v. British Railways Board* and a few other cases. Ultimately, Dworkin singles out the fifth and sixth interpretations as fitting the best to solve this hard case. Briefly, the fifth interpretation makes clear that the claimant has a moral right to compensation for emotional or physical injury caused by careless behavior of the respondent with one exception. The injury committed by the respondent was reasonably foreseeable.[70] The sixth interpretation is similar. It states that a claimant has a moral right to compensation for reasonably foreseeable accidents with one exception. The compensation cannot impose a "massive and destructive financial burden" on the respondent.[71] Ultimately, Dworkin explains that Hercules favors the fifth interpretation to the sixth as long as there is liability insurance in the case of car accidents.[72] Thus, following a relaxed doctrine of precedent, the best interpretation to fit the case is to follow a law that allows "compensation for all emotional injury directly caused by careless driving and foreseeable by a reasonably thoughtful motorist."[73] There are three issues to consider from an ALN point of view. First, we must focus on whether there should be a legal right to emotional and physical injury by the claimant. Second, we must focus on what is psychological harm and whether it is relevant to the case. The last issue is whether anyone who is related to the accident may claim to be harmed in any relevant legal sense.

The ALN principle takes health as one of its central values, which is part of the harm principle. This is so because we are all free and equal, and no one ought to compromise one another's health. Minimally, this means that we should refrain from making others worse off or contributing to significant setbacks to the physical, mental or the social well-being of other persons. That said, while there are obvious examples of physical harm which are too numerous to mention, the issue about psychological harms, despite the rulings of *Chadwick* and *McLoughlin*, remain nebulous.

The examples from both *Chadwick* and *McLoughlin* suggest that their experiences led to severe psychological trauma. Of course, the trauma (and *supposedly* the support of the psychiatric community) led both courts to award the claimant's financial compensation. Certainly, such awards from the court system does not prove that the psychiatric harm the claimant claimed to experience was tangible. The House of Lords raised this issue. In other words, to vote in favor of *McLoughlin* would open the doors to charlatans and the unethical barristers. This is possible because of the lack of physical evidence, essential to verify such mental illnesses. Such mental illnesses are easy to emulate. So, such a ruling may overrun the court system with individuals claiming psychological harm (even uncaring mothers seduced by a large settlement). Thus, while the ALN recognizes the legal relevance of the physical and mental traumas we can cause to one another (as long as they are verified by the successful sciences), it does not do so with the naivety of the House of Lords. The ALN requires evidence of harm.

Dworkin endorses interpretation five: compensation for all emotional injury directly caused by an accident. However, can his view survive critical assessment? It is doubtful. First, Dworkin naturally assumes that psychological harm can be verified. I am not sure such an evaluation of "nervous shock" may be forthcoming even from the American Psychological Association. Second, it is not clear what he means by who is emotionally injured directly. Although the House of Lords limits the scope to the parent-child relationship, Dworkin's claim represents a position whose meaning is at its lowest visibility. Here is what I mean. There are many individuals who, for a lack of a better term, are *directly* involved in an accident. The first responders to the accident, e.g., police officers, fire fighters, EMTs, and so forth, are directly involved. The emergency room staff who care for the injured are also directly involved. Later, is it not true that the surgeons, the ICU staff, if needed, will be directly involved as well? What about the individuals who witnessed the accident and tried to give assistance? Of course, the list may include many others. According to Dworkin's lights, the necessity attached to those directly involved would entail granting anyone of the aforementioned group compensation for psychological injury. However, such a conclusion leads us down a dead-end path of who deserves mental health compensation and who does not. However, the ALN demands more evidence of the successful sciences to establish a strong, causal link. Thus, by using the standard of harm entailed by ALN, spelled out minimally as making someone worse off or contributing to significant setbacks, implies that both Dworkin and the House of Lords assessment are prima facie mistaken.

CONCLUSION AND FINAL THOUGHTS

This chapter represents a modest attempt to address the problem of formulating a standard to address the issue of hard cases. Again, the term "hard cases" represents a space in legal theory which initially invokes a sudden feeling of excitement. It is enticing, especially from a philosophical point of view, to consider such an issue and apply our trade to the legal debate. At first glance, given the obvious commonality between the goals of law and philosophy, such a discussion brings with it the promise of a fruitful debate and a genuine step toward a progressive development of knowledge. That said, after stepping into the waters of this debate, a feeling of near animus replaces the frisson when the complexity of the legal and philosophical issues becomes apparent. To be sure, the issue is exacerbated by the overwhelming number of books, periodicals, and articles dedicated to this dispute. That said, two issues intensify the complexity of this discussion.

The first matter concerns the way debate characteristically proceeds. Anecdotally, I have noticed two different aspects about the treatment of this debate. First, legal scholars speak precisely to the matters of law, but falter when philosophical issues emerge. Second, philosophers who enter this debate typically trained in moral theory and metaethics, talk in clear-cut terms about philosophical issues, but often fail to appreciate the complexity of the legal debate. The result of both efforts is that scholars from both sides end up talking at cross-purposes about the same topic. Certainly, I am no exception to this problem. I fall into the second camp. Be that as it may, what I think I bring to this debate, is what is often missing from this dispute, namely, a historical outlook of the roots of this debate. Personally, I have noticed that, in certain contexts, if a historical outlook is employed, the debate only goes back to David Hume, with codicils to certain individuals like Aquinas. Unlike Rommen and Kelsen, both sides seem to ignore the historical aspect the contemporary debate stems from and, how much a lack of the historical aspects of this debate hinders what we are trying to accomplish.

Thus, following Rommen's lead, my text seeks to illuminate the historical roots of the debate between the legal positivists and the natural law theorists. In particular, one of my contributions to this debate attempts to identify the metaphysical underpinnings to justify normative moral claims, why the groundwork for such justification is missing, and then show why the normative outlook of natural law will fail. In the long run, what I want to argue is this: *There is no room for natural law in legal theory.* If I can establish that, then I am satisfied with my efforts.

The second aspect of this debate presents itself as a dilemma between two sides: the legal positivists and the natural law realists. The debate I enter focuses on the phenomena of "hard cases." The dilemma is no less present in this debate than it is in other theoretical legal disputes. The problem, as I see it, is that both sides present arguments to patch up the dispute which (I argue) represent the tragedy of unfulfillment. Without the metaphysical underpinnings to supply an objective legal or moral standard, the legal positivists cannot supply a convincing argument to supplant the will of the sovereign as the origin and authority of law. The natural law realists sit much piqued by their inability to justify the moral standard of the natural law by the same problem. My ALN position, however, defines and defends a middle position between the two above. On the one hand, ALN exemplifies a basic norm, which is analytic, necessarily true, and known *a posteriori*. So, against the legal positivists, it supplies an objective legal standard which effectively removes (at least for hard cases) the necessity of the will of a sovereign authority. Moreover, against the natural law realists, ALN provides a nonmoral standard which, because of its analyticity and necessity, avoids the need to dredge the bottomless sea of speculation. Finally, ALN provides a standard which brings with it not only the necessity to give it the cross-cultural and trans-historical punch it needs to avoid political subjectivism and political intersubjectivism, but it does so in a conventional manner. This means that the ALN standard does not require a moral or a modal reality as truth-making characteristics. On the contrary, it makes what is legally valuable or disvaluable dependent upon empirically verifiable facts that are legally relevant, facts which can serve to produce the value in question and serve as reasons for justified legal coercion and criminalization.[74]

NOTES

1. My version of legal naturalism has four core elements. First, it begins with a commitment to a realist account of legal statements. Using the categories develop by Geoffrey Sayre-McCord for ethical realism, we may profitably make an analogical case for legal realism: 1. Legal claims, when literally construed, are literally true or false. 2. Some of these legal claims are literally true. That is, sometimes the appropriate truth conditions are satisfied. My use of the term "realism" is in no way an endorsement of what Brian Leiter describes as the "Received View" of legal realism. Brian Leiter, *Naturalizing Jurisprudence*, 16. In fact, from my own perspective, the issue related to the "Received View" is only tangentially related. I argue, for example, that judges, in their decisions about hard cases, may not need to appeal to morality or a moral concept of justice. Ultimately, how judges makes decisions is not within the purview of this discussion.

The second core element is my alignment with foundationalism. Foundationalism is concerned with two types of beliefs, one basic and the other nonbasic. In the simplest terms, basic beliefs are beliefs, which have a certain kind of status for an individual because they are thought to be true in virtue of the fact that there is no conceivable revision to make the individual revise the truth of these beliefs. A non-basic belief is thought to be revisable under certain circumstances. As I noted earlier, the distinction between basic and non-basic beliefs is discussed very early by Amartya K. Sen and later, by Michael DePaul (and other scholars), who develop foundationalism into different versions. Because I align my view to an epistemic foundational structure, I argue that my standard has positive epistemic status. This is so because the legal standard expresses analyticity and necessity between facts (which are legally relevant) and legal properties (which I will explain shortly). There are two qualifications; First, my commitment to foundationalism stands opposed to Quine's Replacement Thesis. In the briefest of terms, following Leiter through this thorny thicket, my legal foundationalism assumes that there is a normative account that justifies the connection between legal reasons and judicial decisions. Thus, a purely descriptive account of judicial decisions provided by the social sciences will not lead to the benefits of a theoretical legal investigation. Consequently, while the social sciences are useful to help us determine issues, say, the relative frequencies of harm associated with accidents, assaults, or even methods of punishment, they cannot establish the normative status of these issues. Leiter, *Naturalizing Jurisprudence*, 37–38, 184–99. Second, my viewpoint advances a limited foundationalism project. This means that not all adjudication must take a foundational methodology. cf. Leiter, *Naturalizing Jurisprudence*, 41. My foundationalism is also consistent with Hans Kelsen's "basic norm." Kelsen, *Pure Theory of Law*, 8; 194–95. This "higher law" is a presupposition, which cannot be derived from a higher authority. According to Kelsen, the "basic norm is the common source for the validity of all norms that belong to the same order—it is their common reason of validity." Of course, while my own concerns are similar, the question of the epistemic status becomes of central focus to stress. According to Covell, Kelsen's agenda of a legitimate legal system required something deeper than Austin's appeal to the dictates of a political superior. Covell, *The Defence of Natural Law*, 19. I share Kelsen's outlook. Nevertheless, even if the basic norm constitutes the unity of legal norms and their validity (as I would also argue), the question of the type of foundationlism still remains profoundly significant. There is one more point about Kelsen.

Kelsen's basic norm, in question, takes initially a historical outlook, and thus, he spells out the process of the creation of a basic norm in roughly two steps or theses. The first thesis states that the basic norm(s) of a constitution are partially generated by the recognition of the culture that there is legal community dedicated to creating such norms. This means that there is a reliance upon the procedures in place to generate the basic norm or a constitution. The second step involves the role of the assembly of the legal community dedicated to this process. Kelsen explains that a basic norm is created by individuals, who are known to be "norm-creating authorities." Ibid., 198–99. Thus, the warrant of the basic norm is not based on a norm created by custom or by sovereign authority (the positivism associated with an act of a legal organization). Rather, the view he defends, after he clears away the copse, reveals that the norm is not a form of legal positivism, but a *presupposed norm* authorized by the legal community. Ibid., 199. Even though I am sympathetic with Kelsen's approach, it still only represents a historical approach to foundationalism. Ultimately, it lacks the objectivity he thinks is attainable and avoids the tough issue of epistemic warrant.

Finally, my foundationalism appears to be at odds in some respects with Richard A. Posner's account of legal pragmatism (and legal pragmatism, in general). In particular, whereas I promote the need for an objective or impersonal legal criteria, Posner makes a peremptory demand to reject such an approach. Richard A. Posner, "What Has Pragmatism to Offer Law?," 63 *Southern California Law Review* 1653 (1990): 1660. Unfortunately, Steven D. Smith robs my claim of tranquility. Smith, for example, makes clear that there are formalistic aspects to Posner's defense of antiformalism. In this context, I gather that Posner's "formalism" refers to a set of immutable legal principles disconnected, in some sense, from experience. Posner, "What Has Pragmatism to Offer Law?," 1656 and 1663. Smith, however, stresses that such persistent rumors that law is just a body of immutable principles and that legal questions may be answered without, at least, a superficial understanding of the world, are blatantly false. Smith, "The Pursuit of Pragmatism," 427. Thus, following Smith's detailed investigation of Posner's pragmatism, the difference between the theory I develop and Posner's pragmatism may be one of emphasis or temperament. So, the pragmatist may demur the need for a coherent and comprehensive theories, the foundationalism I defend does. Ibid., 329.

The third core element concerns the connection between my version of legal naturalism and justice. I follow Kelsen here again. There are two points. First, Kelsen correctly rejects the metaphysical machinery attributed to Plato, Aristotle, and Aquinas, a view that he calls philosophical absolutism. It is "the metaphysical view that there is an absolute reality, i.e., a reality that exists independently of human knowledge. Hence its existence is objective and unlimited in, or beyond, space and time, to which human knowledge is restricted." Hans Kelsen, "Absolutism and Relativism in Philosophy and Politics," *American Political Science Review* 42, no. 5 (October, 1948): 906. Contrasted to this view, Kelsen argues that the basic norm of the positive law "does not provide a standard for justice or injustice of positive law and therefore does provide its ethical-political justification. . . ." Kelsen, *Pure Theory of Law*, 219–20. That said, Kelsen argues that while it is tempting to be critical of this view and reject it in favor of natural law, natural law faces its own intractable problems. Ibid., 220. Rather, he embraces "philosophical relativism, which recognizes only relative truth and relative values." Kelsen, "Absolutism and Relativism in Philosophy and Politics," 906. Covell attributes Kelsen's view to Locke and Hume. Covell, *The Defence of the Natural Law*, 22. Ultimately, Kelsen argues that because there is a link between political absolutism and philosophical absolutism, it is imperative to give up the intolerance of philosophical absolutism and embrace (some version) of relativism. This means that we must disconnect the link between justice and morality. Kelson, "Absolutism and Relativism in Philosophy and Politics," 910–11. Thus, although there are problems with Kelsen's view of relativism and the notion of tolerance linked to it, like Kelsen, I make what is just relative to my analytical legal naturalism.

Finally, the last core element is its Conventionalism. This means three things. First, to say that it is conventionally-based is to point out that it rests on facts which are legally relevant. It is here that my own view falls in line with, what Leiter calls, Results Continuity. This means roughly that philosophical theories should be supported by the results of successful sciences as opposed to just emulating their methods. Leiter, *Naturalizing Jurisprudence*, 34. Second, the facts are logically related to the legal value, which the standard serves to produce. This is the requirement of OPS, EPS, and LPS, stated above. Moreover, three, its normative (legal) status does not depend upon any modal or moral reality whatsoever. My view (contra Fuller) strives to be "utterly indifferent to ethics," Fuller, *The Law in Quest of Itself*, 91.The standard itself is designed to be used in situations at which, as Leiter describes, "the law on some point is rationally indeterminate." Leiter, *Naturalizing Jurisprudence*, 9, 64. Again, by making such a claim, I am not committing my view, to what Leiter later calls, "the Core Claim of Legal Realism," that is, "judges respond primarily to the stimulus of facts." Ibid., 21, 56, 183–99. Rather, my interest is limited, not so much to how judges make decisions, but more importantly, to how they should make decisions.

2. Ronald Dworkin, "Natural Law Revisited," *University of Florida Law Review* 34, no. 2 (Winter, 1982), 165.

3. One extreme position we may face is described by Andrei Marmor, which he calls semantic subjectivism. Roughly speaking, this is the view that there are no legally relevant facts. Thus, the discourse of law by judges or lawyers, whether from the outlook of legal standards or hard cases, is really a disguised discussion about their own subjective preferences. See Andrei Marmor, "An Essay on The Objectivity of Law," in *Analyzing Law: New Essays in Legal Theory*, ed. Brian Bix (Oxford: Clarendon Press, 1998): 8. One may, I imagine, object that the first premise of my (implicit) disjunctive syllogism is false because it fails to mention a viable alternative, viz., legal pragmatism. This is a perplexing issue because while legal experts like Dworkin treat it as a competing theory for judicial adjucation, Steven D. Smith defends persuasively that, in the end, legal pragmatism "is not in the end a theory about law. . . ." Rather, it "is best understood as a kind of exhortation about theorizing. . . ." Smith, "Pursuit of Pragmatism," 411.

4. Elliot D. Cohen, *Making Moral Judgments* (Malabar, FL: Krieger Publishing Co., Inc., 1985), 90–91. Italics are in text.

5. Ibid., 92–94. Italics are in text. Dworkin's discussion of the "Causal Impact Hypothesis" has some bearing on the EPS. It may be tempting to think that EPS falls under thesis of the Causal Impact of moral or legal facts. If it does, then the presence of moral facts, and in my case, the presence of legal facts can cause legal convictions. Thus, on the assumption that such facts exist, the best explanation for some of our true legal evaluations is the presence of these facts. Ronald Dworkin, *Justice for Hedgehogs* (Cambridge and London: The Belknap Press of Harvard University Press, 2011), 70–75. However, EPS does not rely upon such a viewpoint. On the contrary, I reject the Causal Impact Hypothesis in favor of the truth of nominalism. Therefore, the features in question are perceptible or observable according to a theory or set of theories that make the perceptions possible. For an excellent discussion related to the failure of Causal Impact Hypothesis, see Gilbert Harman, "Ethics and Observations," in Geoffrey Sayre-McCord (ed.), *Essays on Moral Realism*, 119–124.

6. Although I initially draw the notions of freedom and equality, historically speaking, from Locke's *Second Treatise*, I also follow, to some extent, Rawls' discussion of the same topic in *A Theory of Justice (Revised Edition)*, (Cambridge: The Belknap Press of Harvard University Press, 1999), 441–49; 475.

7. Here is legal naturalism stated in a logical format: $\Box(x)\{[Px \supset (Fx \,\&\, Ex) \,\&\, (y)(Py \supset (Fy \,\&\, Ey)] \supset ({\sim}Hxy \,\&\, {\sim}Hyx)\}$.

8. My approach resembles the approach outlined in Julie Dickson's excellent text: "In short, analytical jurisprudence is concerned with explaining the nature of law by attempting to isolate and make clear those features which make law into what it is." If this method is successful, then we expect some of our sentences about law to be "necessarily true, and . . . adequately explain the nature of law." Julie Dickson, *Evaluation and Legal Theory* (Oxford and Portland, OR: Hart Publishing, 2001), 17. In this chapter I explain why the principle of analytical legal naturalism is both analytically true and necessarily true.

9. These are the elements mentioned in the first thesis, OPS. Two clarifications of this point should be discussed. First, there is the question of the two antecedents of ALN. In particular, what is the status of the statement "all persons are born free and equal"? Ultimately, I want to maintain is that this statement is analytically true. If this is so, then such a claim depends upon spelling out what the term "person" means. With perceptible hesitation, especially given the scope of this text and the prodigious literature dedicated to this topic, I have little inclination to do so. Nevertheless, given what I know about this discussion, while it may end up being true that all persons are born free and equal, it will demand a close discussion to see why this claim is true. Rather, I am inclined to follow Locke's notion of personhood. For Locke, the notion of "person" is a forensic term, and as such, indicates a public term known to most people. For the majority of usages, it is a quasi-legal term indicating what beings are subject to and capable of following a law. Consistent with this line of discussion, Locke makes clear that "person" refers to the self, namely, a self-conscious being, which attributes to itself praise and blame to its past and present actions. Locke, *An Essay Concerning Human Understanding*, II.xxvii.26. Is it self-evident that such beings are born free and equal? Certainly, not without knowledge defining what the term "person" means which proceeds from observations or experience to the deduction of the consequent.

10. Taking up Locke's notions of freedom and equality leaves us with little to go on. Locke does not discuss either concept at length. The context, of course, remedies some of the ambiguity. Locke's assumption follows directly from his attack of Filmer who argues that some people are not born free and equal. Of course, as I argued earlier, Locke's claim is not just a denial of Filmer's position. On the contrary, Locke grounds the notions of freedom and equality in a corpuscular account of humanity. Such an account then makes certain distinctions meaningful. For example, on the notion of equality, Rawls distinguishes two conceptions of equality. For example, from the point of view of the distribution of goods within society, equality becomes a determining factor when deciding who deserves a portion of a tangible or an intangible good. The other conception, one analogous to my own, conceives of equality as the respect owed to a person regardless of their position within society. Rawls, *A Theory of Justice*, 447. My claim is that all persons are born free and equal makes clear that irrespective of the political culture one might be a part of (e.g., a culture in which certain members are born politically slaves or unequal), the notions of freedom and equality give us prima facie reasons not harm one another. Two observations remain relevant. First, unlike Hobbes and Pufendorf, and to some extent, Rawls, my claim that all people are born free and equal avoids relying on some sort of psychological trait, which serves as a sufficient condition (a capacity of sorts) for equal treatment. On this view, the possession of, say, a moral personality, may give us prima facie reasons for respect and not harming. Ibid., 442. One drawback of such a view is recognized by Rawls. The problem requires us to make some sort of decision about the treatment of humans who lack this capacity; unfortunately, Rawls dismisses this problem. For example, Rawls argues that, at least for his view, such a problem is that only a few people are without this capacity. Ibid., 443. In fact, in those cases of diminished capacities, we still have prima facie reasons to respect their equality. Regrettably, other problems emerge for Rawls and for any approach like this one. First, Rawls' capacity hardly applies to fetuses and infants. What sort of moral personality do these human creatures possess? Additionally, to argue that fetuses and infants possess this

capacity potentially does not avoid the knotty discussions surrounding whether a potential property can warrant the same prima facie reasons for equality, and so forth. So, Rawls is mistaken that his view applies to a group of scattered individuals. The problem gets worse: What are we to do with individuals whose moral personality becomes (non-temporarily) compromised by disease or accidents? What sort of equality do these individual possess without a moral personality? Two more complaints seem appropriate. On the one hand, a part from the individuals in non-temporary comas or persistent vegetative states, where do we draw the cutoff line for humans who possess or do not possess a moral personality? On the other hand, this opens the door for questions about the status of animals. Certainly, the lack of a moral personality has serious implications for the treatment toward animals, implications that many individuals, including many scholars, will disagree with, and seriously so.

11. Joel Feinberg, *Harm to Others: The Moral Limits of the Criminal Law* (Oxford University Press, 1984), 109–10.

12. My goal to separate law and morality does not represent just an attempt to refine our intuitions about the meaning of law. With this in mind, Arie Rosen argues that any serious attempt to maintain the separation faces this objection: "They do not take into account the existence of something that is actually there (i.e. the connection between law and deference which is perceived as legitimate)." Arie Rosen, "The Normative Fallacy Regarding Law's Authority," 93. As a result, such a position, as Rosen makes clear, is inferior to one view that maintains the connection. My response to Rosen's objection is simply to admit that she is right that there is a perception between the connection of law and morality, and its legitimacy is seriously recognized. Unfortunately, this does not demonstrate that there is warrant for the connection. As I will attempt to demonstrate momentarily, if it possible to maintain a position that justifies the separation of law and morality, then the perception of legitimacy spoke of by Rosen is mistaken.

13. Ultimately, I would like to spell out the conventional meaning of "harm." Here I have in mind the limited role of conceptual analysis within a legal context. In particular, given my fondness for conceptual analysis, Natalie Stoljar's article draws my attention: Natalie Stoljar, "What Do We Want Law to Be? Philosophical Analysis and the Concept of Law," in *Philosophical Foundations of The Nature of Law*, ed. Wil Waluchow and Stefan Sciaraffa (Oxford University Press, 2013): 230–53. First, as Stoljar makes clear, we must state the meaning of "harm" in a way which is reflected in ordinary use. Ibid., 234. Additionally, in line with the second thesis of EPS stated earlier, Stoljar explains that we must root our concepts upon an empirical foundation. In my case, then, the notion of "harm" must be attached to a perceptible, legally-relevant fact, or what Stoljar calls the elements within a "The Descriptive Project." Ibid., 235. To accomplish both, even in a limited way, may reduce some of the fuzzy edges with which the notion of "harm" is normally associated with. Of course, both projects are consistent with what logicians call "lexical definitions." On this view, a definition reports the conventional and publically available meaning of a term. Herrick, *The Many Worlds of Logic*, 226. But whether we describe the analysis in the way Stoljar accentuates, or Herrick's explanation, the point is to make sure the concept we are using is true. Thus, to report *correctly* the common or conventional meaning of a term guarantees the concept is true, and if it is not consistent with common usage, we will have strong reasons to think it is false. Such a requirement intends to avoid, what Stoljar calls, "The Ameliorative Project." Ibid., 237–39. The same issue, captured by stipulative definitions, recommends a new proposal for a word. Herrick, *The Many Worlds of Logic*, 226. Of course, while it may be necessary to stipulate the meaning of a term, it is not considered true or false because it does not report the way world commonly is understood. Ibid. In certain cases, if we begin with a word that is established, e.g., harm, but for specific reasons, it becomes vague, conceptual analysis will proceed with a précising definition. Such a definition combats vagueness, while remaining in line with ordinary usage. Ibid., 227. Thus, I constrain my discussion of "harm" to maintain its common usage, and to guarantee that it gets as close to the truth as possible. It is interesting to note that Joseph Raz makes a similar comment about the notion of harm. Of his discussion of harm, Raz writes: "[I] hope that these observations are as uncontroversial as they are intended to be. I have tried to follow the common understanding of harm, but to describe it in terms which bring out the connection between harm and autonomy." Joseph Raz, *The Morality of Freedom* (Oxford: Clarendon

Press, 1986), 414. For an equally excellent discussion, see Leiter, *Naturalizing Jurisprudence*, 196–99. In the same text, Leiter also discusses the notion of conceptual analysis discussed by Ian P. Farrell. In a book review dedicated to H. L. A. Hart's life, written by Nicola Lacey, Farrell explicates what he calls a "modest conceptual analysis." As a legitimate methodology for jurisprudence and one that he attributes to Hart, a modest conceptual analysis "is merely descriptive, and descriptive of the *concept* and not of the *world* (which of course the concept purports to describe, or at least refer to)." Ian P. Farrell, "H. L. A. Hart and the Methodology of Jurisprudence," *Texas Law Review* 84 (2006): 999. In contrast to this, Farrell, following Frank Jackson's discussion of conceptual analysis, highlights immodest conceptual analysis, which "involves drawing conclusions about what the world is like from how we wield our concepts." Ibid.

The inertia of immodest conceptual analysis must be overcome. So, a part from the difficulty of conceptual analysis, with codicils to Quine, conceptual analysis can be a useful tool to pin down, so to speak, important legal and morally relevant terms. At least from my perspective, the conceptual analysis of the relevant kind is, ideally speaking, (following Darwall) both world-corrected and world-correcting. For example, beginning from the common usage of a term, we begin to test whether the term grasps what we normally mean when we use it meaningfully in a sentence. For example, sometimes conceptual analysis is applied to things in the world, say, the concept of a dog. The notion of a dog is a conventionally determined, natural kind. If we suppose (at least from a quasi-scientific account) that a dog is an animal with a snout with non-retractable nails, then, we should be able to do two different things. First, if the description of the (perceptible) physical traits is accurate, it should enable us to discriminate, from a world-corrected point of view, what a dog is. Second, it should also aid us in our ability to point out accurately, from a world-correcting focus, what animals are dogs and which animals are not dogs. In less tangible contexts, conceptual analysis can also be fruitfully applied to controversial terms in legal and medical circumstances. For example, as Herrick makes clear, our own culture struggles to give more precise definitions to terms like obscenity, free-speech, sexual harassment, and even death. Herrick, *The Many Worlds of Logic*, 227. As indicated above, précising definitions aim to reduce the vagueness of a term, which has a culturally (determined) meaning, but which need adjusting to adapt to borderline cases. And, yet, even in these abstract examples, the method of conceptual analysis maintains a sense of fitness. This is especially relevant in cases, e.g., the question of what death means, where the concept in question, as Leiter makes clear, falls within the parameters of a natural kind concept. Leiter, *Naturalizing Jurisprudence*, 172–73. Of course, in certain conditions, an abstract term, e.g., law, may resist the method of conceptual analysis. The immediate problem, as Locke claims about such mixed modes, a part from the minds of other individuals, there is no referent from which to judge whether the meaning is true or false. In other words, world-correctedness is not an option. In the end, as Leiter makes clear, the term "law" plays the role of a "hermeneutic concept," which minimally points (following Raz) "how humans make themselves and their practices intelligible to themselves." Ibid., 173, 186. See Joseph Raz, "Authority, Law and Morality," *The Monist* 68 (1985): 295–327. So, like the notion of justice, from a nominalist point of view, the determination of the meaning of "law" is ultimately determined by our best legal intuitions (or a pragmatic theory approach), and (like the notion of justice) the looming problem of a "strange notions of law objection." Thus, even if this problem draws our attention to a halt, it is not a problem with conceptual analysis. On the contrary, it is a problem with the idealism we must face within an atomistic universe described in nominalists' terms.

14. Hamish Stewart, "The Limits of the Harm Principle," *Criminal Law and Philosophy* 4 (2010): 19.

15. This is merely a partial list of what we may take to be in our interests. Such a list may be too long to spell out. Nevertheless, it is my hope that such examples remain uncontroversial instances of prima facie harm-making characteristics.

16. Making this point is important to avoid a possible objection. For example, on the assumption that a harm occurs only if it recognized by the victim leads to the odd conclusion that if the victim never realizes the harm because of death, no harm will be attributed to the victim. Thus, as long as the victim maintains a desire, at least once prior to death, to continue in an uninterrupted state of homeostasis, we may attribute harm to the victim even after death.

17. Joseph Raz's concept of harm is relevant here. From my own perspective, a neo-Lockeian view of harm, it is natural to align the same notion of harm, as Raz does, to Mill's harm principle. Raz makes clear that his own view revolves around Mill's view of harm, namely, that the only legitimate reason to limit coercively the behavior of an individual is to prevent harm to others. Raz qualifies his view and broadens Mill's view of harm to include harm to oneself (This is missing in Mill). Joseph Raz, *The Morality of Freedom* (Oxford: Clarendon Press, 1986), 412–13. This qualification, no doubt, makes sense in certain abnormal cases, especially in cases of drug and alcohol addiction, severe depressions, age, and mental diminishment. It should be noticed that Locke makes clear that his own principle of harm applies not just to the destruction of other people, but also to the destruction of oneself. Locke, *Treaties*, II.ii.§6. Moreover, as Raz makes clear, the restraint involved applies not just to well meaning individuals but also to the government. So, as Mill's principle of harm implies harms to avoid, it also dictates the kind of freedom all persons deserve. In fact, Raz connects this point to what he designs as the notion of "autonomy-based freedom." Ibid., 314. Thus, to interfere unjustly with an individual's freedom of action, i.e., their autonomy, roughly means that an unjust harm diminishes an individual's prospects to pursue their own goals and projects. Of this point, Raz writes: "Roughly speaking, one harms another when one's action makes the person worse off than he was, or is entitled to be, in a way which affects his future well-being." Joseph Raz, *The Morality of Freedom*, 414.

Another famous and notable account of harm comes from Joel Feinberg. Like Raz, Feinberg seeks to formulate a notion of harm that will determine "when legal interference with a citizen's liberty is morally legitimate." Feinberg, *Harm to Others*, 108. My own efforts in this study face the same issue. Of the notion of harm, Feinberg writes: "Harm . . . is produced by acts of setting back, thwarting, impairing, defeating, and so on, when those acts are wrongful." Ibid., 105. Such harms include intentional acts of commission and (in limited cases) acts of omission (reminiscent of Locke). Ibid., 171. Moreover, harms may apply to obvious cases where neglect or recklessness leads to a wrong (or to what amounts to a setback of someone's interests). Although this is entirely too brief to give Feinberg's view the attention it deserves, two implications should be underscored, one minor and one major implication. First, Feinberg distances the notion of harm from its cousin injury. I quite agree with this point. So, although some injuries may count as a wrong, the concepts are not equivalent. So, it is possible to conceive of a harm that is not an injury or an injury which is not a harm. The former points to an obvious case of, say, theft, where the victim's interests are set back by the loss, but remain uninjured (where injury involves, minimally, the physical compromise of the victim's body). Ibid., 106. The latter may point to the injury obtained in a contact sport because the unintentional, relative frequency rates of injuries may be high, will not count as a harm. Feinberg's analysis of harm also directs our attention to the necessary condition of moral indefensibility. Feinberg's explanation ties this condition to the nature of the set back of someone's interests. The implication, as I understand Feinberg, is that an act will only count as a harm only if the set back of the victim's interest is morally relevant. This makes sense, if I am correct. Thus, on Feinberg's account, unlike my own, morality enters the discussion in order to clarify which harms would then be candidates for the establishment of law and the moral legitimacy of the law. Ibid., 108.

There are two responses that may cast a shadow of doubt on the condition of moral indefensibility. First, the condition of moral indefensibility implies that there is a possibility of using a moral theory to show the act of harm was not morally defensible. If we assume such a claim is true, then what moral theory will we use? Will we use a form of deontology or consequentialism? Many different versions follow under each group. Additionally, on the occasion a legislator or judge assumes such a role, can we expect either one to use the moral theory correctly? What if the judge in question uses Kant's strict deontology or he decides to use Bentham's hedonic consequentialism? What if the judge appeals to the "ancient roots" of natural law to decide the moral relevance of harm? There are other internal problems with each moral theory too numerous to mention now. At least for my part, without admitting that eliminative naturalism is true, i.e., there are no ethical statements or ethical properties or relations, appealing to morality to determine harms seems, at best, a precarious endeavor. Scott, "Five Types of Ethical Naturalism," 269–70. Second, if it is possible to discuss harms (described as the setbacks to someone's interest) without a moral outlook which still confirms our intuitions about the wrongness of a harm, then we could make the case that moral theory in a legal context is irrelevant. Such a procedure, if successful, could maintain the autonomy of each discipline without relegating morality to a story about our non-cognitive sentiments. In the end, this is goal I seek to attain in this text.

18. Following Hamish, the notion of harm, while used as a reason for criminalizing behavior, should not be used as either a necessary or sufficient condition for criminalizing behavior. To establish reasons for harm in a pre-legal situation requires often that we that consult the results of successful sciences dedicated to such endeavors.

19. Leiter, *Naturalizing Jurisprudence*, 34. Here I have in mind cases where an individual may claim to be psychologically harmed because they witnessed a traumatic event. What can the psychological community say, if anything, about the legitimacy of such a complaint? Toward the end of this chapter, I discuss variations of this issue.

20. Locke, *Treatises*, II.ii.§6. I also follow Pufendorf on this same point. See, for example, Pufendorf, *The Whole Duty of Man*, I.VI.ii-iii. Although Locke immediately aligns his argument with a theological account, namely, that we are God's property and workmanship, there is no reason to think that, in light of his commitment to corpuscularism, such an account is necessary to establish our obligation not to harm one another. I follow, to some extent, Dworkin's skepticism about whether a divine authority "can provide a ground for basic human rights." Ronald Dworkin, *Justice for Hedgehogs* (Cambridge and London: The Belknap Press of Harvard University Press, 2011), 340.

21. Locke, *Treatises*, II.ii.§6. Locke's qualification invokes a legal symmetry principle. Such a principle makes clear when not helping is legally symmetrical to harming another individual. The notion of a legal symmetry principle indicates that causing physical harm to an individual may not be the only foundation for the criminalization of such behavior. Of course, concomitant with such a discussion, to speak of harms naturally leads to the discussion of rights. As I pointed out, ALN sets out a partial list of obligations persons have toward one another. All of them are negative obligations. The standard set out will be used to establish, even in a limited fashion, what obligations imply rights that criminal law has a reason to recognize. Naturally, it will be useful to invoke the Hohfeldian notion of rights described as correlative rights and duties. W. N. Hohfeld, *Fundatmental Legal Conceptions*, ed. Walter Wheeler Cook (Clark, NJ: The LawBook Exchange, Ltd., 2010), 38. Original work published 1910. Such rights and their content, like the notion of justice, will be relative to the ALN standard. In other words, the account of rights will not be independent of the account of harms. Hamish, "The Limits of the Harm Principle," 19.

22. I have in mind Plato, Aristotle, the Stoics, Seneca, Aquinas, Grotius, John Finnis, Lon L. Fuller, and in some respects, Dworkin.

23. Alan Sidelle, *Necessity, Essence, and Individuation: A Defense of Conventionalism* (Ithaca and London, Cornell University Press, 1989), 23.

24. Ibid.

25. The Principle of the Indiscernibility of Identicals is expressed in the following manner: If x is identical with y, then whatever is true of x is true of y and whatever is true of y is true of x. Herrick, *The Many Worlds of Logic*, 433.

26. Sidelle, *Necessity, Essence, and Individuality*, 30. Sidelle qualifies this point by making clear that the negations of necessary *a posterior* statements are epistemically possible or imaginable. Thus, as Sidelle explains, on the occasion that historical research revealed that Margaret Truman was not the biological daughter of Bess Truman, but the daughter of a hospital cook due to an administrative foul-up, we would cease to maintain our original view; instead, we would change it to what we believe to be true. Also, see footnote 13 for Sidelle's discussion of whether necessary *a posterior* statements are imaginable or apparently imaginable. Ibid.

27. Ibid., 30–32.

28. Ibid., 32.

29. Ibid., 34.

30. Although Sidelle initially represents this general principle of individuation in this way, he spells out a more detailed GPI where both the specific references to the subject and predicate are removed: "(x)(If x is a chemical compound . . . then (if p is x's chemical structure [deep

explanatory feature], then it is necessary that x has P)). . . ." Ibid., note 20. Sidelle also details a GPI for the origin of biological entities in the same note.

31. Sidelle also explains that the any principle of individuation developed to demonstrate the conventional necessity of a statement must also be analytically true. Such statement is true, not because it mirrors some sort of nonlinguistic modal reality. Rather, it is true because of the meaning of its terms. This will show, then, the instantiated principle that follows will be necessary from a conventional point of view. Unfortunately, I have doubts about whether my own principle of individuation is analytically true. Nevertheless, as Sidelle explains, such a requirement is briefly discussed by other scholars, but there does not appear to be any consensus about this issue. Sidelle, *Necessity, Essence, and Individuation*, 35 and note 22.

32. Sidelle, *Necessity, Essence, and Individuation*, 34–35.

33. For the rule of Universal Generalization, see Herrick, *The Many Worlds of Logic*, 394.

34. Ibid., 387–89.

35. Mill, *Utilitarianism*, 53.

36. Hume, *An Enquiry Concerning the Principles of Morals*, 20–21, 34.

37. Covell, *The Defence of Natural Law*, 2.

38. Again, see Fred Feldman's discussion of what is required to satisfy a moral criterion. Feldman, *Introductory Ethics*, 162–63.

39. Under this view I also include Lon L. Fuller, *The Law in Quest of Itself* and John Finnis, *Natural Law and Natural Rights*, ed. H. L. A. Hart (Oxford: Clarendon Press, 1980).

40. Schauer also describes the same viewpoint: "Under a common conception of legal positivism, the separation thesis consists of the claim that the criteria of legality do not include a criterion of morality." Schauer, "Positivism Through Thick and Thin," 67.

41. Peter J. Henning, "Lawyers, Truth, and Honesty in Representing Clients," *Notre Dame Journal of Legal Ethics & Public Policy* 20, no. 1 (2006): 214.

42. The following discussion is not intended to be a deep account of the cases or the case laws involved which are adjudicated by the Justices. My primary purpose is to highlight the empirical issues involved in case law and the empirical issues identified by ALN. Initially, the cases I discuss may be considered hard cases, not because there is no relevant case law involved. Rather, there is some aspect of the case that creates a puzzle for those adjudicating the case. That is, there is an aspect of the case, i.e., something missing, which needs a legal patch, so to speak (something akin to a software patch), in order to make the case work. Depending upon the degree of difficulty, it can be used to patch a case or it can be used to jumpstart a case when the case sits, so to speak, outside of any relevant case law or the Constitution. And so, in either situation, ALN represents a *principled* approach to solve or to address a problem.

43. Epstein and Walker, *Rights, Liberties, and Justice*, 358.

44. Ibid.

45. The decision to use and evaluate scientific studies is consistent with the notion of Results Continuity doctrine discussed earlier. Leiter, *Naturalizing Jurisprudence*, 34. It is the approach that the ALN takes advantage of in order to evaluate the degree of, say, harm that might be involved in a case. Thus, with the welfare interests of children in mind, contra Feinberg, the USSC decides in favor of *Entertainment Merchants Association* without considering the moral problems, deontological, consequential, or otherwise, associated with violent, interactive games. In other words, the moral indefensibility condition is irrelevant.

46. Epstein and Walker, *Rights, Liberties, and Justice*, 360. The different positions defended by Justice Scalia and Justice Breyer are subtle and should be accentuated. Justice Scalia makes clear that any law that imposes a restriction on protected speech must pass strict scrutiny. Therefore, in a case like this, the State of California must show there is an actual problem that can only be solved by the curtailment of free speech. The actual problem it must prove is that there is a "direct causal link between violent video games and harm to minors." Ibid., 358. Justice Scalia comments that the State of California cannot meet this standard for two prominent reasons. First, the State of California admits that it cannot show a direct link between violent video games and aberrant behavior of minors. Second, the evidence brought forward by the state is not compelling. Rather, the studies suffer significant flaws. Ibid.

Justice Breyer's dissent is significant and complicated. I will pick out two points he makes. First, Justice Breyer agrees with the petitioner's adaptation of the Miller standard (i.e., the obscenity standard) from *Miller v. California* (1973) by the State of California and the application of *Ginsberg v. New York* (1968), which forbids the sale of pornography to minors. To this Justice Breyer adds: "But what sense does it make to forbid selling to a 13-year-old boy a magazine with an image of a nude woman, while protecting a sale to that 13-year-old of an interactive video game in which he actively, but virtually, binds and gags the woman, then tortures and kills her? What kind of First Amendment would permit the government to protect children by restricting sales of that extremely violent video game only when the woman—bound, gagged, tortured, and killed—is also topless?" *Brown v. Entertainment Merchants Association* (2011). Second, Justice Breyer questions the majority's opinion about the social science scholarship dedicated to the topic. The majority opinion views it with a half-hearted interest at best. To counter the majority opinion, even though he recognizes the limitations of such studies, Justice Breyer takes enormous effort to underscore the exceptional value of the sources. This also includes citing the American Psychological Association's recommendation based on the same scholarship. In fact, at the end of his dissent, Justice Breyer list 12 pages of sources in Appendixes A and B, which defend the view that there is causal evidence that violent video games are potentially more harmful than films, books, or television. Of these sources and authorities, Justice Breyer writes: "I, like most judges, lack the social science expertise to say definitively who is right. But associations of public health professionals who do possess that expertise have reviewed many of these studies and found a significant risk that violent video games, when compared with more passive media, are particularly likely to cause children harm." The additional details of Justice Breyer's dissent are taken from the following online source: https://www.supremecourt.gov/opinions/10pdf/08-1448.pdf.

47. Here, again, I have in mind Leiter's discussion of Results Continuity doctrine that requires philosophical theories be supported by successful sciences. Leiter, *Naturalizing Jurisprudence*, 34.

48. Epstein and Walker, eds., *Rights, Liberties, and Justice*, 429.

49. This is the argument Kim Davis, former County Clerk of Rowan County, KY, used when the USSC ruled on *Obergefell v. Hodges*, 576 U.S. __ (2015). Certainly, Martin Luther King Jr. would also have to agree with her assessment of same sex marriages.

50. One qualification should be noted. My assessment may be a little overly simplistic because while harm may be a factor involved which was overlooked, the case itself turns upon other earlier cases which I did not include in my assessment of *Bowers*. For example, it includes *Katz v. United States* (1967) and *Stanley v. Georgia* (1969). For an editorial account of these cases and their relationship to *Bowers*, see Epstein and Walker, eds., *Rights, Liberties, and Justice*, 428.

51. Epstein and Walker, *Rights, Liberties, and Justice*, 433.

52. Ibid., 433.

53. Ibid., 395.

54. Ibid., 396. One noteworthy argument for the recognition of the right of privacy as a fundamental personal right (and one emanating from the Amendments), comes from Justice Goldberg. Justice Goldberg argues that the best foundation for the right to privacy should be the Ninth Amendment. Part of the reason is that the Ninth Amendment was added because the Framers of the Constitution understood clearly that there may be other fundamental rights not mentioned in the first Eight Amendments. What is also interesting and worth mentioning is part of the reason why Justice Goldberg advocated such a personal right. With his arrows aimed at the dissent, Justice Goldberg makes clear that without such a right, the logic of the dissent could not provide a basis to prevent the Government from compulsory birth control. Clearly, even as Goldberg makes clear, such a law would unjustly intrude upon marital privacy. Yet, what seems to remain implicit in Justice Goldberg's opinion is also the harm such a law would create, namely, a harm captured by ALN. That is, not only is such a totalitarian limitation of the marital family unconstitutional, it also represents an unjustified harm against a marital couple who are both free and equal. For the complete opinion of Justice Goldberg, see: https://www.law.cornell.edu/supremecourt/text/381/479. I am indebted to Prof. Frank Colucci for bringing Justice Goldberg's comments to my attention.

55. Ibid., 398.

56. An informal fallacy is due to the logical form of the argument and the content of the reasoning. Herrick, *The Many Worlds of Logic*, 242.

57. Herrick, *The Many Worlds of Logic*, 266–68. The logical form of the fallacy of compositions is as follows: 1. A is part of B. 2. A has property X. Therefore, B has property X.

58. The statute, in question, is this: "USE OF DRUGS OR INSTRUMENTS TO PREVENT CONCEPTION. Any person who uses any drug, medicinal article or instrument for the purpose of preventing conception shall be fined not less than fifty dollars or imprisoned not less than sixty days nor more than one year or be both fined and imprisoned." General Statutes of Connecticut, 1958, 53–32. https://caselaw.findlaw.com/us-supreme-court/367/497.html .

59. The USSC indicates in *Poe v. Ullman* (1961) that there is one exception to the Statute in question, namely, a "test case" that had little impact: *State v. Nelson*, 126 Conn. 412, 11 A. 2d 856. A police raid on a medical clinic seized the clinic's contraception literature and medical equipment and supplies. Later, the legality of the seizure was litigated in *State v. Certain Contraceptive Materials*, 126 Conn. 428, 11 A. 2d 863.

60. Confident of the mistake in the majority opinion, Justice Harlan argues that if such a law can be made to restrict the privacy between a physician and his patients to provide counseling and methods of conception, it can (reminiscent of a slippery slope argument) also violate the privacy of the bedroom to enforce the statute in question. For example, Justice Harlan writes: "Here is the core of my disagreement with the present disposition. As I will develop later in this opinion, the most substantial claim which these married persons press is their right to enjoy the privacy of their marital relations free of the enquiry of the criminal law, whether it be in a prosecution of them or of a doctor whom they have consulted. And I cannot agree that their enjoyment of this privacy is not substantially impinged upon, when they are told that if they use contraceptives, indeed whether they do so or not, the only thing which stands between them and being forced to render criminal account of their marital privacy is the whim of the prosecutor." https://caselaw.findlaw.com/us-supreme-court/367/497.html.

61. There are two other cases that deserve attention: *Roe v. Wade,* 410 U.S. 113 (1973) and *Planned Parenthood of Southeastern Pa. v. Casey,* 505 U.S. 833 (1992). Unfortunately, such a discussion will have to wait for another time. Having said that, it is worth pointing out that, in both rulings, the Justices are already employing elements of ALN which point out legally relevant facts and which bring integrity to the law without employing Hart's viewpoint or Dworkin's view. For example, writing for the majority opinion, Justice Blackmun in *Roe* states plainly that, regardless of the foundation of privacy, the states denial of a woman's right to choose an abortion would lead to numerous and significant harms: physical, mental, psychological, financial, and so forth. Epstein and Walker, *Rights, Liberties, and Justice*, 406. So, to deny a woman's right to an abortion, ignores the freedom and equality all women deserve and unjustifiably harms each woman's choice to make decisions about her life and liberty.

Likewise, Justices O'Connor, Kennedy, and Souter, writing for the majority opinion in *Casey*, state that there is an area of privacy that the state cannot interfere with, viz., the liberty to define one's own existence. Thus, it is for this consideration and others like it, which make the issue of abortion profoundly significant. On the one hand, it is fraught with consequences not only for the woman who chooses an abortion, but for others involved, e.g., the spouse, family, society, and the life of the fetus. On the other hand, advocates for the proscription of abortion by the state fail to understand something important. They fail to appreciate correctly why a woman's liberty to choose an abortion overrides the state's vision of a woman's role in society. To force a woman to carry a pregnancy to full term ignores the choice only a woman can make when faced with the sacrifices a pregnancy bring with it. For a complete transcription of the majority opinion, see https://www.law.cornell.edu/supremecourt/text/505/833 . Thus, like Blackmun's opinion in *Roe*, ALN underscores in a principled manner the majority opinion in *Casey*. The state proscription of abortion directly denies the freedom and equality all women deserve including the liberty to define their own goals and projects, and to define for themselves without the state imposing its own view of life and motherhood. I am indebted to Prof. Frank Colucci for bring these two cases to my attention.

62. Text is taken from http://www.courts.state.ny.us/reporter/archives/riggs_palmer.htm.

63. http://www.courts.state.ny.us/reporter/archives/riggs_palmer.htm.

64. For the entire ruling, see http://www.bailii.org/uk/cases/UKHL/1982/3.html.
65. Dworkin, *Law's Empire*, 26.
66. Ibid., 27.
67. Ibid., 28–29.
68. Additional details of the case including the rule are found here: http://www.bailii.org/uk/cases/UKHL/1982/3.html
69. The six interpretations are listed in Dworkin's *Law's Empire*, 240–41.
70. Ibid., 241.
71. Ibid.
72. Ibid., 258. Later Dworkin confirms the same point, 270.
73. Ibid., 258.
74. Imer B. Flores shares a similar outlook to my approach. She defends a two-tier thesis. For example, Flores writes: "there are features in law and legal rationality which are important or valuable, some morally important or valuable; and, second, that at least some of these features . . . may turn out to be necessary as well." Imer B. Flores, "The Nature of Law vis-à-vis Legal Rationality Revisted," 104. Although I do not share her appeal to the moral value as part of the value-making characteristics of legal claims, her sharpened focus on "features in law" and the possibility of legal "necessity" represent the imperative needs of this debate.

Bibliography

Alexander, Peter. *Ideas, Qualities and Corpuscles: Locke and Boyle on the External World.* Cambridge: Cambridge University Press, 1985.
Annas, Julia. "Ethics in Stoic Philosophy." *Phronesis* 52 (2007): 58–87.
Aquinas, Thomas. *Basic Writings of Saint Thomas Aquinas.* Edited by Anton C. Pegis. Translated by Laurence Shapcote. 2 vols. Indianapolis and Cambridge: Hackett Publishing Co., 1997.
Armstrong, D. M. *Universals: An Opinionated Introduction.* Boulder, CO: Westview Press, 1989.
Aristotle. *Complete Works of Aristotle: The Revised Oxford Translation.* Edited by Jonathan Barnes. 2 vols. Bollingen Series. Princeton, NJ: Princeton University Press, 1984.
———. *Metaphysics.* In *Complete Works of Aristotle: The Revised Oxford Translation.* Edited by Jonathan Barnes. Translated by W. D. Ross. 2 vols. Bollingen Series. Princeton, NJ: Princeton University Press, 1984.
———. *Nicomachean Ethics.* In *Complete Works of Aristotle: The Revised Oxford Translation.* Edited by Jonathan Barnes. Translated by W. D. Ross and revised by J. O. Urmson. 2 vols. Bollingen Series. Princeton, NJ: Princeton University Press, 1984.
———. *Physics.* In *Complete Works of Aristotle: The Revised Oxford Translation.* Edited by Jonathan Barnes. Translated by R. P. Hardie and R. K. Gaye. 2 vols. Bollingen Series. Princeton, NJ: Princeton University Press, 1984.
———. *Politics.* In *Complete Works of Aristotle: The Revised Oxford Translation.* Edited by Jonathan Barnes. Translated by B. Jowett. 2 vols. Bollingen Series. Princeton, NJ: Princeton University Press, 1984.
Audi, Robert. *Moral Knowledge and Ethical* Character. Oxford: Oxford University Press, 1997.
Augustine. *The Essential Augustine.* 2nd ed. Edited by Vernon J. Bourke. Indianapolis, IN: Hackett Publishing Co., 1974.
Austin, John. *The Province of Jurisprudence Determined.* Edited by Wilfrid E. Rumber. Cambridge University Press, 2001.
Bellany, Alastair. *The Politics of Court Scandal in Early Modern England: News Culture and the Overbury Affair, 1603–1660.* Cambridge: Cambridge University Press, 2002.
Bentham, Jeremy. *The Principles of Morals and Legislation.* Amherst, New York: Prometheus Books, 1988.
Bentham, Jeremy. "Anarchical Fallacies; being an examination of the Declaration of Rights issued during the French Revolution." In *'Nonsense upon stilts': Bentham, Burke, and Marx on the Rights of Man*, 46–69. Edited by Jeremy Waldron. London: Methuen, 1987.
Bentham, Jeremy. *A Fragment on Government.* Cambridge: Cambridge University Press, 1988.

Bittle, Celestine N. *Reality and the Mind: Epistemology*. Milwaukee: Bruce Publishing Co., 1936.
Blackburn, Simon. "Supervenience Revisited." In *Essays on Moral Realism*, 59–75. Edited by Geoffrey Sayre-McCord. Ithaca and London: Cornell University Press, 1988.
Brink, David O. "Legal Theory, Legal Interpretation, and Judicial Review." *Philosophy & Public Affairs* 17, no. 2 (Spring 1988): 105–148.
Boyle, Robert. *Selected Philosophical Papers of Robert Boyle*. Edited by M. A. Stewart. Indianapolis and Cambridge: Hackett Publishing Company, Inc., 1991.
Clark, Samuel. *A Discourse Concerning the Unchangeable Obligations of Natural Religion*. In *Moral Philosophy from Montaigne to Kant*, 295–312. Edited by J.B. Schneewind. Cambridge University Press, 2003.
Cohen, Elliot D. *Making Moral Judgements*. Malabar, FL: Krieger Publishing Co., Inc., 1985.
Colman, John. *John Locke's Moral Philosophy*. Edinburgh: Edinburgh University Press, 1983.
Coleman, Jules and Brian Leiter, "Legal Positivism." In *A Compainion to Philosophy of Law and Legal Theory*, 228–248. 2nd ed. Edited by Dennis Patterson. Chichester, West Sussex, UK: Wiley-Blackwell, 2010.
Coleman, Jules L. "Second Thoughts and Other First Impressions." In *Analyzing Law: New Essays in Legal Theory*, 257–322. Edited by Brian Bix. Oxford: Clarendon Press, 1998.
Covell, Charles. *The Defense of Natural Law*. New York: St. Martin's Press, Inc., 1992.
Cox, Richard H. *Locke on War and Peace*. Oxford: Clarendon Press, 1960.
Curd, Patricia. "Knowledge and Unity in Heraclitus." *Monist: An International Quarterly Journal of General Philosophical Inquiry* 74, no. 4 (October 1991): 531–549.
Curley, Edwin. "Reflections on Hobbes: Recent Work on his Moral and Political Philosophy." *Journal of Philosophical Research* 15 (1989–90): 169–250.
Daniels, Norman. "Wide Reflective Equilibrium and Theory Acceptance in Ethics." *The Journal of Philosophy* 76, no. 5 (May 1979): 256–282.
Darwall, Stephen. "Pufendorf on Morality, Sociability, and Moral Powers." *Journal of the History of Philosophy* 50, no. 2 (April 2012): 213–238.
Darwall, Stephen. *Philosophical Ethics*. Boulder, CO: Westview Press, 1998.
Dickson, Julie. *Evaluation and Legal Theory*. Oxford and Portland, OR: Hart Publishing, 2001.
DePaul, Michael R. "Reflective Equilibrium and Foundationalism." *American Philosophical Quarterly* 23, no. 1 (January 1986): 59–69.
Donner, Wendy. "Mill's Utilitarianism." Chap. 7 in *The Cambridge Companion to Mill*. Edited by John Skorupski. Cambridge: Cambridge University Press, 1998.
Dworkin, Ronald. *Taking Rights Seriously*. Cambridge, MA: Harvard University Press, 1978.
———. "Natural Law Revisited," *University of Florida Law Review* 34, no. 2 (Winter 1982): 165–188.
———. *Law's Empire*. The Belknap Press of Harvard University Press, 1986.
———. *Freedom's Law: The Moral Reading of the American Constitution*. Cambridge, MA: Harvard University Press, 1996.
———. *Justice for Hedgehogs*. Cambridge and London: The Belknap Press of Harvard University Press, 2011.
Epstein, Lee and Thomas G. Walker, eds. *Rights, Liberties, and Justice*. 9th ed. Thousand Oaks, CA: CQ Press, 2016.
Farrell, Ian P. "H. L. A. Hart and the Methodology of Jurisprudence," *Texas Law Review* 84 (2006): 983–1011.
Feinberg, Joel. *Harm to Others: The Moral Limits of the Criminal Law*. Oxford: Oxford University Press, 1984.
Filmer, Sir Robert. *Patriarcha and Other Writings*. Edited by Johann P. Sommerville. Cambridge: Cambridge University Press, 1991.
Finnis, John. *Natural Law and Natural Rights*. Oxford: Clarendon Press, 1980.
Finnis, J. M. "Blackstone's Theoretical Intentions; Note." *Natural Law Forum* 12 (1967): 163–183.
Flores, Imer B. "The Nature of Law vis-à-vis Legal Rationality Revisited." In *Philosophical Foundations of The Nature of Law*, 101–126. Edited by Wil Waluchow and Stefan Sciaraffa. Oxford University Press, 2013.

Frankena, William. *Ethics*. 2nd ed. Upper Saddle River, NJ: Prentice Hall, 1973.
Fuller, Lon L. *The Law in Quest of Itself*. Clark, NJ: The Lawbook Exchange, LTD, 2012.
Grotius, Hugo. *The Rights of War and Peace*. Edited by Richard Tuck. 3 vols. Indianapolis, IN: Liberty Fund, 2005.
Grotius, Hugo. *Commentary on the Law of Prize and Booty*. Edited by Martine Julia van Ittersum. Indianapolis, IN: Liberty Fund, 2006.
Grube, G. M. A. *Plato's Thought*. Indianapolis, IN: Hackett Publishing Co., Inc., 1980.
Haakonssen, Knud. *Natural Law and Moral Philosophy: From Grotius to the Scottish Enlightenment*. Cambridge University Press, 1996.
Harman, Gilbert. "Ethics and Observation." In *Essays on Moral Realism*, 119–124. Edited by Geoffrey Sayre-McCord. Ithaca and London: Cornell University Press, 1988.
———. "The Nonexistence of Character Traits." *Proceedings of the Aristotelian Society* 100 (2000): 223–226.
———. "Skepticism about Character Traits." *Journal of Ethics* 13 (2009): 235–242.
Hart, H. L. A. *The Concept of Law*. 3rd ed. Oxford: Oxford University Press, 2012.
Harvey, Martin. "Grotius and Hobbes." *British Journal for the History of Philosophy* 14, no. 1 (2006): 27–50.
Henning, Peter J. "Lawyers, Truth, and Honesty in Representing Clients." *Notre Dame Journal of Law, Ethics & Public Policy* 20, no. 1 (2006): 209–278.
Hobbes, Thomas. *Leviathan: with selected variants from the Latin edition of 1668*. Edited by Edwin Curley. Indianapolis and Cambridge: Hackett Publishing Co., Inc., 1994.
Hohfeld, W. N. *Fundamental Legal Conceptions*. Edited by Walter Wheeler Cook. Clark, NJ: The LawBook Exchange, Ltd., 2010.
Holmes, Oliver Wendell. "The Path of the Law." *Harvard Law Review* 110, no. 5 (March 1997): 991–1009.
Hughes, Robert C. "Law and the Entitlement to Coerce." In *Philosophical Foundations of The Nature of Law*, 183–206. Edited by Wil Waluchow and Stefan Sciaraffa. Oxford: Oxford University Press, 2013.
Hume, David. *A Treatise of Human Nature*. 2nd ed. Oxford: Oxford University Press, 1978.
———. *An Enquiry Concerning the Principle of Morals*. Edited by J. B. Schneewind. Indianapolis and Cambridge: Hackett Publishing Company, 1983.
———. "Of the Original Contract." In *Essays: Moral, Political and Literary*, 465–487. Edited by Eugene F. Miller. Indianapolis, IN: Liberty Fund, 1985.
Irwin, Terrance. *Plato Ethics*. Oxford University Press, 1995.
———. "Mill and the Classical world." Chap. 12 in *The Cambridge Companion to Mill*. Edited by John Skorupski. Cambridge: Cambridge University Press, 1998.
———, ed. *Nicomachean Ethics*. 2nd ed. By Aristotle. Translated by Terrance Irwin. Indianapolis and Cambridge: Hackett Publishing Company, Inc., 1999.
Ittersum, Martine Julia van, ed. "Note on the Text." In *Commentary on the Law of Prize and Booty*. By Hugo Grotius. Edited by Martine Julia van Ittersum. Indianapolis, IN: Liberty Fund, 2006.
Kelsen, Hans. "Absolutism and Relativism in Philosophy and Politics." *American Political Science Review* 42, no. 5 (October 1948): 906–914.
———. *Pure Theory of Law*. Clark, NJ: The Lawbook Exchange, 2009.
Keys, Mary M. "Aquinas's Two Pedagogies: A Reconstruction of the Relation between Law and Moral Virtue." *American Journal of Political Science* 45, no. 3 (July 2001): 519–531.
King, Jr., Martin Luther. " Letter from Birmingham Jail." Stanford: The Martin Luther King, Jr., Research and Education Institute, 1963. https://kinginstitute.stanford.edu/king-papers/documents/letter-birmingham-jail.
Kripke, Saul. *Naming and Necessity*. Cambridge: Harvard University Press, 1980.
Laslett, Peter, ed. Introduction to *Two Treatises of Government*. By John Locke. Cambridge: Cambridge University Press, 1988.
Leiter, Brian. *Naturalizing Jurisprudence*. Oxford: Oxford University Press, 2007.
Liddell, H. G. and Robert Scott. *An Intermediate Greek-English Lexicon*. 7th ed. Oxford: Oxford University Press, 1999.

Locke, John. *Essays on the Law of Nature, together with transcripts of Locke's shorthand in his journal of 1676*. Edited by W. von Leyden. Oxford: Clarendon Press, 1965.

———. *An Essay Concerning Human Understanding*. Edited by Peter H. Nidditch. Clarendon Press, Oxford, 1975.

———. *Two Treatises of Government*. 3rd ed. Edited by Peter Laslett. Cambridge: Cambridge University Press, 1960.

Loux, Michael J. *Metaphysics: A Contemporary Introduction*. 2nd ed. London and New York: Routledge, 1998.

Mackie, J. L. "The Subjectivity of Values." In *Essays on Moral Realism*, 95–118. Edited by Geoffrey Sayre-McCord. Ithaca and London: Cornell University Press, 1988.

Marmor, Andrei. "An Essay on the Objectivity of Law." In *Analyzing Law: New Essays in Legal Theory* 3–31. Edited by Brian Bix. Oxford: Clarendon Press, 1998.

McDowell, John. "Values and Secondary Qualities." In *Essays on Moral Realism*, 166–180. Edited by Geoffrey Sayre-McCord. Ithaca and London: Cornell University Press, 1988.

Mill, John Stuart. *On Liberty*. Edited by Elizabeth Rapaport. Indianapolis and Cambridge: Hackett Publishing Company, Inc., 1978.

———. *Utilitarianism*. 2nd ed. Edited by George Sher. Indianapolis and Cambridge: Hackett Publishing Co., 1979.

———. "Remarks on Betham's Philosophy." In *Ultimate Collection: Works on Philosophy, Politics & Economy (Including Memoirs & Essays)*. Madison & Adams Press, 2017). Kindle.

———. *Three Essays on Religion*. In *Ultimate Collection: Works on Philosophy, Politics & Economy (Including Memoirs & Essays*). Madison & Adams Press, 2017. Kindle.

Mintz, Samuel I. *The Hunting of Leviathan*. Cambridge: Cambridge University Press, 1962.

Mitsis, Phillip. "The Stoics and Aquinas on Virtue and Natural Law." *The Studia Philonica Annual* 15 (2003): 35–53.

Moss, Jessica. "Right Reason in Plato and Aristotle: On the Meaning of *Logos*." *Phronesis* 59 (2014): 181–230.

Plantinga, Alvin. *Warranted Christian Belief*. Oxford: Oxford University Press, 2000.

Plato. *Plato: Complete Works*. Edited by John M. Cooper. Indianapolis and Cambridge: Hackett Publishing Company, 1997.

———. *Parmenides*. In *Plato: Complete Works*. Edited by John M. Cooper. Translated by Mary Louise Gill and Paul Ryan. Indianapolis and Cambridge: Hackett Publishing Company, 1997.

———. *Phaedo*. In *Plato: Complete Works*. Edited by John M. Cooper. Translated by G.M.A. Grube. Indianapolis and Cambridge: Hackett Publishing Company, 1997.

———. *Philebus*. In *Plato: Complete Works*. Edited John M. Cooper. Translated by Dorothea Frede. Indianapolis and Cambridge: Hackett Publishing Company, 1997.

———. *Republic*. In *Plato: Complete Works*. Edited by John M. Cooper. Translated by G.M.A. Grube and revised by C.D.C. Reeve. Indianapolis and Cambridge: Hackett Publishing Company, 1997.

Posner, Richard A. "What Has Pragmatism to Offer Law?" 63 *Southern California Law Review* 1653 (1990): 1653–1670.

Pratt, James Bissett. "The Ethics of St. Augustine." *International Journal of Ethics* 13, no. 2 (January 1903): 222–235.

Pufendorf, Samuel. *The Whole Duty of Man, According to the Law of Nature*. Edited by Ian Hunter and David Saunders. Indianapolis: Liberty Fund, Inc., 2003.

———. *The Law of Nature and Nations*. In *Moral Philosophy from Montaigne to Kant*, 170–182. Edited by J. B. Schneewind. Cambridge: Cambridge University Press, 2003.

Rawls, John. *A Theory of Justice (Revised Edition)*. Cambridge: The Belknap Press of Harvard University Press, 1999.

———. *Lectures on the History of Political Philosophy*. Edited by Samuel Freeman. Cambridge and London: The Belknap Press of Harvard University Press, 2007.

Raz, Joseph. "Authority, Law and Morality." *The Monist* 68 (1985): 295–327.

———. *The Morality of Freedom*. Oxford: Clarendon Press, 1986.

Rosen, Arie. "The Normative Fallacy Regarding Law's Authority." In *Philosophical Foundations of The Nature of Law*, 75–100. Edited by Wil Waluchow and Stefan Sciaraffa. Oxford: Oxford University Press, 2013.

Rommen, Heinrich A. *The Natural Law: A Study in Legal and Social History and Philosophy*. Translated by Thomas R. Hanley. Indianapolis, IN: Liberty Fund, 1998.

Rudan, Paola. "Society as a Code: Bentham and the Fabric of Order." *History of European Ideas* 42, no. 1 (2016): 39–54.

Rumble, Wilfrid E., ed. Introduction to *The Province of Jurisprudence Determined*. By John Austin, vii–xxiv. Cambridge: Cambridge University Press, 2001.

Sayre-McCord, Geoffrey. "Introduction: The Many Moral Realisms." In *Essays on Moral Realism*, 1–23. Ithaca and London: Cornell University Press, 1988.

Schneewind, J. B., ed. Introduction to *Moral Philosophy: from Montaigne to Kant*, 1–34. Cambridge: Cambridge University Press, 2003.

Schauer, Frederick. "Positivism Before Hart." *Canadian Journal of Law & Jurisprudence* 24, no. 2 (July 2011): 455–471.

Schauer, Frederick. "Postivism Through Thick and Thin." In *Analyzing Law: New Essays in Legal Theory*, 65–78. Edited by Brian Bix. Oxford: Clarendon Press, 1998.

Scott, Jr., Robert B. "Five Types of Ethical Naturalism." *American Philosophical Quarterly* 17, no. 4 (October 1980): 261–270.

Sen, Amartya K. "The Nature and Classes of Prescriptive Judgments." *Philosophical Quarterly* 17, no. 66 (1967): 46–62.

Shiner, Roger A. "Law and Its Normativity." In *A Companion to Philosophy of Law and Legal Theory*, 417–445. 2nd ed. Edited by Dennis Patterson. Chichester, West Sussex, UK: Blackwell Publishing, Ltd., 2010.

Sidelle, Alan. *Necessity, Essence, and Individuation: A Defense of Conventionalism*. Ithaca and London, Cornell University Press, 1989.

Smith, Munroe. *Jurisprudence*. New York: Columbia University Press, 1909.

Smith, Steven D. "The Pursuit of Pragmatism." *Yale Law Journal* 100 (1990): 409–449.

Spinoza, Benedict de. *The Theological-Political Tractate*. In *Spinoza: Complete works*. Edited Michael L. Morgan. Translated by Samuel Shirley. Indianapolis and Cambridge: Hackett Publishing Co., Inc., 2002.

Stecker, Robert. *Aesthetics and the Philosophy of Art: An Introduction*. 2nd ed. Lanham, MD: Rowman & Littlefield, 2010.

Stewart, Hamish. "The Limits of the Harm Principle." *Criminal Law and Philosophy* 4 (2010): 17–35.

The Stoics Reader: Selected Writings and Testimonia. Translated by Brad Inwood and Lloyd P Gerson. Indianapolis and Cambridge: Hackett Publishing Co., Inc., 2008.

Stoljar, Natalie. "What Do We Want Law to Be? Philosophical Analysis and the Concept of Law." In *Philosophical Foundations of The Nature of Law*, 230–253. Edited by Wil Waluchow and Stefan Sciaraffa. Oxford: Oxford University Press, 2013.

Sturgeon, Nicholas L. "Moral Explanations." In *Essays on Moral Realism*, 229–255. Edited by Geoffrey Sayre-McCord. Ithaca and London: Cornell University Press, 1988.

Tocqueville, Alexis de. *Democracy in America*. Edited by Eduardo Nolla. Translated by James T. Schleifer. 4 vol. Indianapolis, Liberty Fund, Inc., 2010.

Tuck, Richard, ed. *The Rights of War and Peace*. By Hugo Grotius. 3 vols. Indianapolis, IN: Liberty Fund, 2005.

Waldron, Jeremy, ed. *'Nonsense upon stilts': Bentham, Burke, and Marx on the Rights of Man*. London: Methuen, 1987.

White, F. C. "The Compresence of Opposites in *Phaedo* 102." *The Classical Quarterly* 27, no. 2 (1977): 303–311.

Wilson, Catherine. "Matter, Mortality, and the Changing Ideal of Science." In *Scientia in Early Modern Philosophy, Studies in History and Philosophy of Science* 24, 35–51. Edited by T. Sorell et al. Springer Science+Business Media B.V., 2010.

Zinaich, Samuel. "John Locke's Moral Revolution: from Natural Law to Moral Relativism." *The Locke Newsletter* 31 (2000): 79–114. (Journal now known as *Locke Studies*).

———. "The Internal Coherency of Locke's Moral Views in the Questions Concerning the Law of Nature." *Interpretation: A Journal of Political Philosophy* 29, no. 1 (Fall 2001): 55–73.

———. *Locke's Moral Revolution: from Natural Law to Moral Relativism*. Lanham, MD: University Press of America, Inc., 2006.

Index

About the Author

S. Zinaich Jr., PhD, is associate professor of philosophy in the department of History and Philosophy at Purdue University Northwest. His interests include the moral views of John Locke (1632–1704), the history of natural law and virtue theory, constitutional theory, applied and professional ethics, and philosophical counseling.

www.ingramcontent.com/pod-product-compliance
Ingram Content Group UK Ltd.
Pitfield, Milton Keynes, MK11 3LW, UK
UKHW041842031026
15587UKWH00002B/964

9 781498 598798